MANAGING DOWNSIDE RISK IN FINANCIAL MARKETS

Butterworth-Heinemann Finance

aims and objectives

- books based on the work of financial market practitioners, and academics
- presenting cutting edge research to the professional/practitioner market
- combining intellectual rigour and practical application
- covering the interaction between mathematical theory and financial practice
- to improve portfolio performance, risk management and trading book performance
- covering quantitative techniques

market

Brokers/Traders; Actuaries; Consultants; Asset Managers; Fund Managers; Regulators; Central Bankers; Treasury Officials; Technical Analysts; and Academics for Masters in Finance and MBA market.

series titles

Return Distributions in Finance
Derivative Instruments: theory, valuation, analysis
Managing Downside Risk in Financial Markets: theory, practice and implementation
Economics for Financial Markets
Global Tactical Asset Allocation: theory and practice
Performance Measurement in Finance: firms, funds and managers
Real R&D Options

series editor

Dr Stephen Satchell

Dr Satchell is Reader in Financial Econometrics at Trinity College, Cambridge; Visiting Professor at Birkbeck College, City University Business School and University of Technology, Sydney. He also works in a consultative capacity to many firms, and edits the journal *Derivatives: use, trading and regulations*.

MANAGING DOWNSIDE RISK IN FINANCIAL MARKETS: THEORY, PRACTICE AND IMPLEMENTATION

Edited by

Frank A. Sortino

Stephen E. Satchell

OXFORD   AUCKLAND   BOSTON   JOHANNESBURG   MELBOURNE   NEW DELHI

Butterworth-Heinemann
Linacre House, Jordan Hill, Oxford OX2 8DP
225 Wildwood Avenue, Woburn, MA 01801-2041
A division of Reed Educational and Professional Publishing Ltd

A member of the Reed Elsevier plc group

First published 2001

British Library Cataloguing in Publication Data

Managing downside risk in financial markets: theory,
    practice and implementation. – (Quantitative finance series)
    1. Investment analysis   2. Investment analysis – Statistical methods
    3. Risk management – Statistical methods
    I. Sortino, Frank A.   II. Satchell, Stephen E.
    332.6'0151954

Library of Congress Cataloguing in Publication Data

A catalogue record for this book is available from the Library of Congress

ISBN 0 7506 4863 5

For information on all Butterworth-Heinemann publications visit our website at
www.bh.com and specifically finance titles: www.bh.com/finance

Typeset by Laser Words, Chennai, India
Printed and bound in Great Britain by Biddles Ltd
www.biddles.co.uk

Contents

List of contributors   vii
Preface   xi

Part 1   Applications of Downside Risk   1

 1   From alpha to omega   3
     Frank A. Sortino

 2   The Dutch view: developing a strategic benchmark in an
     ALM framework   26
     Robert van der Meer

 3   The consultant/financial planner's view: a new paradigm for
     advising individual accounts   41
     Sally Atwater

 4   The mathematician's view: modelling uncertainty with the
     three parameter lognormal   51
     Hal Forsey

 5   A software developer's view: using Post-Modern Portfolio
     Theory to improve investment performance measurement   59
     Brian M. Rom and Kathleen W. Ferguson

 6   An evaluation of value at risk and the information ratio (for
     investors concerned with downside risk)   74
     Joseph Messina

 7   A portfolio manager's view of downside risk   93
     Neil Riddles

Part 2   Underlying Theory   101

   8   Investment risk: a unified approach to upside and downside
       returns   103
       Leslie A. Balzer

   9   Lower partial-moment capital asset pricing models: a
       re-examination   156
       Stephen E. Satchell

  10   Preference functions and risk-adjusted performance
       measures   169
       Auke Plantinga and Sebastiaan de Groot

  11   Building a mean-downside risk portfolio frontier   194
       Gustavo M. de Athayde

  12   FARM: a financial actuarial risk model   212
       Robert S. Clarkson

Appendix The Forsey–Sortino model tutorial   245

Index   253

Contributors

Sally Atwater is the Vice President of the Financial Planning Business Unit for CheckFree Investment Services, North Carolina, USA. Sally has over fifteen years of experience in the financial arena. She began her career in accounting and financial management, and as a result of an interest in retirement and estate planning, she accepted the position of Chief Operating Officer for Leonard Financial Planning in 1993. Sally joined Möbius Group in April of 1995 and became Vice President in 1996. Soon after the acquisition of Möbius by Check-Free in 1998, Sally became Vice President of the Financial Planning Business Unit. She is currently responsible for business, product, and market development in the personal financial planning market for CheckFree Investment Services. Sally holds an undergraduate degree in management sciences from Duke University and an MBA from the Duke University Fuqua School of Business.

Leslie A. Balzer, PhD (Cantab), BE(Hons), BSc (NSW), Grad Dip Appl Fin & Inv (SIA), FSIA, FIMA, FIEAust, FAICD, AFAIM, Cmath, CPEng, is Senior Portfolio Manager for State Street Global Advisors in Sydney, Australia. His experience covers industry, commerce, academia and includes periods as Investment Manager for Lend Lease Investment Management, as Principal of consulting actuaries William M. Mercer Inc. and as Dean of Engineering at the Royal Melbourne Institute of Technology. Dr Balzer holds a BE in Mechanical Engineering with First Class Honours and a BSc in Mathematics & Physics from the University of New South Wales, Australia. His PhD is from the Control and Management Systems Division of the University of Cambridge, England. He also holds a Graduate Diploma in Applied Finance and Investment from the Securities Institute of Australia. He has published widely in scientific and financial literature and was awarded the prestigious Halmstad Memorial Prize from the American Actuarial Education and Research Fund for the best research contribution to the international actuarial literature in 1982. He was the first non-American to win the Paper of the Year award from the *Journal of Investing*.

Robert Clarkson – after reading mathematics at the University of Glasgow, Scotland, UK, Robert Clarkson trained as an actuary and then followed a career in investment management at Scottish Mutual Assurance, latterly as General Manager (Investment). Over the past twelve years he has carried out extensive research into the theoretical foundations of finance and investment, particularly in the areas of financial risk and stockmarket efficiency. He has presented numerous papers on finance and investment to actuarial and other audiences both in the UK and abroad, and he is currently a Visiting Professor of Actuarial Science at City University, London.

Gustavo M. de Athayde is a Senior Quantitative Manager with Banco Itaú S.A. at São Paulo, Brazil. He has consulting experience in econometrics and finance models for the Brazilian Government and financial market. He holds a PhD in Economics, and his present research interests are portfolio design, in static and dynamic settings, econometrics of risk management models and exotic derivatives.

Kathleen Ferguson is currently Principal of Investment Technologies. She has experience of consulting to both plan sponsors and investment consultants in matters relating to investment policy and asset management, with particular emphasis on asset allocation. Ms Ferguson has broad experience in areas relating to investment management for employee benefit plans including investment policy, strategies, and guidelines, selection and monitoring investment managers, and performance measurement and ranking. She has contributed to the *Journal of Investing* and *Investment Consultant's Review* and is a member of the Investment Management Consultants Association and the National Association of Female Executives. She holds an MBA in Finance from New York University, New York, USA.

Hal Forsey is Professor of Mathematics emeritus from San Francisco State University, USA. He has worked with Frank Sortino and the Pension Research Institute for the last ten years. He has degrees in Business (A.A. San Francisco City College), Statistics (B.S. San Francisco State), Mathematics (PhD University of Southern California) and Operations Research (MS University of California, Berkeley), and presently lives on an island north of Seattle.

Sebastiaan de Groot currently works as an Investment Analyst for Acam Advisors LLC, a hedge funds manager in New York. Previously, he worked as an Assistant Professor and PhD student at the University of Groningen, The Netherlands. His research includes work on behavioural finance and decision models, primarily applied to asset management.

Robert van der Meer holds a degree in Quantitative Business Economics, is a Dutch CPA (registered accountant) and has a PhD in Economics from the Erasmus University Rotterdam.

His business career started in 1972 with Pakhoed (international storage and transport) in The Netherlands, and from 1976 until 1989 he worked with Royal Dutch/Shell in several positions in The Netherlands and abroad. During this time, he was also Managing Director of Investments of the Royal Dutch Pension Fund. From 1989 until 1995 Robert van der Meer was with AEGON as a member of the Executive Board, responsible for Investments and Treasury.

In March 1995 he joined Fortis as a member of the Executive Committee of Fortis and Member of the Board of Fortis AMEV N.V. In January 1999 he was appointed member of the Management Committee of Fortis Insurance and of the Board of Directors of Fortis Insurance, Fortis Investment Management and Fortis Bank.

Robert van der Meer is also a part-time Professor of Finance at the University of Groningen, The Netherlands.

Joseph Messina is Professor of Finance and Director of the Executive Development Center (EDC) at San Francisco State University, USA. Prior to assuming his position as Director of EDC, Dr Messina was Chairman of the Finance Department at San Francisco State University. Dr Messina received his PhD in Financial Economics from the University of California at Berkeley and his Masters Degree in Stochastic Control Theory from Purdue University.

Dr Messina has carried out research and consulting in the areas of the term structure of interest rates, interest rate forecasting, risk analysis, asset allocation, performance measurement, and behavioural finance. His behavioural finance research has revolved around the theme of calibrating experts and how information is exchanged between experts (money managers, staff analysts) and decision makers (pension plan sponsors, portfolio managers). His research and consulting reports have been presented and published in many proceedings and journals.

Auke Plantinga is an Associate Professor at the University of Groningen, The Netherlands. He is currently conducting research in the field of performance measurement and asset-liability management.

Neil Riddles serves as Chief Operating Officer with Hansberger Global Investors, Inc., USA, where he oversees the performance measurement, portfolio accounting, and other operational areas. He has a Master of Business Administration degree from the Hagan School of Business at Iona College, and he is a Chartered Financial Analyst (CFA) and a member of the Financial Analysts Society of South Florida, Inc.

Mr Riddles is a member of the AIMR Performance Presentation Standards Implementation Committee, After-Tax Subcommittee, GIPS Interpretations Sub-committee and is an affiliate member of the Investment Performance Council. He is on the advisory board of the *Journal of Performance Measurement* and is a frequent speaker on performance measurement related topics.

Brian Rom is President and founder of Investment Technologies (1986) a software development firm specializing in Internet-based investment advice, asset allocation, performance measurement, and risk assessment software for institutional investors. He developed the first commercial applications of post-modem portfolio theory and downside risk in collaboration with Dr Frank Sortino, Director, Pension Research Institute. Mr Rom is Adjunct Professor of Finance, Columbia University Graduate School of Business. Over the past 23 years he has published many articles and spoken at more than 50 investment conferences on investment advice, asset allocation, behavioural finance, downside risk, performance measurement and international hedge fund and derivatives investing. He holds an MBA from Columbia University, an MBA from Cape Town University, South Africa and a MS in Computer Science and Mathematics from Cape Town University.

Editors:

Dr Stephen Satchell is a Fellow of Trinity College, a Reader in Financial Econometrics at the University of Cambridge and a Visiting Professor at Birk-beck College, City University Business School, London and at the University of Technology, Sydney. He provides consultancy for a range of city institutions in the broad area of quantitative finance. He has published papers in many journals and has a particular interest in risk.

Dr Frank Sortino founded the Pension Research Institute (PRI) in the USA in 1980 and has conducted many research projects since, the results of which have been published in leading journals of finance. For several years, he has written a quarterly analysis of mutual fund performance for *Pensions & Investments Magazine*. Dr Sortino recently retired from San Francisco State University as Professor of Finance to devote himself full time to his position as Director of Research at the PRI.

Preface

This book is dedicated to the many students we have taught over the years, whose thought-provoking questions led us to rethink what we had learned as graduate students. For all such questioning minds, we offer the research efforts of scholars around the world who have come to the conclusion that uncertainty can be decomposed into a risk component and a reward component; that all uncertainty is not bad.

Risk has to do with those returns that cause one to not accomplish their goal, which is the downside of any investment. How to conceptualize downside risk has a strong theoretical foundation that has been evolving for the past 40 years. However, a better concept is of little value to the practitioner unless it is possible to obtain reasonable estimates of downside risk. Developing powerful estimation procedures is the domain of applied statistics, which has also been undergoing major improvements during this time frame.

Part 1 of this book deals with applications of downside risk, which is the primary concern of the knowledgeable practitioner. Part 2 examines the theory that supports the applications. You will notice some differences of opinion among the authors with respect to both theory and its application.

The differences are generally due to the assumptions of the authors. Theories are a thing of beauty to their creators and their devotees. But the assumptions underlying any theory cannot perfectly fit the complexity of the real world, and applying any theory requires yet another set of assumptions to twist and bend the theory into a working model. We believe that quantitative models should not be the decision-maker, they should merely provide helpful insights to decision-makers.

APPLICATIONS

The first chapter is an overview of the research conducted at the Pension Research Institute (PRI) in San Francisco, California, USA. References are made to chapters by other authors that either enlarge on the findings at PRI, or offer opposing views.

The second chapter, by Robert van der Meer, deals with developing goals for large defined benefit plans at Fortis Group in The Netherlands. The next chapter, by Sally Atwater, who developed the financial planning software at Checkfree Inc., proposes a new paradigm for establishing goals for defined contribution plans, such as the burgeoning 401(k) market in the US. Sally offers new insights for financial planners and consultants to 401(k) plans.

Chapter 4 by Hal Forsey explains how to use the latest developments in statistical methodology to obtain more reliable estimates of downside risk. Hal also wrote the source code for the Forsey–Sortino model on the CD enclosed with this book.

Chapter 5 by Brian Rom and Kathleen Ferguson illustrates the importance of skewness in the calculation of downside risk. Brian developed the first commercial version of an asset allocation model developed at PRI in the early 1980s.

Chapter 6 examines alternative risk measures that are gaining popularity. Joseph Messina, chairman of the Finance Department at San Francisco State University, evaluates the Information Ratio and Value at Risk measures in light of the concept of downside deviations. Joseph points out both the strengths and weaknesses of these alternative performance standards.

The final chapter in the applications part presents the case for measuring downside risk on a relative basis. Neil Riddles was responsible for performance measurement at the venerable Templeton funds. Neil is currently Chief Operating Officer at Hansberger Global Advisors. While PRI takes the contrary view expressed in Chapter 2 by van der Meer, we think Neil presents his arguments well, and this perspective should be heard.

THEORY

The theory part begins with a chapter by Leslie Balzer, a Senior Portfolio Manager with State Street Global Advisors in Australia, and a former academic. He develops a set of properties for an ideal risk measure and then uses them to present a probing review of most of the commonly used or proposed risk measures. Les confronts the confusion of 'uncertainty' with 'risk' by developing a unified theory, which separates upside and downside utility relative to the benchmark. Benchmark relative downside risk measures emerge naturally from the theory, complemented by novel concepts such as 'upside utility leakage'.

In Chapter 9, Stephen Satchell expands the class of asset pricing models based on lower-partial moments and presents a unifying structure for these models. Stephen derives some new results on the equilibrium choice of a target return, and uncovers a representative agent in downside risk models.

Next, Auke Plantinga and Sebastiaan de Groot relate prospect theory, value functions, and risk adjusted returns to utility theory. They examine the Sharpe ratio, Sortino ratio, Fouse index and upside-potential (U-P) ratio to point out similarities and dissimilarities.

Our colleague in Brazil, Gustavo de Athayde, offers an algorithm in Chapter 11 to calculate downside risk.

Finally, Robert Clarkson proposes what he believes to be a new theory for portfolio management. This may be the most controversial chapter in the book. While we may not share all of Robert's views, we welcome new ideas that make us think anew about the problem of assessing the risk-return trade off in portfolio management.

A tutorial for installing and running the Forsey–Sortino model is provided in the Appendix. This tutorial walks the reader through each step of the installation and demonstrates how to use the model. The CD provided with this book offers two different views of how to measure downside risk in practice. The program, written by Hal Forsey in Visual Basic, presents the view of PRI. The Excel spreadsheet by Neil Riddles presents the view of the money manager.

It is our sincere hope that this book will provide you with information that will allow you to make better decisions. It will not eliminate uncertainty, but it should allow you to manage uncertainty with greater skill and professionalism.

Frank A. Sortino
Stephen E. Satchell

P.S.: The woman petting the rhino is Karen Sortino, and the unaltered picture on the following page was taken on safari in Kenya.

Just because you got away with it doesn't mean you didn't take any risk

Part 1

Applications of Downside Risk

Chapter 1

From alpha to omega

FRANK A. SORTINO

SUMMARY

This chapter is intended to provide a brief history of the research carried out at the Pension Research Institute (PRI) and some important developments surrounding it. According to Karl Borch (1969), the first person to propose a mean-risk efficient ranking procedure was a British actuary named Tetens in 1789. However, it was Harry Markowitz (1952) who first formalized this relationship in his articles on portfolio theory. This was the beginning of the theoretical foundation, commonly referred to as Modern Portfolio Theory (MPT). MPT caused a schism amongst academics in the United States that exists to this day. As a result, Finance Departments in the School of Business in most US universities stress the mean-variance (M-V) framework of Markowitz, while economists, statisticians and mathematicians offer competing theories. I have singled out a few of the conflicting views I think are particularly relevant for the practitioner.

1.1 MODERN PORTFOLIO THEORY (MPT)

MPT has come to be viewed as a combination of the work for which Harry Markowitz and Bill Sharpe received the Nobel Prize in 1990. It is a theory that explains how all assets should be priced in equilibrium, so that, on a risk-adjusted basis, all returns are equal. The implicit goal is to beat the market portfolio, and of course, in equilibrium, one cannot beat the market. It would be hard to overestimate the importance of this body of work. Before Markowitz, there was no attempt to quantify risk. The M-V framework was an excellent beginning, but that was almost 40 years ago. This book identifies some of the

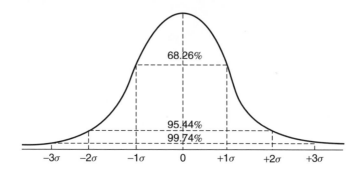

Figure 1.1   *The normal distribution*

advancements that have been made and how to implement them in portfolio management.

Jensen (1968) was the first to calculate the return the manager earned in excess of the market. He regressed the returns of the manager against the returns of the market to calculate the intercept, which he called alpha. Sharpe (1981) proposed measuring the performance of managers in terms of both the excess return they earned relative to a benchmark, and the standard error of the excess return. This has come to be called the 'information ratio'. The excess return in the numerator of the information ratio is also called alpha by most consultants (see Messina's contribution in Chapter 6 for a detailed critique of the information ratio).

MPT assumes investors make their decisions based solely on the first and second moments of a probability distribution, i.e. the mean and the variance, and that uncertainty always has the same shape, a bell-shaped curve. Whether markets are at a peak or a trough, low returns are just as likely as high returns, i.e. the distribution is symmetric (see Figure 1.1). Of course, there isn't any knowing what the true shape of uncertainty is, but we know what it isn't, and it isn't symmetric. Since all you can lose is all your money, the distribution cannot go to minus infinity. In the long run, it has to be truncated on the downside, and therefore, positively skewed.

1.2   STOCHASTIC DOMINANCE RULES

This was an important development in the evolution of risk measurement that most practitioners find tedious and boring. So, I am going to replace mathematical rigour with pictures that capture the essence of these rules. I urge those who want a complete and rigorous development of risk measures to read Chapter 8 by Leslie Balzer.

Hadar and Russell (1969) were the first to offer a competing theory to M-V. They claimed that expected utility theory is a function of all the moments of the probability distribution. Therefore, rules for ranking distributions under conditions of uncertainty that involve only two moments, are valid only for a limited class of utility functions, or for special distributions. They proposed two rules for determining when one distribution dominates another, which are more powerful than the M-V method. The stochastic dominance rules hold for all distributions and require less restrictive assumptions about the investor's utility function.

First degree stochastic dominance states that all investors viewing assets A and C in Figure 1.2 would choose C over A, regardless of the degree of risk aversion, because one could always do better with C than with A. In an M-V framework there would not be a clear choice because asset A has less variance than asset C. M-V is blind to the fact that all of the variance in A is lower than C.

Second order stochastic dominance states that all risk-averse investors who must earn the rate of return indicated by the line marked MAR in Figure 1.3,[1] would prefer investing in C rather than A. As noted elsewhere in the book, *MAR stands for the minimal acceptable return.* Again, M-V rules could not make this distinction.

Hanock and Levy (1969) applied the rules of stochastic dominance to rectangular distributions to show that variance may not adequately capture the concept

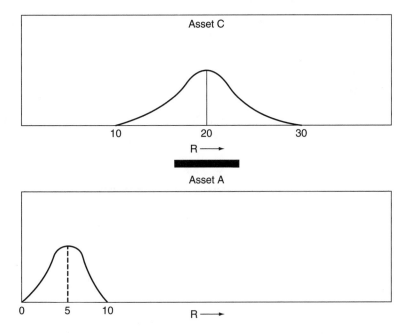

Figure 1.2 *C dominates A by first degree stochastic dominance*

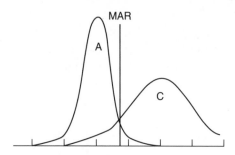

Figure 1.3 *C dominates A by second degree stochastic dominance*

of risk, no matter what the degree of risk aversion. They conclude that the identification of risk with variance is clearly unsound, and that more dispersion may
be desirable if it is accompanied by an upward shift in the location of the distribution or by positive asymmetry. Rom and Ferguson provide some empirical
evidence to support this in Chapter 5.

These are, of course, extreme examples, and one could argue that these examples do not take into consideration investor's preferences. Most performance
measures do not incorporate utility theory, but that will be discussed in detail
in Chapter 10 by Plantinga and de Groot. The larger question is whether or not
these factors really matter in the real world. We will examine some empirical
results later in this chapter. But for now, let's simplify the real world with an
example that allows you to see the importance of asymmetry and downside risk.
Figure 1.4 shows statistics for three assets from a mean-variance optimizer.

The S&P 500 has an expected return of 17% and a standard deviation
of 19.9%. This implies the distribution is symmetric. The second asset is a
diversified portfolio of stocks plus a put option (S + P) that truncates the distribution and causes it to be asymmetric, or positively skewed. S + P has a higher
expected return than the S&P 500 but after the cost of the put it has the same
mean and standard deviation as the S&P 500. Figure 1.5 shows us what these
distributions would look like.

Clearly, S + P is a better choice than the S&P 500. The third asset is treasury
bills. A mean-variance optimizer produced the results shown in Figure 1.6.

The optimizer allocated 53% to T-bills and split the other half equally
between S + P and the S&P 500 for the first efficient portfolio with an expected

Asset	Mean	Standard deviation	Low 10th percentile	High 10th percentile	Skewness
S&P 500	17%	19.9%	−8.5%	42.5%	1
S + P	17%	19.9%	0	40%	2.47
T-bills	4%	0.8%	3%	5%	1

Figure 1.4 *Optimizer inputs*

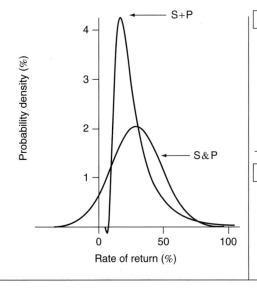

Stock + Put	
Expected return	29.5%
Standard deviation	19.5%
Low 10th %ile	13.7%
High 10th %ile	51.2%
Median	24.0%
Skewness	2.65
Alpha	0.0%
Beta	1.0%

S&P 500	
Expected return	29.5%
Standard deviation	19.5%
Low 10th %ile	4.5%
High 10th %ile	54.5%
Skewness	1.00

Figure 1.5 *Distributions of inputs*

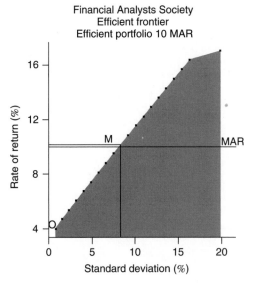

Expected return	10.2
Standard deviation	8.4
Sharpe ratio (ER/SD)	1.21
HP skew 1.03 marg. risk	1.3
Downside probability	49.7
Av. downside deviation	6.59

Asset class	Adj. ER	EFF10 Mix	EFF11 Mix
S&P 500	17.0	24	27
Stk+Put	17.0	23	26
Cash	4.0	53	47

Compared portfolio:		Eff 11
	ER	SD
Value	10.8	9.3
Point change	+0.7	+0.9
% change	+6.7	+10.5

Figure 1.6 *Mean-variance optimizer output*

return higher than the MAR. Notice this is almost half way up the efficient frontier. Why? The large allocation to cash is because M-V optimizers love assets with tight distributions, even if they all but guarantee failure to achieve the investor's MAR.

The split between the S + P and S&P 500 is because M-V optimizers are blind to skewness. The optimizer thinks the S + P and S&P 500 are the same because they both have the same mean and standard deviation. Yes, this is a straw man. But if a mean-variance optimizer won't give you the right answer when you know what the right answer is ... how reliable is it in a complex, realistic situation, when nobody knows what the right answer is? The output from a mean downside risk optimizer PRI designed for Brian Rom at Investtech produced the correct answer (see Figure 1.7): that is, if there was such an asset as S + P, everyone should prefer it to the others shown in Figure 1.6.

One hundred per cent is allocated to the S + P. It is true that the M-V optimizer eventually reaches the same solution. Figure 1.8 shows how assets come into solution. The lowest point on the efficient frontier is 100% to T-bills, even though that would guarantee failure to achieve the MAR. The optimizer quickly diversifies until at some point the allocation to S + P begins to accelerate. The highest risk portfolio is 100% to S + P, and that choice would require a utility function that was tangent at the extreme end of the efficient frontier.

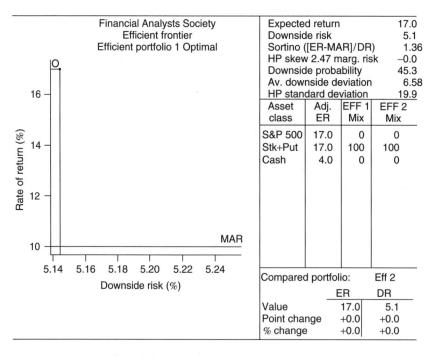

Figure 1.7   *Mean-downside risk optimizer output*

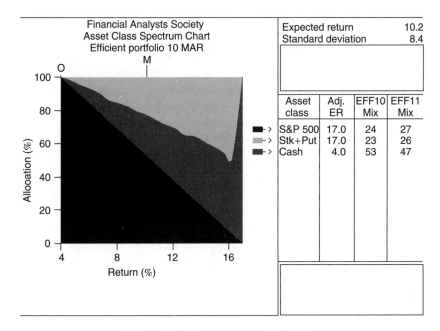

Figure 1.8 *How assets come into solution*

Robicheck (1970) was the first researcher I am aware of who related risk with failure to accomplish an investor's goal, acknowledging that all investors are not trying to beat the market. Unfortunately, he only considered the probability of failing to accomplish the goal, not the magnitude of regret that would accompany returns that fall further and further below the MAR.

Peter Fishburn (1977) was one of the first to capture the magnitude effect. His path-breaking paper is the cornerstone of the research at the Pension Research Institute. It should be read by all serious researchers on the subject of downside risk. Fishburn shows how the rigour of stochastic dominance can be married to MPT in a unifying mean downside framework called the α-*t* model (see Equation 1.1). While Markowitz and Sharpe attempted to solve the investment problem for all investors simultaneously, Fishburn developed a framework suitable for the individual investor.

$$\int_{-\infty}^{t} (t - X)^{\alpha} \, df(X) \alpha > 0 \tag{1.1}$$

where $F(x)$ = the cumulative probability distribution of x

t = the target rate of return

α = a proxy for the investor's degree of risk aversion

When I first began publishing research on applications of downside risk I also used t and referred to the investor's target rate of return. Unfortunately, I found that pension managers frequently thought they should set an arbitrarily high target rate of return so that their managers would strive to get a high rate of return for them. They failed to associate the target with their goal of funding their pension plan. Consequently, I started using the term 'minimal acceptable return' (MAR) and stressed this was the return that must be earned at minimum to accomplish the goal of funding the plan within cost constraints.

Fishburn called this risk measure a 'probability weighted function of deviations below a specified target return'. Others have referred to it as the lower partial moment (Bawa, 1977). I have called it downside risk. There are a number of other downside risk measures, some of which are examined by Messina in Chapter 6, but when the term downside risk is used in this chapter *without qualification*, it will refer to Equation 1.1.

When Fishburn's α has the value of 2 it is called below target variance. I chose to let α only take on the value of 2, because it was difficult enough to explain why one should square the differences below some MAR instead of the mean; let alone, discuss why the exponent could also be less than or greater than 2. Also, I found a lot of resistance to the use of squared differences. People wanted the risk measure to be in percent, not squared percent. So I took the square root of the squared differences, as shown in Equation 1.2.

Because the formulation for a continuous distribution is confusing to many practitioners, I used the discrete version of Fishburn's $\alpha - t$ model shown in Figure 1.2 to explain the calculation of downside risk.

$$\left[\sum_{-\infty}^{\text{mar}} (R - \text{MAR})^2 P_r \right]^{1/2} \tag{1.2}$$

This may give the impression that all returns above the MAR are ignored. This was not Fishburn's intention. It is intended to be a probability weighted function of deviations below the MAR. Which means we should be concerned with the probability of falling below the MAR as well as how far the return falls below the MAR. Therefore, we need to know how many observations were above and below the MAR. Observations above the MAR are recognized but their value is not. This is more easily understood in the continuous form shown in Equation 1.1. Fishburn's formulation would be read as: integrate over all returns in the continuous distribution, square all returns below the MAR and weight them by the probability of their occurrence. Both the probability and the magnitude are captured in one number.

Markowitz also discussed a measure of downside risk he called semi-variance. Many people have misinterpreted semi-variance to mean risk should *only* be measured as squared deviations below the mean (the bottom half of a symmetric distribution). Markowitz made it clear that the mean is just one of many possible points from which to measure risk. Markowitz did point out that when the

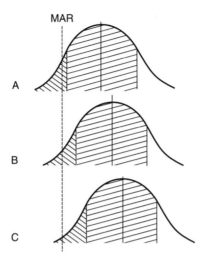

Figure 1.9   *Relative rankings*

location point from which risk is measured is the mean, and the distribution is normal, variance and semi-variance give the same rankings. This has erroneously been construed to mean that standard deviation and downside risk always give the same information.

Even if the assets have exactly the same symmetric distribution, but the MAR is not the mean (see Figure 1.9), the rankings will be the same with variance and downside risk, but the perception of relative risk will be quite different. If assets A, B and C in Figure 1.9 were ranked by M-V rules, B would be preferred to A because B has a higher mean expected return for the same risk. Similarly C would be preferred to B and A. If ranked by mean downside risk rules, B would also be ranked higher than A because the expected return is higher *and the downside risk is lower.* Asset C has the least risk and the highest expected return. If assets A, B and C were mutual funds, I am sure fund manager C would want credit for both lower risk and higher return.

Of course, when the MAR is not the mean and the distributions are not identically symmetric, rankings can be very different with standard deviation than with downside risk. What is more, *downside risk will always provide the more correct ranking, if the estimates are reliable.*

1.3   BETTER ESTIMATES OF RISK

It is one thing to have a more correct concept of risk, it is quite another to obtain reliable estimates empirically. In the early 1990s I began to grow concerned about the way I was calculating downside risk. As the market soared upward, estimates of downside risk for mutual funds I tracked for *Pensions and Investments* magazine got smaller. I was bootstrapping five years of monthly returns to generate 2000 years of annual returns. Standard deviation was also shrinking from its average of over 20% to a mere 5%. I became concerned that investors would obtain estimates that risk was very small ... just before a crash in the market. While theory assumes the underlying distribution is stable, the way risk was estimated by everyone at that time provided very unstable estimates.

The cause of the problem is twofold: looking at too short an interval of time, and looking only at what did happen instead of what could have happened. The bootstrap procedure developed by Bradley Effron (Effron and Tibshirani, 1993) addresses the latter part of the problem, but only a longer interval of time can correct for the former. What is needed is 20 years or more of monthly returns, yet, many portfolio managers have only been in existence for a few years. A detailed description of the bootstrap procedure and how it is used to generate a more reliable distribution of returns is offered by Hal Forsey in Chapter 4.

A solution to the short time interval is offered by a procedure called 'returns based style analysis' proposed by Bill Sharpe of Stanford University (1992). This statistical procedure attempts to replicate the style of an active manager with a set of passive indexes called a style benchmark, e.g. a large cap growth index, large cap value index, small cap growth index, small cap value index and cash. Sharpe has shown that a style benchmark accounts for over 90% of the variance in returns for most stocks. Research at PRI confirms this, not only for US mutual funds, but for mutual funds in Europe and South Africa as well.

1.3.1 The omega return

This raised another problem. How to measure a manager's ability to out-perform a style benchmark on a risk-adjusted basis? The solution chosen in Sortino, Miller and Messina (1997) was to create a risk-adjusted return for the manager and then subtract the risk-adjusted return of the benchmark. We called this the omega excess return. The idea of using a utility function to calculate a manager's risk-adjusted return was suggested to me by Bill Fouse at Mellon Capital Management. This is an extension of that idea.

Equation 1.3 provides an example of how the omega return is calculated. The manager's return for the period was 35%. To obtain a risk-adjusted return in the manner of a utility function, we must subtract the downside variance of the manager's style benchmark (0.0231). We assume the average risk-averse investor requires 3 units of return to take on one unit of risk. Without any further adjustments, this would be a straightforward adaptation of the Fouse Index to style analysis.

However, if an active manager could get a higher return than the style benchmark, why couldn't the manager also take less risk? In an effort to accommodate this possibility of taking more or less risk than the style benchmark, I introduce a style beta (the downside risk of the manager divided by the downside risk of the style benchmark). The style beta of 1.25 indicates the manager systematically took 25% more downside risk than the benchmark.

The style beta times the downside variance of the manager's style benchmark is called the style-adjusted downside risk, or SAD risk.

$$
\begin{aligned}
\text{Omega} &= R - A[\text{style}\beta(DVAR_{\text{style}})] \\
&= 0.35 - 3[1.25(0.0231)] \\
&= 0.35 - 0.0866 \\
&= 26.34\%
\end{aligned}
\tag{1.3}
$$

The omega return is found by subtracting three times the SAD risk from the realized return of 35%. It is a risk-adjusted return that is easily interpreted: the manager earned 26.34% on a risk-adjusted basis.

The fact that it requires some mathematical expertise to calculate the downside variance and the style beta should not deter investors from using it. One doesn't have to know how to build an airplane in order to fly a large jet plane; and one doesn't have to be a pilot in order to travel by air to far-off places. Computer models can make the omega calculations in a nanosecond, and many consultants know how to use the models.

Subtracting the omega return for the manager's style benchmark from the omega return of the manager yields the omega excess return. Suppose the omega return for the manager's style benchmark was 20%. The omega excess would be 6.34%, which is the value added by the manager's skill.

1.3.2 Behavioural finance

Recent research in the behavioral finance area claims that investors do not seek the highest return for a given level of risk, as portfolio theory assumes. According to Hersh Shefrin (1999) investors seek upside potential with downside protection. Olsen (1998) says, 'investors desire consistency of return and therefore choose decision processes that preserve appropriate future financial flexibility'. Rather than maximize the expected return, they want to maximize a 'satisfying' strategy.

Sebastiaan de Groot (1998) studied one hundred wealthy investors to determine if they made decisions in a manner consistent with expected utility theory or behavioural finance theory. He found that approximately half the questions were answered in a manner consistent with utility theory and the other questions were answered in a manner consistent with behavioural finance. But most of these investors said they wanted 'wealth growth that is as stable as possible where a trade-off between risk and return has been made'. De Groot also

	Fund 1	Upside	Fund 2	Upside
Year 1	11	3	4	0
Year 2	10	2	6	0
Year 3	10	2	9	1
Year 4	10	2	14	6
Year 5	11	3	6	0
Year 6	11	3	7	0
Year 7	11	3	11	3
Year 8	7	0	10	2
Year 9	7	0	14	6
Year 10	8	0	15	7
Mean	9.6		9.6	
Potential	1.8	18/10	2.5	25/10
Probability	70%		60%	

Figure 1.10   *Upside potential for MAR = 8%*

made some interesting observations on the relationship between utility functions proposed by Harry Markowitz and those proposed by Sortino and van der Meer.[2] Plantinga and de Groot will elaborate on how downside risk relates to utility theory and behavioral finance in Chapter 10.

The example in Figure 1.10 illustrates how upside potential should be calculated and how it differs from the mean, or average return.

Both fund 1 and 2 have an average return of 9.6%, but fund 1 had returns above the MAR 70% of the time while fund 2 was only above the MAR 60% of the time. But how often the funds were above the MAR does not tell the whole story. Fund 1 never exceeded the MAR by more than 3%, while fund 2 exceeded the MAR by twice that amount on a number of occasions.

In keeping with the formula for downside risk, upside potential should take into consideration both frequency and magnitude. Therefore, the sum of the excess returns are divided by 10 instead of 7. Dividing by 7 would provide an average excess return, which would capture magnitude, but not probability of exceeding the MAR.[3] Upside potential combines both probability and magnitude into one statistic. Technically, *upside potential is the probability weighted function of returns in excess of the MAR.* It is not the average return above the MAR, e.g. $(11 + 10 + 10 + 10 + +11 + 11 + 11)/7$ for fund 1, and it is not the average excess return above the MAR (18/7). It is another statistic that captures the potential for exceeding the minimal acceptable return (MAR) necessary to accomplish your goal.

As shown in Figure 1.10, fund 2 has the potential to do 2.5% more than the MAR of 8%, while fund 1's upside potential was only 1.8%. The formula for upside potential is similar to the formula for downside risk, with two exceptions:

we are concerned with returns above the MAR instead of below, and we take the simple differences instead of squaring the differences (see the numerator of Equation 1.4).

A risk/return tradeoff that incorporates the concept of upside potential is shown in Figure 1.9. The numerator of the U-P ratio is the probability weighted function of returns above the MAR and can be thought of as the *potential for success*. The denominator is downside risk as calculated in Sortino and van der Meer (1991) and can be thought of as the *risk of failure*.

$$\frac{\sum_{mar}^{+\infty} (R - MAR)^1 P_r}{\left[\sum_{-\infty}^{mar} (R - MAR)^2 P_r \right]^{1/2}} \qquad (1.4)$$

As with the downside risk calculation, estimates should be obtained from a continuous probability distribution generated with the bootstrap procedure (see Appendix in Chapter 4 for equations).

Figure 1.11 shows how 2000 annual returns that could have happened were generated from 20 years of monthly returns. Unlike Figure 1.1, this picture of uncertainty is not symmetric. It is positively skewed. All the returns are uncertain, but only those below the MAR contribute to risk. The better one can describe uncertainty, the better one can manage it.

To obtain more accurate estimates of risk and return, a three parameter lognormal distribution was used to fit a curve to the discreet distribution so that integral calculus could be used to estimate downside risk and upside potential from a continuous distribution. Many people confuse the third moment, skewness, with the concept of a third parameter that allows one to shift the distribution to include negative returns and/or flip it to allow for negative skewness.

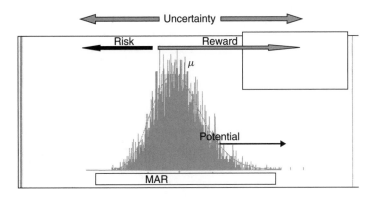

Figure 1.11

The theoretical foundation for a three parameter lognormal distribution was developed by Aitchison and Brown at Cambridge University. But it was Larry Siegal, now with the Ford Foundation, who first brought this concept to my attention. For more details see Chapter 4 by Hal Forsey.

1.3.3   Absolute versus relative performance

Should the MAR for both equity and fixed income components be the same, or should performance for equity managers be measured relative to an equity index, and performance for bond managers measured relative to a fixed income index? Peter Bernstein (2000) made a plea for returns to be measured in terms of what the manager is 'contributing in excess of the required return', instead of measuring returns relative to a benchmark like the S&P 500.

In 'The Dutch Triangle' (Sortino, van der Meer and Plantinga, 1999) we also make a case for measuring risk relative to the required return, which we call the MAR. However, it is more popular to measure performance of bond managers relative to a bond index and equity managers relative to an equity index. The argument in favour of this popular view is presented by Neil Riddles with Templeton funds in Chapter 7 and Les Balzer in Chapter 8.

Figure 1.12 shows the distribution for a bond index, an equity index and a bond manager who earns a constant return. The MAR is represented by a broken line. Suppose one decided to measure the performance of equity managers

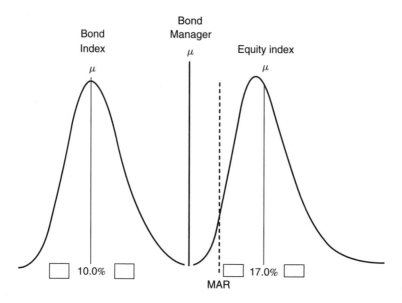

Figure 1.12   *Relative versus absolute rankings*

relative to the mean of the equity index, and bond managers relative to the mean of the bond index. If the bond manager invested only in government notes and earned a constant return represented by the spiked line, the downside risk for the manager measured relative to the mean of the bond index is zero. It is also true that the standard deviation of returns for the manager is zero, and that government notes have no default risk. All three measures confirm the riskless nature of the strategy pursued by the manager. But, what about the risk of not accomplishing the goal? Only by measuring risk relative to the return necessary to fund the plan within their cost constraints (the MAR) would management be aware of the investment risk that was incurred.

I am not suggesting bond managers be compared with equity managers. The performance of a bond manager should be compared with an appropriate bond index and/or other bond portfolio managers, but risk and return for all indexes and all managers should be measured relative to the MAR of the investor's total portfolio. Using the same MAR for all managers keeps everyone focused on the return necessary to accomplish the goal of the pension plan and clearly identifies the returns from each manager that will contribute to the risk of not achieving the client's goal.

Of course, this does not take into consideration the covariance relationship between stocks and bonds. Neither does the Sharpe ratio or the information ratio. Covariance is an important aspect of asset allocation, but is not commonly used for performance measurement.

1.4　EMPIRICAL RESEARCH RESULTS

There was very little interest in using downside risk until Robert van der Meer, who was then at Shell Pension Funds in the Netherlands, started to use it. This decision was the result of extensive tests conducted by van der Meer and his staff while he and I taught a class at his alma mater, Erasmus University in Rotterdam. Some of this research was published in a joint article by Robert and myself in the *Journal of Portfolio Management*, Summer 1991.

There were two important findings in this paper. (1) T-bills, or their European equivalent, are not riskless assets. In fact, they guarantee failure to accomplish financial goals for most investors. (2) Using downside risk produced better results than a mean-variance optimizer or a naïve strategy that maintained a 60/40 mix of stocks to bonds. This was in keeping with the theoretical findings of the late Vijay Bawa (1977).

1.4.1　Tests of style analysis

If style analysis is a powerful tool for explaining the returns generating mechanism for equity portfolios, why couldn't it be used to explain how much risk

Fund Name	R-Sqd	90 day	LG-Dutch	LV-Dutch	SG-Dutch	SV-Dutch	UK	France	Germany	Japan	Pac X	USA
ABN-Amro	93	0	17	21	25	20	0	3	0	0	4	11
Holland	92	7	3	24	27	19	0	0	0	2	6	12
ING	94	4	23	22	20	17	0	4	5	0	2	3
AXA	83	12	9	5	18	39	11	0	0	0	5	0
EOE	95	0	19	37	8	27	0	0	0	4	5	0
Orange	66	22	20	0	0	43	0	9	0	2	0	4

Figure 1.13 *Sharpe's style analysis: The Netherlands style analysis*

Fund Name	R^2	Cash	Bond	Large Cap	Mid Cap	Small	MSCI
NIB Prime	90%	0	0	23%	50%	16%	11%
BOE Equity	87%	0	9%	40%	46%	0	5%
Sage Fund	95%	1%	13%	62%	9%	8%	8%
GuardBank Growth	96%	0	22%	78%	0	0	0
Standard BK	91%	0	24%	54%	20%	2%	1%
FedSure Growth	90%	0	3%	36%	34%	20%	7%
Marriott Growth	92%	0	15%	49%	35%	0	2%
RMB Equity	90%	0	12%	54%	34%	0	0
Met. Gen. Equity	84%	0	8%	48%	44%	0	0
SanLam General	92%	0	5%	61%	29%	1%	3%
Investek Equity	90%	0	3%	49%	47%	0	1%

Figure 1.14 *Sharpe's style analysis: South Africa style analysis*

is involved in a particular style of portfolio management? We decided to test this notion at PRI by using Sharpe's style analyser to construct a benchmark of passive indexes for each mutual fund. We then bootstrapped the returns for each fund's benchmark and calculated the downside risk for each fund from that distribution. The result was a much more stable estimate of downside risk.

Some have questioned the application of Sharpe's style analysis to non-US markets, particularly, small or emerging markets. Figures 1.13 and 1.14 indicate otherwise.

Passive Dutch indexes explained over 90% of the variance in returns for all but the Orange funds. Professor Roger Otten at Maastricht University said that might have been improved by including a micro cap index.

The passive indexes for South Africa were selected by Etienne de Waal at Momentum Advisory Services, Centurion, South Africa. Style analysis also explained approximately 90% of the returns for most funds.

1.4.2   Tests of omega excess

An unpublished study done by Bernardo Kuan of DAL Investment Company indicated Omega excess was a risk-adjusted return that seemed to have strong

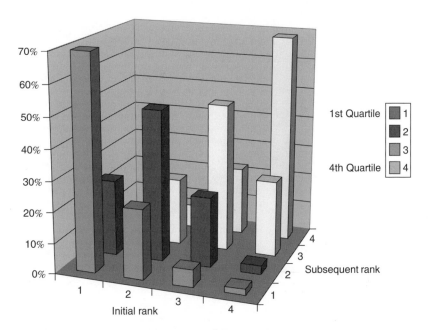

Figure 1.15   *Predictive power of the Omega excess: omega excess return 1981–1996*

predictive power. Kuan's study (see Figure 1.15) showed managers with the highest omega excess in period one, were also in the top quartile in the following period almost 70% of the time. Those managers were least likely to fall in the fourth quartile. The opposite was true for the worst performing managers (back row).

1.4.3   An ex ante test of the U-P ratio

In January of 2000, the U-P ratio was used to rank mutual funds for *Pensions and Investments* magazine. From the funds in the top half of the rankings, the omega excess was used to select the top funds. The subsequent market decline from 10 March to 31 May provided an excellent opportunity to test the efficacy of these performance measures to provide upside potential with downside protection. The performance of the three funds identified in the P&I report were compared with the three funds with the highest return the previous year. The results are shown in Figure 1.16. The three funds chosen with the U-P ratio and omega excess were up an average of 13% while the funds with the highest return the previous year were down an average of 37%.

A second, more severe decline in the stock market occurred in September of 2000, with the results shown in Figure 1.17. The three funds chosen with the U-P ratio and omega excess were up slightly on average (0.4%). While the funds with the highest returns the previous year were down an average of −44%.

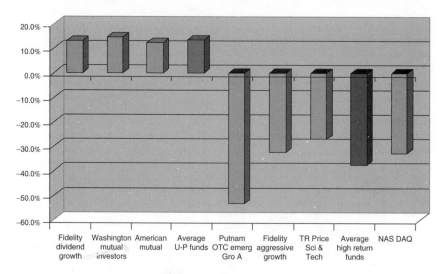

Figure 1.16   *Application of upside potential and omega excess: gain/loss 10 March to 31 May 2000*

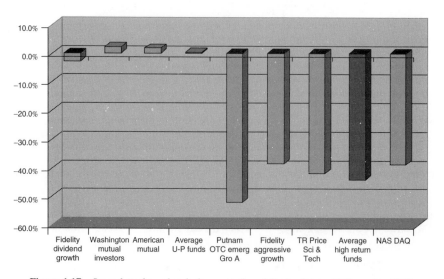

Figure 1.17   *Second stock market decline: gain/loss 1 September to 30 November 2000*

We also tested this paradigm on various styles to see if it could identify top performers from poor performers in each style category. The results are shown in Figure 1.18. The top ranked U-P funds did better in all three style categories, and on average, did approximately four times better than the bottom ranked funds. The results are particularly striking for the small cap category where the highest ranked fund was down only 1% while the lowest ranked fund was off 31%. Of course, past performance is no guarantee of future performance. But

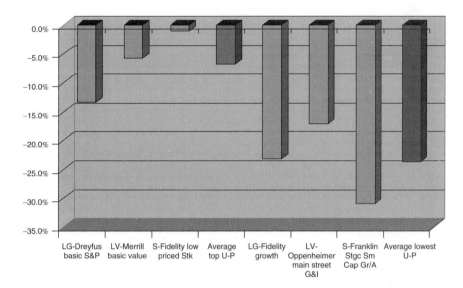

Figure 1.18   *Style rankings: gain/loss 1 September to 30 November 2000*

how long can organizations reporting performance continue to ignore the U-P ratio and the omega excess?

1.5   THE INTERNET APPLICATION

With the advent of the Internet, many investors are seeking help in managing their self-directed retirement plans. It was Bill Sharpe's launch of Financial Engines.com that first called my attention to the possibility of providing very sophisticated technology to help ordinary investors. My vision of how this could be accomplished is a two-stage process.

The first stage is to find those fund managers whose style has the highest upside potential relative to its downside risk. It begins by ranking all mutual funds available to the 401(k) investor by the upside potential ratio. Up to 6 mutual funds in each style category are chosen for asset allocation consideration.

Figure 1.19 shows a listing of mutual funds ranked by U-P ratio. Wells Fargo Diversified Equity has the highest U-P ratio, but it has a negative omega excess return, so it is rejected. The first fund with a positive omega excess is T. Rowe Price Growth Stock fund.

The second stage is to allocate resources to each asset category in accordance with some predetermined asset allocation strategy that is appropriate for investors with a particular MAR. Figure 1.20 shows such an allocation strategy. The bar chart at the bottom indicates the diversification across style categories (19% large cap growth ... 4% T-bills). Each bar in the graph can be thought

Fund name	Select	R-Squared	U-P ratio	Omega excess
Wells Fargo Diversified Equity		0.99	1.4	−0.80%
Fidelity Adv Grth Opp/T		0.93	1.38	−9.70%
BGI Masterworks S&P 500		0.99	1.36	−0.90%
One Group Equity Index		0.99	1.36	−1.00%
T Rowe Price Growth Stock	X	0.98	1.36	3.10%
Amer Cnt Income & Gr/Inv		0.98	1.36	−1.20%
Vanguard Growth & Income	X	0.96	1.35	0.30%
Fidelity Spartan US Eq Indx		0.99	1.35	−0.70%
Dreyfus Basic S&P		0.99	1.35	−0.80%
Vanguard 500 Index	X	0.99	1.35	−0.50%
T Rowe Price Blue Chip Gr	X	0.98	1.34	0.10%
Cap Research AMCAP	X	0.92	1.33	8.00%
Fidelity Magellan Fund		0.97	1.31	−0.90%
American Century Select	X	0.96	1.3	0.20%
Wells Fargo Large Growth		0.94	1.3	−2.70%
AXP Stock		0.97	1.29	−6.90%
MFS Research Fund/A		0.97	1.29	−2.40%
Fidelity		0.95	1.28	−0.10%
MFS Emerging Growth		0.68	1.26	−11.60%
Vanguard U.S. Growth		0.96	1.26	−3.40%
Fidelity Advisor Equity Growth		0.89	1.26	−5.00%
AIM Value Fund/A		0.92	1.25	−1.30%
Putnam Investors		0.94	1.25	−3.30%
AXP New Dimensions		0.98	1.25	−1.00%
Kemper Growth		0.92	1.25	−8.40%
Fidelity Blue Chip Growth		0.99	1.24	−1.90%
Mainstay Capital Appreciation		0.95	1.23	−2.90%
Amer Cnt Ultra/Inv		0.92	1.23	−4.80%
Amer Cnt Growth/Inv		0.94	1.21	3.20%
Fidelity Contrafund		0.91	1.2	0.40%
Janus Inv Twenty		0.79	1.2	14.70%
Janus Inv Janus		0.9	1.19	6.90%
Fidelity Capital Appreciation		0.93	1.18	1.30%
MFS Mass Inv Growth Stock/A		0.96	1.16	11.30%
Dreyfus Founders Growth		0.92	1.16	−5.40%
Cap Res New Economy		0.93	1.13	12.00%
Putnam Voyager/A		0.95	1.1	7.00%
Janus Mercury	?	0.83	1.1	26.50%
AIM Constellation Fund/A		0.92	1.1	−2.70%
Cap ResGrowth Fund of America		0.93	1.09	16.20%
Fidelity Aggressive Growth	?	0.84	1.07	23.60%
Putnam New Opportunity/A		0.9	1.06	12.00%
Fidelity OTC Portfolio		0.86	1.03	11.50%
Fidelity Retirement Growth		0.87	1.01	9.30%

Figure 1.19 *Ranking by U-P ratio*

of as a bucket to be filled with combinations of mutual funds and indexes that will maximize the omega excess return for the portfolio.

If I would have allowed all funds ranked by U-P ratio to be considered for solution in the asset allocation, Janus Mercury would have replaced some of the AMCAP and New Economy allocation and there would have been no

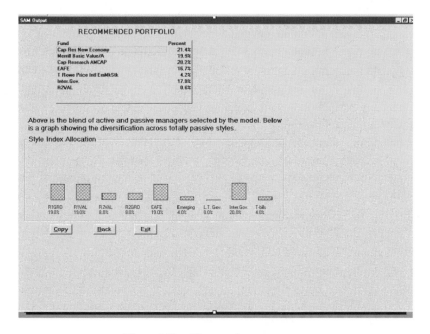

Figure 1.20   *Allocation by omega excess*

point in ranking by U-P ratio. The rationale for this two-stage process is that the distribution generated by 25 years of data on the manager's style is more stable than the distribution generated by three years of manager data. Therefore, information about the upside potential of the manager's style relative to its downside risk should determine the ranking in stage 1. In stage 2, allocate money to managers who can beat their top-ranked style benchmark, i.e. have a positive omega excess. To the extent that the buckets cannot be filled, allocate money to the style index, e.g. 16.7% is allocated to the EAFE because only 2.3% of the required 19% could be allocated to active management.

The 401(k) participant doesn't have to know that the allocation shown at the top of Figure 1.20 involved bootstrapping data generated by a style analyser, fitting a three parameter lognormal distribution to the data, using integral calculus to calculate each fund's upside potential and downside risk, and using linear programming to allocate funds based on their omega excess return. All it takes is a couple of clicks on a web page. An updated list of the websites that offer this methodology is available at www.sortino.com.

1.6   CONCLUSION

The three most important questions to answer when attempting to manage a portfolio of securities are:

(1)   What is the goal, i.e. what are you trying to accomplish?
(2)   What rate of return do you have to realize at minimum in order to accomplish the goal? This will determine the risk and return character-istics of every investment opportunity.
(3)   What diversified portfolio provides the best risk/return tradeoff relative to my MAR?

For any performance measure to be oriented toward an investor's goal, risk and return must be measured relative to the MAR that will achieve that goal. Similarly, asset allocation should focus on those portfolios that provide the highest upside potential for a given level of risk of falling below the MAR.

Therefore, I believe the single most important step in developing a successful investment strategy is to identify the appropriate MAR. This requires a finan-cial planner or financial planning software, as described in Chapter 3 by Sally Atwater.

NOTES

1.   For ease of understanding, the probability density function is shown instead of the cumulative.
2.   De Groot used a generalized value function: $(x - k)^\alpha$ if $x \geq k$, $-\lambda(k - x)^\alpha$ if $x < k$. He then shows how this is different than the piecewise linear value func-tion presented by Markowitz (1991), who assumed $k = 0$ and that losses do not become more important when they are further away from k. De Groot shows that tests of prospect theory assumed $\lambda = 0.88$, whereas Sortino and van der Meer (1991) assumed $\lambda = 3$.
3.   I am grateful to Jared Shope and Mike Wilkinson at LCG for helping me to clarify this point.

REFERENCES

Bawa, Vijay S. (1977) Mean-lower partial moments and asset prices, *Journal of Finan-cial Economics*, June.

Bernstein, Peter L. (2000) *Pensions and Investments*, 7 August, p. 53.

Borch, Karl (1969) A note on uncertainty and indifference curves, *Review of Economic Studies*, 36.

De Groot, J. Sebastiaan (1998) *Behavioral Aspects of Decision Models in Asset Man-agement*, The Netherlands: Labyrint Publications.

Effron, Bradley and Tibshirani, Robert J. (1993) *An Introduction to the Bootstrap*, London: Chapman and Hall.

Fishburn, Peter C. (1977) Mean-risk analysis with risk associated with below target returns, *American Economic Review*, March.

Hadar, J. and Russell, W. (1969) Rules for ordering uncertain prospects, *American Economic Review*, March.

Hanock, G. and Levy, H. (1969) The efficiency analysis of choices involving risk, *Review of Economic Studies*, 36.

Jensen, Michael C. (1968) The performance of mutual funds in the period 1945–1964, *Journal of Finance*, May.

Markowitz, H. (1952) Portfolio selection, *Journal of Finance*, 6.

Markowitz, H. (1991) *Portfolio Selection: Efficient Diversification of Investments*, 2nd edn, Oxford: Blackwell.

Olsen, Robert A. (1998) Behavioural finance and its implications for stock-price volatility, *Financial Analysts Journal*, March.

Robicheck, Alexander (1970) Risk and the value of securities, *Journal of Financial and Quantitative Analysis*, IV.

Sharpe, William F. (1981) Decentralized investment management, *Journal of Finance*, 36.

Sharpe, William F. (1992) Asset allocation: management style and performance measurement, *Journal of Portfolio Management*, Winter.

Shefrin, Hersh (1999) *Beyond Greed and Fear*, Boston, MA: Harvard Business School Press.

Sortino, F. and van der Meer, R.A.H. (1991) Downside risk, *Journal of Portfolio Management*, Summer.

Sortino, F.A., Miller, G. and Messina, J. (1997) Short term risk-adjusted performance: a style based analysis, *Journal of Investing*, Summer.

Sortino, F., van der Meer, R.A.H. and Plantinga, A. (1999) The Dutch Triangle, *Journal of Portfolio Management*, Fall.

Chapter 2

The Dutch view: developing a strategic benchmark in an ALM framework

ROBERT VAN DER MEER

SUMMARY

A critical factor in management and control of the investment process is the determination of appropriate benchmarks. This chapter discusses how benchmarks for investments by pension funds can be established. Practical evidence is taken from the Dutch pension fund industry. The approach relies on asset liability simulation and market valuation of plan assets and liabilities and their correlation. In the framework of a pension fund, benchmarks are a result of policy decisions with respect to:

- the desired level of premium contributions
- the security of the future indexing of benefits
- the financial risk to the plan sponsor and the beneficiaries.

In order to evaluate alternatives, it is essential to obtain a correct understanding of the economic cost of alternatives.

2.1 ASSET ALLOCATION OF DUTCH PENSION FUNDS

Since the 1980s there has been a consistent trend in portfolio allocation. The average proportion of equities in a typical Dutch pension portfolio has risen from 5% in 1980 to more than 30% in 2000. It is expected that this international trend will continue. This is primarily the result of the recognition that equities produce higher average results in the long run and that pension funds, because of their long-term planning horizon, are able to sustain the increased level of investment risk which is revealed in a higher volatility.

Some argue that this is related to the improved quality of the investment decisions made by the individual pension funds. However, one should be aware that one can only fully appreciate the quality of policy decisions after proper recognition of the differences among the individual pension funds. These differences apply to two aspects of pension fund investment policy. First of all, investment decisions are based not only on the expected rate of return, but also on the risk of investment returns as well. Unless pension funds are identical, the risks of alternative asset portfolios will differ as the result of interactions between the assets and liabilities. For not every pension fund has an identical liability structure. Secondly, even when the risks and returns of the portfolios are identical across pension funds, the risk tolerance may vary. The risk tolerance primarily follows as the outcome of an internal decision process that involves all of the funds' stakeholders. These stakeholders are the plan's sponsor(s), the plan's participants, both active and retired, and the plan's supervisory bodies.

With respect to the asset allocation, it is remarkable that especially the allocations to fixed income investment instruments in Holland range from a minimum of 25% to a maximum of 100%. The combined effect of asset allocation and the particular characteristics of the pension funds, including their appetite for risk, lead to dramatic differences in the investment portfolio. These differences have a strong hold on the portfolio allocations and are therefore of great importance in the determination of the relevant performance measurement.

Similar to earlier studies, a major part of performance is explained by the portfolio allocation decision. However, in general the asset allocation decision is complex. It not only involves the tradeoff between the various investment categories, it also involves the interaction with pension liabilities. Moreover, the asset allocation involves the allocation and balancing of risks and returns among several of the pension fund's interest groups.

2.2   PENSION FUND ASSET LIABILITY MANAGEMENT

With respect to the pension plan there is flexibility in the vesting and indexing of benefits. Dutch pension funds typically aim to compensate beneficiaries fully for the effects of inflation on their pensions. There can, however, be restrictions as to the level of indexing. With respect to premium policy, alternative contribution schemes exist that primarily affect the timing and level of regular contributions, conditional on the solvency of the pension fund. When the fund is confronted with a solvency shortfall, additional premium contributions are mandated by the fund's regulators. If the fund reduces the average level of premium contributions by assuming that the investment production increases by a more active investment policy, then the so-called pension risk increases. Indeed, for the participants the risk increases because there is a corresponding risk of insolvency. To the plan sponsor, increases in risk result because the possibility of mandatory premium contributions increases as well. As a consequence, the sponsors face higher contribution rate volatility. These are just examples of the relationships between the different policy aspects that are involved in pension fund risks. Therefore in order to evaluate these decisions, a comprehensive analysis of the effects to the various interest groups is required. This is where an asset liability management (ALM) analysis may support the decision-making process. The objective of an ALM analysis is to identify the risk and return tradeoffs to the various interest groups in relation to their constraints. It should indicate whether a satisfactory mix of policy decisions, which deals with the level and volatility of premium contributions, the indexing of future benefits and the funding level or solvency of the pension fund, can be accomplished. Of course, the interests of the different stakeholders can be of a more or less conflicting nature.

Further, the analysis is complex due to the fact that it involves multiple periods with many uncertain outcomes. Even though the conditions of each pension fund are unique, some important determinants can be indicated. First of all, the nature of the pension contract is important. Pension fund liabilities are characterized by the actuarial and accounting conventions involving the level and vesting of liabilities and the future indexing of benefits. Further, pension fund liabilities are characterized by the number of participants per category, the maturity of the workforce and demographic trends. Secondly, the characteristics of the plan's sponsor are of importance. Depending on the percentage of premium to be paid by the sponsor versus the wage-level, a different view on risk and return may exist. As a result, the tolerance with respect to premium, i.e. contribution volatility, will vary per fund. Of notable relevance to the plan's participants, and to a lesser extent to the fund's regulators, is the financial strength of the sponsor.

2.3   THE DUTCH TRIANGLE

Even though the conditions of each pension fund are unique, there are similarities with respect to the main issues. Pension fund liabilities are characterized by the actuarial and accounting conventions involving the level and vesting of liabilities and the future indexing of benefits. Further, pension fund liabilities are characterized by the number of participants, the maturity of the workforce, and the plan sponsor's policy with respect to hiring new employees and demographic trends. The characteristics of the pension plan's sponsor are also important. Depending on the percentage premium to be paid by the plan sponsor versus the wage level, there may be different views on risk and return. Tolerance with respect to contribution volatility will vary accordingly. Of particular relevance to the plan's participants, and to a lesser extent to the fund's regulators, is the financial strength of the plan sponsor. Default risk affects tolerance of the

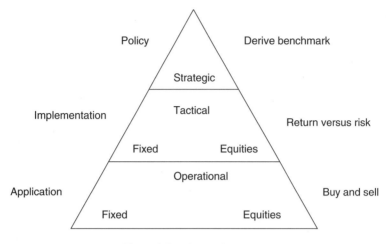

Figure 2.1   *The Dutch Triangle*

parties with respect to the timing and volatility of contributions as well. To manage this process the following three-tiered management structure has been proposed by Sortino, van der Meer and Plantinga (1999):

- *the strategic level*, where policy determines the information needed at all levels
- *the tactical level*, where policy is implemented and actions are concerned with risk-return tradeoffs
- *the operational level*, where the execution of buy and sell orders takes place.

The three levels are shown in Figure 2.1.

Dutch pension funds typically aim to compensate beneficiaries fully for the effects of inflation on their pensions, although there may be restrictions related to the maximum level of indexing or to the solvency of the fund. With respect to premium policy, alternative contribution schemes exist that primarily affect the timing and level of regular contributions, conditioned on the solvency of the pension funds. When a fund is confronted with a solvency shortfall, the fund's regulators mandate additional premium contributions.

2.3.1   The strategic level

The allocation of risk and return across the fund's stakeholders are critically affected by volatility of premium contributions, indexing of future benefits, and funding level or solvency of the pension fund. If the plan sponsor reduces the average level of premium contributions by pursuing a more aggressive investment policy, risk increases. To the participants, increases in risk result because there is a correspondingly higher probability of insolvency. To the plan sponsor, increases in risk result because the possibility of mandatory premium contributions increases as well. As a consequence, the sponsors face higher contribution rate volatility. The main threat to all stakeholders is a shortfall relative to the minimum funding requirements, either now or in future time periods. For the plan sponsor this calls for additional premium contributions. For the plan participants, this allows for the possibility of lower future benefits. It is therefore suggested to use downside risk measures with respect to these shortfalls. Since several future periods are involved, the traditional downside risk measure in Sortino and van der Meer (1991) is extended to the discounted downside risk described in van der Meer and Smink (1998).

To evaluate these policy decisions, a comprehensive approach that identifies the impact on the various interest groups is required. An asset liability management (ALM) analysis is admirably suited to the task. It will identify those asset allocations across asset categories that best accommodate the various decisions dealing with the level and volatility of premium contributions, the indexing of future benefits, and the funding level or solvency of the pension fund.

The strategic mix of assets in the ALM study will have an expected return, which is a valuable estimate of the return that must be earned at a minimum in order to accomplish the policy goals of the plan. This is referred to as the minimal acceptable return (MAR).

The MAR is what links the decisions of top level management at the strategic level to the management decisions at the tactical level and the operational level. It is also the MAR that serves as the point from which risk is measured for both performance measurement and asset allocation, thus linking performance measurement with asset allocation. It is this crucial link that distinguishes the Dutch Triangle from more traditional approaches for pension fund management. This structure shapes the policy statements as follows:

(1)   The goal is to fund the pension plan within the constraints identified in the ALM study.
(2)   The investment objective is to maximize the expected return above the MAR, subject to the risk of falling below the MAR.

Notice that the objective supports the goal, in that, if the object is achieved, the goal will be accomplished. The rate of return that separates success from failure to accomplish the goal is the MAR. Only returns equal to or greater than the MAR assure success. The goal is not to make money. Making money is how one accomplishes the goal. The MAR identifies how much money is needed at a minimum. Unless the MAR is established at the strategic level, there is a danger that it will either be absent from the performance measurement and asset allocation decisions, or it will be misspecified. Without a directive from above, those responsible for implementing policy usually look outside the organization for advice on what tools to use for performance measurement and asset allocation. If the MAR decision gets pushed down to the operational level, the consultants or portfolio managers may select a substitute for the MAR that presents their results in the most favourable light, but has little or nothing to do with the return necessary to accomplish the stated goal of the pension plan.

2.3.2   The tactical level

At the tactical level, management is concerned with implementation of policy. Actions are concerned with risk-return tradeoffs with respect to performance measurement and asset allocation. The task is to determine what combination of active managers and passive indexes to hold in portfolio. It is the responsibility of the chief investment officer of the pension fund to obtain the tools for accomplishing this task in a manner that is consistent with established policy. This process begins with performance measurement relative to the MAR.

Should the MAR for both equities and fixed income portfolios be the mean of the benchmark identified in the ALM study, or should equity managers be measured relative to the equity component, and bond managers measured relative to the fixed income component? I believe the performance of all managers should be measured relative to the strategic MAR identified in the ALM framework shown below. (For details on this reasoning see Figure 1.12 in Chapter 1 by Sortino.)

The link between performance measurement and tactical asset allocation is the mean of the strategic benchmark, which is the MAR. In the first stage of tactical asset allocation, an efficient frontier consisting solely of passive indexes is generated. The benchmark establishes that segment of the efficient frontier that is most often relevant for implementing policy decisions (see Figure 2.2). This segment lies between the efficient portfolio that has the highest return for the same risk as the strategic benchmark (vertical arrow), and the efficient portfolio that has the least risk for the same return as the strategic benchmark (horizontal arrow).

For active managers to replace passive indexes, they would have to lie beyond the passive efficient frontier, i.e. they would have to add value. One procedure for accomplishing this is to calculate alphas for managers to see if they provide a higher return for the same level of risk. This procedure results in a different mix of styles for each portfolio on the efficient frontier in the first stage of the optimization process. A linear programming model is used to keep the style mix constant. Each vertical line that extends above the efficient frontier represents a combination of active managers and passive indexes that have the same style mix as the point on the original frontier, but have a higher return.

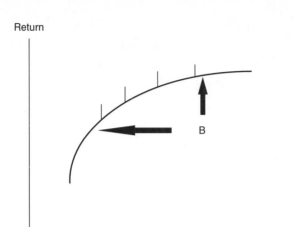

Figure 2.2 *Return versus downside risk*

2.3.3 The operational level

To make the tactical decisions operational, active and passive management firms must now be hired in accordance with the results gathered at the tactical level. Funds are transferred to each manager and purchases of securities are made. Each manager should be informed as to the risk-return procedures that will be used to evaluate their management style and their future performance. *The active managers should understand that their goal is the same as the plan sponsor's which is the same as that of the participants*: to maximize consistency and magnitude of returns above the MAR. They incur risk of failing to accomplish the client's goal if they fall below the MAR.

2.4 MEASURING ALM RISK

Clearly, risk measurement depends on the perspective of the particular interest group. Plan participants are primarily interested in the expected level of real benefits, whereas to the plan sponsor the level of contributions and the present value of contributions may be of a higher concern. Moreover, the perception of risk involves preferences that can be highly individual. Several aspects of the risk involved should be considered.

Once we have established the nature of the pension plan and its premium and investment policy, the main threat to all stakeholders is a shortfall relative to the minimum funding requirements, either now or in future time periods. For the plan participants, this calls for additional premium contributions. For the plan participants, this also involves the risk of lower future benefits. This calls for the use of downside risk measures. In particular the measurement of:

- shortfall probability – indicating the probability that shortfalls in solvency may occur in a particular period;
- risk capital – indicating the expected cash value of the shortfalls in the period under consideration, similar to Merton and Perold (1993); and
- discounted downside risk – indicating the discounted volatility of the present value of the shortfalls are the important elements.

As the fund's solvency over time is the major issue, discounted downside risk is employed (see Sortino and van der Meer, 1991). In all cases the present (cash) value for various periods and scenarios according to an option-pricing technique has to be determined (see Merton and Perold, 1993). The use of present values enables the comparison of the effects of different sets of policy parameters. Alternative policy assumptions produce different results with respect to contribution rates, real level of benefits and funding risks. The costs of alternative pension schemes with different indexing clauses and different contribution rates has to be evaluated.

2.5   CASE STUDY: PENSION FUND XYZ

The foregoing will be illustrated by a case study, based on practical experience in a Dutch pension industry environment. Characteristic for this firm is its relatively young and dynamic workforce. As a result, the turnover rate of employees is rather high. The firm XYZ regards its pension benefits as an important ingredient in its overall employee benefits package. On the one hand, the objective of pension fund XYZ is to secure the value of future benefits to a maximum extent. The level of indexing of contributions and benefits, however, is, to a considerable extent, at the discretion of the XYZ company. On the other hand, the company seeks to stabilize its premium contribution rate by assuming a dynamically calculated premium level reflecting the expectations for the coming 30 years (the analysis in this study starts in 1996).

As an illustration of the evolution of the fund over time, the development of the technical provisions is shown in Figure 2.3, assuming no growth in the number of employees. Despite the zero growth, the population of employees changes and the number of former employees increases rapidly.[1]

Since the population is rather young on average, the actual number of pensioners increases only slowly until the year 2025. Of course the main part of the provisions are those corresponding to the regular retirement pensions of the employees. The next part corresponds to the reserves held for the partners' pensions. The reserve held for additional and temporary pensions (which is not shown) accounts for the next largest part. The reserves of former employees are included in reserved values. Given the strong growth in this number, the turnover rate of employees has an important effect on the total value of the liabilities.

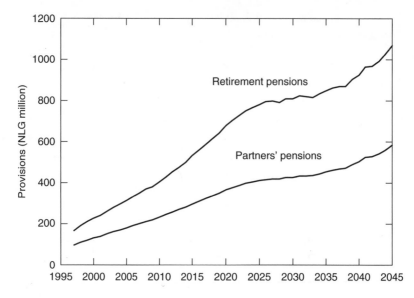

Figure 2.3   *Pension fund of Company XYZ*

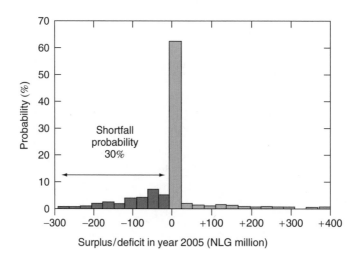

Figure 2.4   *Shortfall probability*

2.5.1   Shortfall probability

Let us now take a look at the risk and returns of the pension fund XYZ. The probability of attaining a particular shortfall or surplus level ten years from now should be analysed. An annually rebalanced asset mix, including 70% long-term government bonds and 30% equities, is considered. As can be observed from

Figure 2.4, the probability of a shortfall in the year 2005 is about 30%. This includes all levels of shortfalls ranging from minus NLG 300 million to zero and assumes that possible previous shortfalls have been funded. If the entire probability distribution is known, the shortfall probabilities corresponding to certain pre-specified target levels can easily be determined.

For instance, the probability of a shortfall in excess of NLG 200 million is less than 5%, under the policy assumptions made. If the fund's management feels that a shortfall over NLG 200 million is unacceptable, then strategies can be designed to avoid this possibility.

In section 2.4 above, reference is made to the expected present value of shortfalls as 'risk capital', and to the scenario-weighted volatility of the present shortfalls as 'discounted downside risk'. The probability distribution of the shortfalls is non-symmetric as a result of the interactions between several policy and plan characteristics. This increases the relevance of downside risk measures.

2.5.2   Level of indexing

As was mentioned at the start of this case study, the level of guaranteed indexing is one of the determinants. By limiting the level of indexing, the costs of pension liabilities can be reduced. However, limiting the level of indexing also affects the future level of benefits and thereby determines the quality of the pension scheme to the participants. Consider how a cap on the indexing of future benefits affects their relative purchasing power: by capping indexing, i.e. indexing occurs if the inflation rate is below the cap; whereas, in case of an inflation rate higher than the cap, the level of indexing equals that of the cap rate. For very low levels on the index cap, the purchasing power of the benefits declines rapidly with the length of time under consideration (see Figure 2.5). For instance, the thick line in this figure shows that after 15 years (in 2010) the average purchasing power value will be 63% in terms if its current counterpart, when the cap on inflation equals 0% and no indexing occurs. By increasing the level of the cap, the average purchasing power of the benefits rises, until the cap is sufficiently high to ensure that inflation will not rise above the cap rate. Clearly, the level of indexing is one important aspect in the design of the pension plan that critically affects the quality of the plan to the participants.

The three-dimensional Figure 2.5 shows that by putting together the 1996 purchasing power of premiums (see vertical axes) and the level of inflation-resistance (see horizontal axes with index cap at 15%), the time-related consequences of the index policy can be analysed. The next step is to relate the index cap to the two other important determinants of the pension policy, i.e. premium contributions as a percentage of wages and the discounted downside risk (see section 2.4). Thus the important dimensions of pension fund risk can be joined.

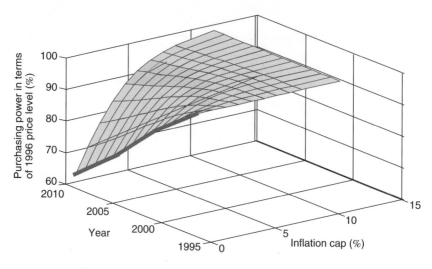

Figure 2.5   *Development and purchasing power versus inflation*

2.5.3   Coherent determinants of the pension fund policy

In Figure 2.6, the mentioned dimensions are shown in their relative coherence. The time dimension that is visible in Figure 2.5 is implicit in Figure 2.6. This has been incorporated in the discounted downside risk by means of the real value determination of the relevant shortfalls.[2] The discounted downside risk, shown on the horizontal field, is thus a crucial determinant. If for instance we look at the vertical 'rear wall' of the figure (i.e. for a given index cap of 10%), the declining line at the back of the projected surface indicates that the premium contributions decline when the discounted downside risk increases. This decline is even stronger at a lower level of the index cap.

The connection between premium contributions and index cap for a given level of discounted downside risk can be made. As was to be expected, a reduction of the index cap causes a decline in premium contributions (shown in the 'grid' by means of lines that move from the back downwards to the front). Thus a graphical depiction of a kind of risk universe for the case study of pension fund XYZ can be achieved.

Of course, the shape of the risk universe depends on the investment policy and the involved risks. In this respect, each point in the downside risk universe, i.e. each point of the curved surface, hides an optimum investment portfolio. In order to determine the surface for this specific situation the minimum risk strategy based on (annually rebalanced) portfolios of investment in two asset categories, i.e. fixed income and equities has to be considered. Thereby risk is measured by the previously defined discounted downside risk measure, based on

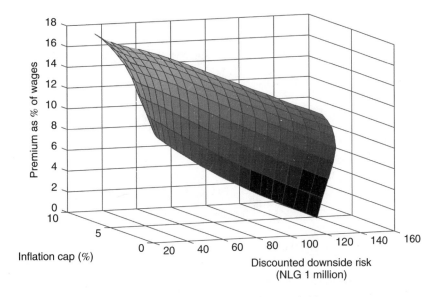

Figure 2.6   *Premiums, inflation cap and risk*

the projection period covering the next 15 years. Low risk portfolios obviously include a high proportion of fixed income.

Figure 2.6 illustrates that the average required contribution rate can be reduced by assuming an additional risk. Moving to the right-hand side of the universe, the level of discounted downside risk increases by adopting alternative investment strategies for a particular level of the index cap. In other words, by changing the level of the discounted downside risk determinant, the strategic asset allocation will change. From the bell-shaped line on the right-hand side of the universe, one can deduce that the risk increases non-proportionally as the contribution level decreases, as an increase in the index cap also corresponds to an increasing risk.

2.6   ALM AT THE LEVEL OF THE PLAN SPONSOR

Until now, only limited attention has been addressed to the solvency aspect of the fund in relation to the solvency of the fund's sponsor. In the case of the imaginary pension fund XYZ, this in the corporation XYZ. It has been argued by interest groups representing the fund retirees, that part of the gains should be kept within the funds in terms of a lower contribution level, in order to secure the level of future indexing against termination of premium payments by the sponsor as a result of financial distress.

There are four alternative conditions the fund may be in. When both the fund and the fund's sponsor are solvent, there are no problems. When the fund is insolvent, whereas the sponsor is solvent, additional payments by the fund's sponsor are demanded by the fund's regulator. Although this can be undesirable to the sponsor, the payments can be met since the sponsor is solvent. When the fund is solvent whereas the sponsor is not, indexing of the fund is secured as yet by the solvency of the fund. In general, however, this situation will frequently result in a fourth possibility, where both the fund and the sponsor are insolvent. The risk involved in this situation is called default risk.

The reason for this transition is that the solvability of the fund, as measured by the regulators, is generally based on current benefits, not on indexed benefits. Therefore, what plan participants typically stand to lose is the level of indexing. Additional ALM risks due to aggressive portfolio strategies generally result in asymmetric risk to the plan participants. Where the main gains in terms of lower premium contributions accrue to the sponsor, the risk in terms of losing indexing primarily accrue to the participants (in this argumentation the default risk is partly based on the meaning of the definition of the solvability of the fund).

To analyse the effect of credit risk in future premium contributions, the universe indicating the relation between indexing, premium contributions and investment policy, has to be redrawn. The universe is therefore limited by taking into account the present value of the pension liabilities, adjusted to the default risk.

Of course this default risk-adjusted present value depends on the particular term structure of the solvency pressure for the sponsor during the period considered. By determining the universe in this way, it links directly to the present value of the liabilities. Here, one should think of the present value as a best estimate of the market value of the liabilities. Figure 2.7 shows that for the case study, the universe is limited (compared to the universe of Figure 2.6). By assuming more ALM risk the present value declines, albeit at a slower rate, than the average contribution rate; the decline in present value corresponds with a small increase in the level of indexing.

2.7 DETERMINATION OF THE STRATEGIC INVESTMENT PORTFOLIO

The final element in the analysis of the pension fund universe concerns the actual determination of the strategic investment portfolio. As already indicated, each point on the risk universe represents a particular strategic portfolio mix. Therefore, one can analyse any point of the universe in relation to the corresponding strategic investment portfolio. See for instance the dot 'P' in Figure 2.7. The (annually rebalanced) portfolio that is represented by this dot consists of 15% in equities and 85% in fixed income. This investment policy results in a minimal discounted risk of NLG 34 million, a contribution level of 13% premium (as a percentage of salaries) and a 3% cap on indexing.

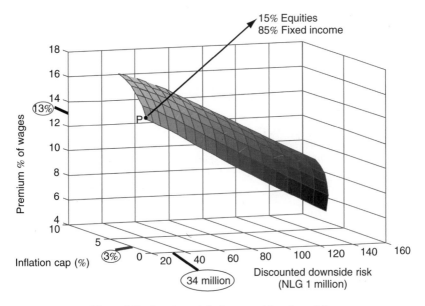

Figure 2.7   *Premiums, inflation cap, risk and portfolio*

2.8   CONCLUSION

The importance of the asset allocation decision to the investment performance of pension funds has been demonstrated. Decisions regarding the strategic investment portfolio indeed warrant close attention. It is, however, inappropriate to base these decisions solely on the risk and return characteristics of the individual asset classes, the so-called asset-only framework. In determining the optimum asset allocation for pension funds a comprehensive analysis of risks and returns is required for all parties involved. Such an analysis, however, is complicated by the fact that several periods have to be considered and have to include the effects of this uncertainty in the results. A set of criteria based on the downside risk concept has to be defined that enables analysis of the pension fund while allowing for adjustments for deviations in shortfalls in timing and scenario. The relationships that exist between the nature of the pension plan, the premium policy and the investment policy have been illustrated by a case study. In this so-called asset liability framework these three determinants are closely connected. It is of major importance to determine an optimal balance between these determinants. Thus the so-called strategic benchmark is generated, a guideline for the investment activities and thus a standard for performance measurement in an asset liability framework. By integrating the various elements of an pension fund policy into a coherent structure, an optimum blueprint for the investment policy and liability policy can be determined. This blueprint should provide a cost effective balance to the interests of both the plan sponsor and the plan participants.

NOTES

1. The probability distribution for the future inflation rates depends on the current state of the economy and requires sophisticated modelling based on all available information. Assumptions are: average inflation of 3%, a return on cash of 1%, a return on longer maturity bonds of 2% and a return on equities of 6%. Historical volatilities on Dutch market returns and inflation (1949–96) are used.
2. See section 2.5 where reference is made to the corresponding method of Merton and Perold (1993).

REFERENCES

Merton, R.C. and Perold, A. (1993) The theory of risk capital for financial institutions, *Journal of Applied Corporate Finance*.

Sortino, F. and van der Meer, R.A.H. (1991) Downside risk, *Journal of Portfolio Management*, Summer.

Sortino, F., van der Meer, R.A.H. and Plantinga, A. (1999) The Dutch Triangle, *Journal of Portfolio Management*, Fall.

Van der Meer, R.A.H. and Smink, M. (1998) Applying downside risk to asset-liability management: a pension fund case study, *Journal of Performance Measurement*, Spring.

Chapter 3

The consultant/financial planner's view: a new paradigm for advising individual accounts

SUMMARY

In this chapter two paradigms are identified for the implementation of financial services by consultants to defined benefit (DB) plans on the one hand, and financial planners for individuals on the other. The investment consultant paradigm focuses on who will manage the money, while the financial planning paradigm focuses on the client's lifestyle goal. The blending of these two paradigms will likely be the result of the explosive growth of capital into 401(k) type plans.

3.1 THE INVESTMENT CONSULTANT PARADIGM

The investment consulting business developed in the late 1960s and early 1970s to meet the demands of plan sponsors of defined benefit (DB) plans. Plan sponsors hired consultants to assist them in meeting the fiduciary responsibilities mandated by ERISA, enacted in 1974. Their foremost need was to hire external money managers. An external focus on performance evaluation grew out of the competitive strategy of employing the best portfolio managers in the market place. Actuaries were hired to deal with the liabilities and consultants were hired to deal with the assets; hence the term asset manager became interchangeable with portfolio manager.

Implementation in the investment consulting arena has generally been with separate accounts. Because the large account sizes could meet the required high minimums for separate account management, competition for clients drove this implementation. The selection of an asset manager from hundreds, and later thousands of qualified managers, required quantitative tools for data gathering of qualitative and quantitative data on separate account managers. A side benefit is that the due diligence process for manager selection and monitoring became well defined.

The early quantitative models developed in the academic community in the 1950s measured how individual managers performed relative to the market. Soon, standard deviation, beta and expected return became an essential part of the consultant's tool kit of financial services. Performance relative to the market became the standard, and beating the market return on a risk-adjusted basis became the goal.

Since the late 1970s, measuring performance relative to a peer group has gained in popularity. In this peer group analysis, a manager's investment style is measured by the returns relative to style indexes over time. Since 1992, one of the primary performance measurement tools for accomplishing this has been returns-based style analysis, developed by William F. Sharpe (1992). Prior to that, style analysis was based only on the actual securities in the portfolio and their average fundamental characteristics such as the price to book and price to earnings ratios. Consultants can now provide answers to these questions: Is the manager really taking on more risk? Is he/she managing within the investment parameters stated? Are we comparing this manager to the right universe?

Beginning in the mid-1980s, many of the principles that had been used for institutional consulting were applied to the management of smaller individual investor portfolios. Initially these portfolios had minimum sizes of at least $1 million. But, with the introduction of the 'wrap' programmes, access to the separate account managers was reduced to accounts with as little as $100 000 per manager. Today, the estimated average 'wrap' account is around $300 000 – it may, in fact, be as low as $200 000 – and there are well over 1 million accounts in the United States, mostly managing individual investor assets in separate accounts.

The focus of performance measurement remains primarily market oriented. How is a manager doing relative to an index or blended index? Or how is a manager doing relative to other managers out there in the market place? Asset managers have learned how to get on the consultants' recommended list – beat the market. However, if they can't beat the market, then at least they aim to beat the others who didn't beat the market.

Figure 3.1 summarizes the investment consultant paradigm.

(1)   Analyse the current investments.
(2)   Design the optimal portfolio, asset allocation based on time horizon, expected return, and risk tolerance.

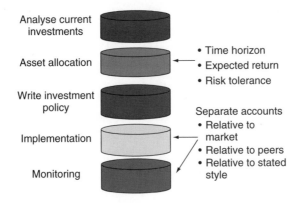

Analyse current
investments

Asset allocation   • Time horizon
   • Expected return
   • Risk tolerance

Write investment
policy   Separate accounts
   • Relative to
Implementation   market
   • Relative to peers
   • Relative to stated
Monitoring   style

Figure 3.1   *The investment consultant paradigm*

(3) Write the investment policy. The investment policy is a written state-
ment that includes the time horizon, the risk tolerance defined, the asset
allocation implemented, and the benchmarks to which performance will
be compared.

(4) Implementation is generally with separate accounts.

(5) In the monitoring process, the manager's performance is measured relative to the market, the peers, and the manager's stated style.

(6) The focus of the old paradigm is on *who manages* the money.

3.2 THE FINANCIAL PLANNING PARADIGM

Now consider the contrast between the institutional investment consultant and
the financial planner. Financial planners focus on the individual client rather
than on market activities external to the institution. They spend considerably
more effort identifying personal goals and doing needs analysis relative to those
goals. Financial planning models focus on achieving the client's desired lifestyle
or financial goals as the basis of the plan, as opposed to seeking only higher
returns relative to the market or among their peers in the profession. Considerable attention is given to understanding the impact of financial choices on an
individual's income tax situation and on the individual's desired time frame and
tradeoffs for certain financial goals. It seems that financial planners are broader
in their scope of services that they provide to their clients, and that they focus
on individuals rather than accounts. Financial planners are primarily concerned
with how the investment performance impacts the individual's financial goals.

Historically, financial planners have implemented investment strategies with
mutual funds. The availability of mutual funds and the lower minimums allow
clients to diversify even with small portfolios. The ability to report across fund
families in the 1980s drove even greater attraction to mutual funds. Because

mutual funds companies advertise heavily and have been promoted in the financial services arena, clients read and hear about them, and understand mutual funds.

The comprehensive approach in financial planning has always included strategic income tax analysis. Planners often work with a client's CPA to provide detailed tax advice. Many planners target high net worth clients with value-added services. However, the market is rapidly moving to middle income families to advise them on their individual retirement accounts and/or 401(k) plans.

Performance measurement in the financial planning market has been driven by client expectations. Many planners spend their time trying to prevent their clients from chasing returns, buying when the market is high and selling when it is low, and helping them to understand financial concepts, e.g. the risk–return tradeoff, diversification and long-term investing versus short-term volatility. The quarterly brokerage statements, along with basic portfolio accounting reports, are the typical performance measurement tools.

Because financial planners must focus on the client's goals and needs for the future, the financial planning analysis is forecast oriented. The initial and key element of a financial plan is a detailed forecast of the client's financial future, given certain assumed investment strategies and actions on the part of the client. This drives detailed forecasting models, calculations of the capital requirement to meet the goal, as well as detailed taxation analysis for short-term investing and value-added services. Financial planning disciplines are goal and needs oriented: retirement, education funding for the children, life insurance planning, estate planning.

Traditional financial planning forecast models use an estimated growth rate for assets with little or no incorporation of risk analysis into the model. The steps in the traditional retirement models are:

(1) Project the gross income needs for the period of analysis (i.e. retirement years).
(2) Discount each of these annual needs using present value formulas to the date the need will begin (i.e. retirement date).
(3) Forecast the valuation of the current assets and future investing program to the same date (i.e. retirement date). This forecast is based on expected return.
(4) Subtract the 'expected' value of the assets from the discounted gross needs to get a shortfall or surplus.
(5) Adjust the variables to reach the discounted needs goal.

The variables that are usually adjusted to reach a calculated surplus or $0 shortfall in financial planning are: return, amount of future investing, years to retirement, and lifestyle goal. When adjustments are proposed, they are typically addressed in this order.

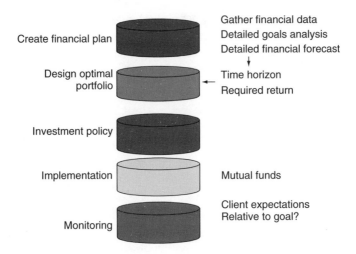

Create financial plan

Gather financial data
Detailed goals analysis
Detailed financial forecast

Design optimal portfolio

Time horizon
Required return

Investment policy

Implementation

Mutual funds

Monitoring

Client expectations
Relative to goal?

Figure 3.2   *The financial planning paradigm*

The implied variable in this methodology is risk. Let's say the following variables are fixed: cash flow available for investing, years to retirement, years of retirement, and the lifestyle goal based on client input. The return is then adjusted to solve for the desired surplus, and the implied variable is risk.

Figure 3.2 summarizes the financial planning paradigm.

The differences in the paradigms can be summarized as follows:

Investment Consultant	**Financial Planner**
• Risk tolerance drives investment policy and lifestyle limits are the implied variable	• Lifestyle goal drives required return and risk tolerance is the implied variable
• Measure performance of the manager and/or the portfolio against market and peers	• Measure performance of the client portfolio against client expectations
• In-depth risk analysis	• In-depth goals and needs analysis
• Sophisticated performance measurement with narrow focus	• Detailed forecasting with taxation and broad focus

The investment consulting paradigm focuses on *who* will manage the money. The financial planning paradigm focuses on *what* is the client's lifestyle goal. In the investment planning process, risk tolerance drives investment policy, and lifestyle limits are the implied variable. We measure manager performance against a benchmark to determine if our implementation maximizes return, given risk. In the planning process, we set the lifestyle goal, which drives the required return. Risk is the implied variable. Measurement is against the return the client needs to earn at minimum in order to accomplish the goal.

3.3   NEW PARADIGM

Three factors are driving demand for a new paradigm. The exponential growth in 401(k) plans should cause asset managers and consultants to focus on the plan participant, who now controls the money. Using the same paradigm that applied to the external focus of DB plans is no longer applicable. Instead of having one client who is trying to meet fiduciary standards for the management of one pension fund, consultants will have to provide a customized service to thousands of clients on a regular basis.

Secondly, the move toward compensation based on fees focuses the financial consultant on asset gathering. The financial plan is the ideal instrument for gathering information about all of a client's assets and the financial planning process is the ideal way to provide value-added service and become the 'trusted advisor' of the client, rather than simply the investment consultant or broker.

Additionally, the far-reaching potential of interactive Internet communication lends itself to this demand for 'mass-customization' and value-added services beyond completion of a transaction.

The ideal process for the investor would be to take the best from both worlds and create a process that relates the financial goals analysis with the investment planning process, and measure progress toward that goal. The key elements required for implementation of this new paradigm are as follows:

- Defined, efficient data gathering process
- Forecast model that incorporates asset depletion, impact of tax deferred assets, and risk into the valuation of the goal
- Risk analysis around the goal valuation
- Determination of the return required to meet the goal valuation
- Risk analysis around that required return
- Goal relative performance measurement along with peer and market relative measurement

The first of these elements is a defined data gathering process that incorporates the needs of the financial plan with the needs of investment performance measurement. Once this data gathering is defined and incorporated into the financial advisor's process, the potential for mining this data is enormous.

In addition to a combined data gathering process, there are some analysis concepts surfacing that the process might use to its advantage. Management of an individual retirement account requires recognizing the uncertainty in the assets, the liabilities and the goal itself. The uncertainty associated with the accumulation of assets is obvious, and has been studied for years. Analytical tools are available to quantify this risk, and continuing research by the investment consulting industry is making those tools better and better.

As illustrated in Figure 3.3, there is also great uncertainty associated with the liability stream to be paid out after retirement.

Inflation, changes in interest rates, and other financial and economic factors are going to affect the actual future income stream dramatically. Most of the current simulation models ignore risk during retirement, and do not capture the volatility associated with the available income stream during retirement.

In addition to ignoring or making gross assumptions about the uncertainty associated with the retirement period, current models also ignore the interdependencies and changing valuation of the goal, relative to the accumulation and depletion periods. The accepted models assume that the amount of money needed to retire can be calculated independent of the accumulation and depletion of assets. However, in reality, the tax nature and amount of each of the assets impacts the valuation of the goal. The amount required at retirement is dependent upon the type and amount of assets you have at retirement, which drives depletion order and timing of taxation during retirement. Therefore, a model that calculates the 'capital required' at retirement based on assumed gross income need during retirement ignores major fluctuations in relative taxes associated with depletion of different types of assets. Current models do not incorporate

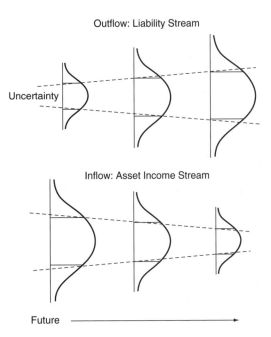

Figure 3.3   *Simulation model uncertainties*

the risk through the depletion period, nor do they recognize that the amount needed is completely dependent upon the amount of deferred taxes and the timing of the payment of those deferred taxes.

The uncertainty of what cash flows will be needed after retirement probably increases as the uncertainty associated with the future value of the assets decreases, and the uncertainty associated with how much of which type of tax-deferred asset will be available. We need a model that would give us some insight as to what these distributions might look like in each period. What happens in period 2 is not independent of what happens in period 1. In addition to analysing the risk that the individual will accumulate a given amount of money by a certain date, we must analyse the risk that the given amount of money is in fact the amount needed.

It would seem that a forecast that could simulate the uncertainty in both assets and liabilities would be preferable to the standard models currently in use. The models currently on the market calculate the value required at a date to meet a discounted value of assumed before tax need. Some models even simulate a probability distribution around this calculated valuation of need at retirement date. However, this is not the same as the probability that the goal will be met. It is the probability that a given amount of assets will grow to a given amount by a certain date, given the underlying correlations of the model are correct.

There are other practical issues that must be addressed. First, to be valid, simulation requires the correlation equations for the underlying factors. The variables and factors in a financial plan are numerous, complex, interrelated and driven by the economy, the investment environment and other external factors. Correlation of these variables requires significant research and data that is not generally available. Second, in order to be useful, the number of factors should be large enough to matter. If the simulation is done varying only investment return, for example, it is probably not much more useful than a single point estimate using expected returns.

The models that include risk analysis only include it on the accumulation or asset side of the model. They ignore variable taxation during asset depletion, and some do not have the research that validates the underlying correlations between factors. Additional research is required to create a model and a process that meets the needs of the current defined contribution and deferred taxation environment, and meets the demands of the client of the new century – a client that demands customized advice based on his or her personal financial goals.

3.4   CONCLUSION

Is there a way to put the best aspects of the financial planning model and the investment consultant model together into one process model to meet the demands of the new paradigm? Can we use financial planning techniques to

improve the investment consulting process? Can we use sophisticated investment consulting analysis to improve the financial planning process? Is there a
way to link portfolio performance to the goal as well as to the market and the
investment policy?

The answer to all of these questions is, not yet, but soon. The drive toward a
financial planning model in the investment community has already begun. The
recognition of the need for inclusion of risk in the financial planning forecast
model has already begun. Perhaps the next step will be the widespread adoption
and industry validation of a new forecasting model for financial planning that
incorporates the depletion side of the picture. What if the academic institutions
teaching financial planning recognized the shortcoming of the current capital
needs model in a tax deferred instrument environment and developed an iterative
depletion model?

Or perhaps the investment consulting community will adopt 'goal relative
performance measurement.' What if performance of each manager is measured
relative to every other manager in the market with respect to the goals of
the client, and risk is defined as failure to accomplish the goal? Performance
measures proposed by Sortino in Chapter 1 using downside risk may be on
target for this analysis.

We currently have the financial planning forecast model, that includes depletion, developed and in place. We also have all of the elements for the new
paradigm. The building blocks that we at CheckFree believe are important are
shown in Figure 3.4. This is the new paradigm that we will follow to implement
the ideas discussed above.

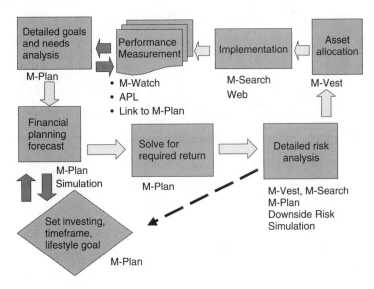

Figure 3.4   *The new paradigm*

REFERENCE

Sharpe, William F. (1992) Asset allocation: management style and performance measurement, *Journal of Portfolio Management*, Winter.

Source: This chapter was developed from a presentation the author made at a client conference for CheckFree Investment Services.

Chapter 4

The mathematician's view: modelling uncertainty with the three parameter lognormal

HAL FORSEY

SUMMARY

This chapter describes the technical underpinnings to Chapter 1 by Sortino. To facilitate the broader use of the quantitative procedures developed at the Pension Research Institute, we are providing this detailed description of these procedures, a computer program for making the calculations, and the source code to enable financial institutions to incorporate the methodology into their existing software, subject to an agreement to recognize the source of the programs.

4.1 ESTIMATING NEXT YEAR'S UNCERTAINTY

Figure 4.1 contains the last three years of monthly returns from a fund you are considering buying. You think that these returns are representative of what could happen in any given month. What is the best way to estimate the range of returns that could happen next year and calculate appropriate risk and return measures for this fund?

The worst year that actually occurred was the second year. Since returns compound it is natural to consider $(1.0076)(1.0101)(0.8761) \cdots (0.9485) - 1 = 0.043465$ or 4.3465% as the worst we might expect in the future. But it is clear that the worst return that might happen in the future could be quite different from 4.3%. Why limit ourselves to what did happen to predict what could happen. Why not take into consideration what could have happened. One way to accomplish this is called the bootstrap procedure proposed by

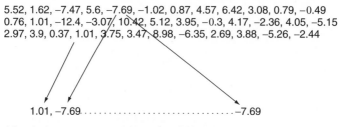

Historical worst year = + 4.35% what did happen

Bootstrap worst year = − 60% what could happen

Figure 4.1   *The bootstrap procedure*

Efron and Tibshirani (1993) at Stanford University. Let's assume that next year's return is made by compounding a random sample of 12 of the monthly returns from Figure 4.1. Our first random draw might be 1.01%, drawn from the fourth month of the third year (see arrow). The first draw is replaced and a second return is randomly selected, in this case, −7.69%. Notice this same return is again selected for the last month of one year that could have happened.

It is easy to program a computer to make lots of these random samples and organize the results in a histogram (see Figure 4.2) of 2500 of these random samples of 12 monthly returns. The returns range from −60% to 80%, with most falling around 12.7%.

The assumption that returns are uncorrelated may seem naive, but is supported by the efficient markets theorem and empirical research (Kendall, 1953; Malkiel, 1985). While there is some evidence that sequential prices tend to follow a submartingale, the correlation between every other return (e.g. 1 and 3) tends toward zero. Therefore, the bootstrapped returns are very likely uncorrelated.

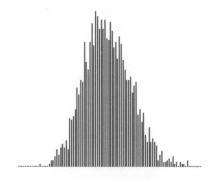

Figure 4.2   *Bootstrap returns from Figure 4.1: histogram of 2500 annual returns*

4.2 DESCRIBING THE HISTOGRAM WITH THE LOGNORMAL CURVE

Since the histogram gives a close approximation to all 2500 return values, we can approximate any useful statistic about the sample from the histogram. For example, we can calculate the mean, the standard deviation and any other useful measure of risk and return. The only information missing is the order in which the returns were generated. Since this histogram contains 100 bars it takes 102 numbers (the lowest value, the width of a bar, and the 100 heights) to define the histogram. This is quite a saving from the original 2500 returns, without any real loss of information. But we can accomplish even more with only three numbers. The basic idea is to approximate the histogram with a curve described by an equation defined with three numbers or, more technically, three parameters. As we will explain later, we will be able to compute the desired statistics about the risk and rewards of an asset from just these three parameters. To understand the nature of the curve-fitting procedure, look at the graphs in Figure 4.3.

The histogram on the left is a smoothed version of the histogram in Figure 4.2. The smoothed version was obtained by averaging bars, so it is a histogram of moving averages. We do this to bring out the underlying regularity of the returns. It is apparent that this regularity can be described with a curve. As you can see from the middle graph, we have found a curve that does a good job. The curve is not a normal curve, although it looks similar to one. If you look carefully you will notice our curve is a little skewed to the right. The normal curve is always symmetrical.

The normal curve often does a good job in describing data when each data point can be considered as the sum of terms. In our problem, each year's return was constructed as a product of monthly returns, not as a sum. So, although a normal curve might fit reasonably well, the fact that we have a product leads us to look at another curve. Statisticians have provided us with a good candidate, the lognormal (Aitchinson and Brown, 1957). Remember, logarithms translate a product into a sum. So the basic idea is simple. If data points are constructed as a product then their logarithms will often follow fairly closely a normal distribution. Rather than working with logarithms of data, we can do some

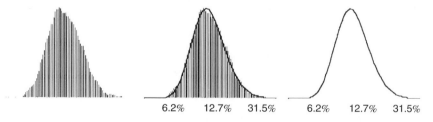

Figure 4.3 *Fitting the three parameter lognormal: smoothed histogram, smoothed histogram with lognormal curve and the lognormal curve*

mathematics and translate the normal curve to another curve, the lognormal, which describes the data directly. Here we use a three parameter version of the lognormal for our curve, not the basic two parameter lognormal. This allows us a great deal more flexibility. As you see, it fits quite well in our example. We have found that it gives an excellent fit to bootstrapped data in all but the most extreme situations.

4.3 SOME DETAILS OF THE THREE PARAMETER LOGNORMAL

The formulas for the lognormal are not pretty. They are generally described in terms of the parameters for the underlying normal. So, with the logarithmic translations, they can get a bit involved. The basic formulas are collected in the Appendix to this chapter. Also in the Appendix is information about computer code for doing these calculations. So we will not concern ourselves here with these technical details. What we will do is describe the essentials.

First, what are the three parameters? There is some choice in selecting the parameters. We made these selections so that the meanings of the parameters would be easily understood in terms of the annual returns. The parameters are the mean, the standard deviation and the extreme value of the annual returns. You are probably already familiar with the mean and standard deviation. The mean is a measure of the central tendency and the standard deviation a measure of the spread of the curve. These two parameters are enough to describe a normal and the standard lognormal. But the three parameter version of the lognormal uses another parameter. A lognormal curve has either a largest value or a smallest value (see Figure 4.4). This third parameter, the extreme value, allows us to shift and flip the distribution.

The next step is to express all the basic formulas in terms of our parameters. The mathematical derivation of these formulas is not important for understanding their use and so will not be given here. However the important final formulas are collected in the Appendix. Now we must find a way of estimating the parameters from a sample. We choose to solve this problem by using the sample mean and

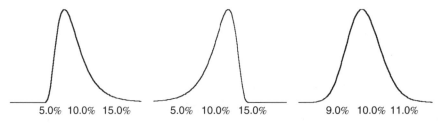

Figure 4.4 *The third parameter. Notice that the first curve has a minimum at about 0%, the middle curve has a maximum at about 20%, and the third curve is a normal curve and theoretically has no maximum or minimum*

sample standard deviation to estimate the mean and standard deviation of the underlying lognormal. Our estimate of the extreme value was selected on the basis of simulations. These simulations showed that only a rough estimate of the extreme value is required to obtain a reasonable lognormal fit. We estimate it as follows. First, calculate the minimum and the maximum of the sample and take the one closest to the mean. The extreme value is obtained from this value by moving it four standard deviations further from the mean. For example, if the mean, standard deviation, minimum, and maximum of a sample are 12%, 8%, −15%, and 70%, respectively, then the extreme value is (−15%) − (7)(8%) = −71%, since the minimum is closer to the mean than the maximum.

4.4   MEASUREMENTS BASED ON THE MAR

The minimum acceptable return, or MAR, is described in Frank Sortino's chapter 'From alpha to omega' (Chapter 1). We describe here four measurements based on the MAR. They are:

- *Upside probability*: the probability that a return exceeds the MAR.
- *Downside deviation*: a measure similar to the standard deviation but measures only deviations below the MAR.
- *Upside potential*: the probable return in excess of the MAR.
- *Upside potential ratio*: the ratio of upside potential to downside deviation.

Each of these measurements requires that the uncertainty of investment returns be described with a probability distribution like the lognormal. The formal definitions are given in the Appendix. The statistics in Figure 4.5 can be quickly calculated with the software described below.

The first two examples in Figure 4.5 differ only in extreme values. One is a maximum and the other a minimum. Please notice how different these two examples are even though they have the same mean and standard deviation. These differences cannot be captured by the normal curve. The third example is similar to the first but with a higher MAR. (Please refer to Chapter 1 for further discussion.)

Parameters and Statistics	Example 1	Example 2	Example 3
Mean	12%	12%	12%
Standard deviation	22%	22%	22%
Extreme value	−50%	74%	−50%
MAR	7.5%	7.5%	13.5%
Upside probability	51.9%	74%	40.4%
Downside deviation	10.5%	15.5%	14.3%
Upside potential	10.6%	11.2%	7.8%
Upside potential ratio	1.01	0.73	0.55

Figure 4.5

4.5   FITTING PORTFOLIOS WITH THE LOGNORMAL

Portfolios are made up of assets. Ultimately we are concerned with the return and risk of our portfolio, not with the return and risk of the individual assets. We have modelled the returns of assets with the lognormal. Can we make use of these models to fit a lognormal to a portfolio? From our choice of parameters, it is fairly clear how to proceed. We can calculate both the mean and the standard deviation of the returns of a portfolio from the means and standard deviations of the assets comprising the portfolio. All we need are some basic formulas from portfolio theory provided in every textbook in finance (e.g. Bodie, Kane and Marcus, 1993). Our problem then reduces to finding a reasonable estimate of the extreme value. Again, we used simulation and found that, if the minimum for the portfolio is taken to be the weighted combination of the minimum of the assets, and similarly for the maximum, we get an estimate for the extreme value using the same method as for individual assets.

It is an important fact that the lognormal approaches the normal as the extreme value moves further from the mean. The above estimation method for the extreme value will often result in a lognormal fit to a portfolio that is close to normal. This is reasonable since the returns of a portfolio are a weighted sum of the returns of its constituent assets, and therefore might be expected to be close to a normal distribution. Figure 4.6 shows how the lognormal approaches the normal as the extreme value moves further from the mean.

4.6   EXTENSION USING SCENARIOS

We know that next year's returns are dependent on economic and market forces that are changing. What can be done to include these changing conditions into our model? We briefly describe one approach, based on market scenarios. The idea is to divide past returns into a handful of groups based on the market scenario existing when they were generated. We then use our bootstrap approach to fit a lognormal curve to each asset for each scenario. Finally, we obtain a probability model for next year's return by using a mixture of these lognormal models with weights chosen according to our beliefs about next year's scenario.

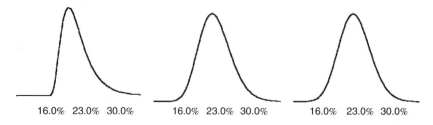

16.0%	23.0%	30.0%	16.0%	23.0%	30.0%	16.0%	23.0%	30.0%

Figure 4.6   *Lognormal graphs with identical mean and standard deviation. The extreme values are 2, 9 and 16 standard deviations below the mean. Note that the graphs approach a normal curve*

4.7   DESCRIPTION OF LOGNORMAL SOFTWARE

Included with this book is a CD containing the Visual Basic source code I wrote for a program that will allow you to become familiar with the relationship between the shape of the lognormal curve and the three parameters. You will also be able to test with your own data the bootstrap and the lognormal fit. Included on the software is the computation of many of the risk–return measures defined in terms of the minimum acceptable return described by Frank Sortino in Chapter 1. Only purchasers of this book are authorized to use this source code for commercial purposes.

APPENDIX: BASIC MATHEMATICAL FORMULAS FOR THE THREE PARAMETER LOGNORMAL

The three basic parameters estimated from the sample

$$\text{Mean} = \text{sample mean}$$
$$\text{SD} = \text{sample standard deviation}$$
$$\tau = \text{extreme value computed as described above}$$

Some auxiliary parameters

$$\text{Dif} = |\text{Mean} - \tau|$$

$$\sigma = \ln\left(\left(\frac{\text{SD}}{\text{Dif}}\right)^2 + 1\right)$$

$$\mu = \ln(\text{Dif}) - \sigma^2$$

$$\alpha = \frac{1}{(\sqrt{2\pi} \cdot \sigma)}$$

$$\beta = -\frac{1}{(2\sigma^2)}$$

Formula for the lognormal curve $f(x)$

If the extreme value is a minimum and x is greater than the extreme value then

$$f(x) = \frac{\alpha}{x - \tau} \cdot \exp(\beta \cdot (\ln(x - \tau) - \mu))$$

If the extreme value is a maximum and x is less than the extreme value then

$$f(x) = \frac{\alpha}{\tau - x} \cdot \exp(\beta \cdot (\ln(\tau - x) - \mu))$$

Formula for the lognormal cumulative distribution function $F(x)$

If the extreme value is a minimum and x is greater than the extreme value then

$$F(x) = 1 - \frac{erfc(\ln(x - \tau) - \mu)}{2\sqrt{2} \cdot \sigma}$$

If the extreme value is a maximum and x is less than the extreme value then

$$F(x) = 1 - \frac{erfc(\ln(\tau - x) - \mu)}{2\sqrt{2} \cdot \sigma}$$

Note   *erfc* is the complementary error function.

Statistics based on the MAR

$$\text{Upside probability} = 1 - F(\text{MAR})$$

$$\text{Downside deviation} = \sqrt{\int_{-\infty}^{\text{MAR}} (\text{MAR} - x)^2 f(x)\, dx}$$

$$\text{Upside potential} = \int_{\text{MAR}}^{\infty} (x - \text{MAR}) f(x)\, dx$$

$$\text{Upside potential ratio} = \frac{\text{Upside Potential}}{\text{Downside Deviation}}$$

Note   Analytic expressions for these statistics are given in the software included with this book.

REFERENCES

Aitchinson, J. and Brown, J.A.C. (1957) *The Lognormal Distribution*, Cambridge University Press: Cambridge.

Bodie, Zvi, Kane, Alex and Marcus, Alan (1993) *Investments*, Richard D. Irwin: Homewood, IL.

Efron, Bradley and Tibshirani, Robert J. (1993) *An Introduction to the Bootstrap*, Chapman and Hall: London.

Kendall, Maurice (1953) The analysis of economic time series, *Journal of the Royal Statistical Society*, 96.

Malkiel, B. (1985) *A Random Walk Down Wall Street*, W.W. Norton: New York.

Chapter 5

A software developer's view: using Post-Modern Portfolio Theory to improve investment performance measurement

BRIAN M. ROM AND KATHLEEN W. FERGUSON

Reprinted with permission of the *Journal of Portfolio Management*,
The Spaulding Group, NY, USA.

SUMMARY

Originally used to improve portfolio optimization and asset allocation, Post-Modern Portfolio Theory (PMPT) is increasingly being applied to measuring the investment performance of portfolios, investment managers and mutual funds. This chapter offers a primer on PMPT, with particular emphasis on performance measurement. Relevant research studies and performance-related case studies are presented together with a response to some of the criticisms and misconceptions that have arisen with regard to these techniques.

5.1 POST-MODERN PORTFOLIO THEORY

The foundations of traditional Modern Portfolio Theory (MPT), the standard for much of the portfolio analysis of the past four decades, are standard deviation and normal distribution. These two measures have a major limitation in common – they are symmetrical. Using standard deviation implies that better-than-expected returns are just as risky as those returns that are worse than expected. Furthermore, using the normal distribution to model the pattern of investment returns makes managers with more upside than downside returns appear more risky than they really are, and vice-versa for portfolios with more downside returns. The result is that using traditional MPT techniques for measuring investment performance frequently obscures important performance information.

It has long been recognized that investors typically do not view as risky those returns above the minimum they must earn in order to achieve their investment objectives. They believe that risk has to do with the bad outcomes (i.e. returns below a required target), not the good outcomes (i.e. returns in excess of the target) and that losses weigh more heavily than gains. This view has been noted by researchers in finance, economics and psychology for many years.[1] Noteworthy among these are Sharpe (1964):

> *Under certain conditions, the mean-variance approach can be shown to lead to unsatisfactory predictions of behavior. Markowitz suggests that models based on semi-variance would be preferable; in light of the formidable computational problems, however, he bases his analysis on the variance and standard deviation.*

and Kaplan (1997):

> *The appeal of below-target semi-variance[2] as a risk measure is that it looks only at the dispersion of bad outcomes. Variance (and therefore also standard deviation) looks instead at the dispersion of all outcomes, whether good or bad.*

In 1987, Frank A. Sortino, director of the Pension Research Institute at San Francisco State University, developed the practical mathematical algorithms of PMPT that are in use today. These methods provide a framework that recognizes investors' preferences for upside over downside volatility. At the same time, a more robust model for the pattern of investment returns, the three-parameter lognormal distribution, was introduced.

5.1.1   The tools of PMPT

5.1.1.1   Downside risk

Downside risk is measured by target semi-deviation (the square root of target semi-variance) and is termed downside deviation. It is expressed in percentages and therefore allows for rankings in the same way as standard deviation.

A familiar way to view downside risk is the annualized standard deviation of returns below the target. Another is the square root of the probability-weighted squared below-target returns. The squaring of the below-target returns has the effect of penalizing failures at an exponential rate. This is consistent with observations made on the behaviour of individual decision-making under uncertainty.[3]

There are two formulas for downside risk.

The *continuous* form:

$$\sqrt{\int_{-\infty}^{t} (t - r)^2 f(r) \, dr}$$

where,

> t is the annual target return,
>
> r is the random variable representing the return for the distribution of annual returns $f(r)$,

$f(r)$ is a normal or three-parameter lognormal distribution.

The *discrete* form:

$$3.464^* \sqrt{\frac{E(t-r)^2}{n}}$$

where

3.464 is the square root of 12, the factor used to annualize the monthly downside risk,

> E is the mathematical expectations operator;
>
> t is the monthly target return,
>
> r is the random variable representing monthly return,
>
> n is the total number of monthly returns observed.

Although more difficult to calculate, the continuous form is preferable for the following reasons.

(1) The continuous form permits all calculations to be made using *annual* returns, the natural way for investors to specify their investment goals. The discrete form requires monthly returns for there to be sufficient data points to make a meaningful calculation, which in turn requires converting the annual target into a monthly target. This significantly affects the amount of risk that is identified. For example, a goal of earning 1% each and every month results in greater risk than a goal of earning 12% each and every year.

(2) A second reason for preferring the continuous form to the discrete form has been proposed by Sortino (1997):

> *Before we make an investment, we don't know what the outcome will be ... After the investment is made, and we want to measure its performance, all we know is what the outcome was, not what it could have been. To cope with this uncertainty, we assume that a reasonable estimate of the range of possible returns, as well as the probabilities associated with those returns can be estimated ... In statistical terms, the shape of [this] uncertainty is called a probability distribution.*
>
> *In other words, looking at just the discrete monthly values does not tell the whole story. Instead, these values need to be used to help identify a distribution of all the values that could have been earned. From this distribution, we then can measure the risk that was taken.*

Using the observed points to create a distribution is a staple of conventional performance measurement. For example, monthly returns are used to calculate a fund's mean and standard deviation. Using these values *and the properties of the normal distribution*, we can make statements such as the likelihood of losing money (even though no negative returns may actually have been observed), or the range within which two-thirds of all returns lie (even though the returns identified in this way do not necessarily have to have actually occurred). Our ability to make these statements comes from the process of assuming the continuous form of the normal distribution and certain of its well-known properties.

In PMPT an analogous process is followed:

(1) observe the monthly returns,
(2) fit a distribution[4] that permits asymmetry to the observations,
(3) annualize the monthly returns, making sure the shape characteristics of the distribution are retained,
(4) apply integral calculus to the resultant distribution to calculate the appropriate statistics.

Figure 5.1 highlights the fact that downside risk is a *relative* risk measure, dependent upon the investor's investment goal which is specified as the target rate of return.

5.1.1.2 *Downside frequency and average downside deviation. . . how often and by how much?*

Just as standard deviation uses the properties of the normal distribution to calculate probabilities and ranges of returns, the properties of PMPT can be used to provide additional insights in interpreting performance results. From the continuous form, two components of downside risk can be calculated: downside frequency and average downside deviation.

Downside frequency measures the frequency with which the returns have fallen below a target. Average downside deviation is the average shortfall below the target – *in those instances in which the* **target** *was not achieved*. With these, we can measure the frequency and magnitude of the failure. This information can provide useful insights as to the source of the risk.

Table 5.1 illustrates this for a 9% target. The Russell 2000 shows a substantially lower failure rate (as measured by downside frequency) than EAFE, but the average shortfall (as measured by the average downside deviation) is higher. Overall, the Russell 2000 is the riskier of the two (as measured by downside deviation) because of the exponential weighting of the average downside deviation in the downside deviation calculation. A similar pattern is seen when comparing the S&P and Lehman indexes. Of course, different results will be found when using different targets and time periods.

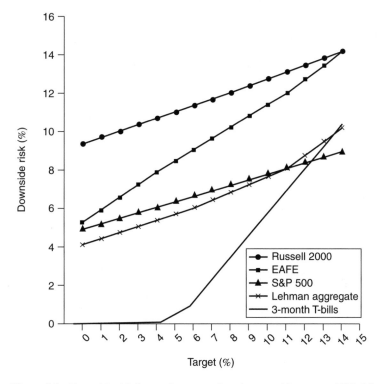

Figure 5.1 *Downside risk for varying targets based on monthly returns, 1992–96*

Table 5.1 *PMPT statistics[a] for 9.0% target for five years, 1992–96*

Index	Downside deviation (%)	Downside frequency (%)	Average downside deviation (%)
90-day T-bill	4.64	100.00	4.63
Lehman aggregate	6.85	49.67	5.38
S&P 500	7.37	21.42	9.95
MSCI EAFE	10.36	55.98	11.54
Russell 2000	12.15	24.15	14.95

[a]Care must be taken with these statistics, since using them independently of each other can lead to erroneous conclusions. For an excellent review of this topic, see Balzer (1994).

5.1.1.3 Sortino ratio

The Sortino ratio measures returns adjusted for the target and downside risk. It is defined as:

$$\frac{r - t}{d}$$

where

r = the annualized rate of return,
t = the target return,
d = downside risk.

This ratio replaces the traditional Sharpe ratio as a means for ranking investment results. Table 5.2 shows risk-adjusted performance for several major indexes using both Sortino and Sharpe ratios. Notice how the Lehman aggregate and MSCI EAFE compare – the Lehman ranks higher using the Sharpe ratio whereas EAFE ranks higher using the Sortino ratio. In many cases, manager or index rankings will be different, depending on the risk-adjusted measure used. This is illustrated in more detail later in this chapter.

5.1.1.4 Volatility skewness

Volatility skewness is the ratio of a distribution's upside variance to its downside variance, where the variances are measured relative to the mean. If the distribution is symmetrical, it has a skewness of 1.00. Values greater than 1.00 indicate positive skewness and values less than 1.00 indicate negative skewness.

Table 5.3 shows the skewness and variance components of several major indexes. Only the T-bill index has approximately equal upside and downside variance – all the others are significantly positively or negatively skewed.

Skewness does not appear to be related to the overall market environment. One might expect that bull markets produce positive skewness and bear markets negative skewness. For the period analysed in Table 5.3, the S&P 500 returned in excess of 15% per year; yet it is significantly negatively skewed. The shape of this index is confirmed by the statistical skewness.

Figure 5.2 shows the actual distribution of the S&P 500 for this period compared to its normal approximation. The significant negative skewness is clearly evident.

Table 5.2 *Risk-adjusted ratios for five years, 1992–96*

Index	Sortino ratio*	Sharpe ratio
90-day T-bill	−1.00	0.00
Lehman aggregate	−0.29	0.63
MSCI EAFE	−0.05	0.30
Russell 2000	0.55	0.93
S&P 500	0.84	1.25

*Based on monthly returns vs. 9.0% annual target.

Table 5.3   *Skewness statistics for five years, 1992–96*

Index	Volatility skewness	% of total variance from returns above the mean	% of total variance from returns below the mean	Statistical skewness*
Lehman aggregate	0.48	32.35	67.65	−0.18
Russell 2000	0.59	37.19	62.81	0.59
S&P 500	0.63	38.63	61.37	−0.28
90-day T-bill	0.93	48.26	51.74	−0.01
MSCI EAFE	1.21	54.67	45.33	0.13

*This is the usual statistical measure of skewness (the third moment of the distribution). Zero skewness represents symmetry while positive and negative values indicate positive and negative skewness, respectively.

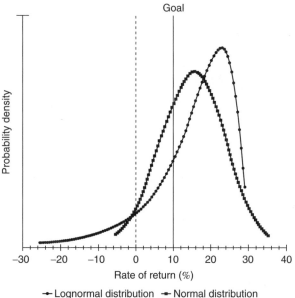

Figure 5.2   *Distribution of S&P 500 lognormal fit to monthly returns, 1992–96*

Figure 5.3 shows the results of a more comprehensive statistical analysis on return distributions.

We tested the hypothesis that the normal distribution is an accurate representation of the distributions of several major asset classes over a wide range of time periods.[5] The results, summarized in Figure 5.3, are dramatic. Overall, returns for the five indexes are not normally distributed more than 60% of the time. The frequency of non-normality ranged from 45.5% for EAFE to 85.7% for the Russell 2000. This finding has significant implications for investors using standard deviation to measure the riskiness of their portfolios.

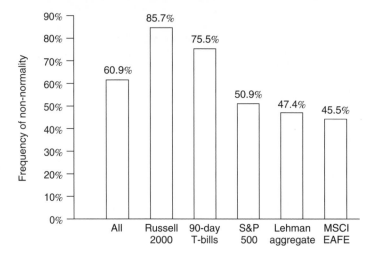

Figure 5.3   *Frequency of non-normal returns for major asset classes*

5.2   PMPT IN PRACTICE

The tools of PMPT have many practical applications in performance measurement today. Used together, they can help investors understand how performance results were achieved and whether there was compensation for the level of risk taken. The following case studies demonstrate two different approaches to using PMPT for performance measurement.

5.2.1   Ranking managers by risk-adjusted return

The Sortino and Sharpe ratios both measure risk-adjusted performance. They differ in the selection of reference return (target and risk-free rate, respectively), and risk measure (downside deviation and standard deviation, respectively). The following example illustrates how the rankings of investment managers can be affected by the choice of the risk-adjusted measure.

Thirty equity managers were randomly selected from the Bankers Trust/ Independent Consultants Consortium database.[6] The managers were ranked according to Sortino and Sharpe ratios for the ten-year period through 1995. The average changes in rankings for each manager are shown in Figure 5.4.

The ranking changes due to the selection of both risk-adjusted measure and target returns are clearly significant. In fact, we found in some cases individual firms tended to rank better or worse depending on the target selected, suggesting that some firms are better suited for certain investment assignments than others. This is particularly important for practitioners. Furthermore, using the Sortino ratio in this way is an effective screening mechanism to help identify managers

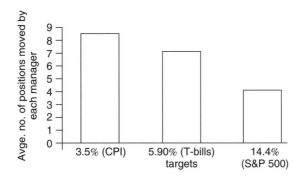

Figure 5.4 *Effect of manager rankings due to use of Sortino vs. Sharpe ratio (30 manager sample: annual returns, 1986–95)*

who should be further evaluated for a particular assignment. It can also be used to complement a style analysis being used for manager screening.

5.2.2 Comparing two managers

Additional analysis using downside frequency, average downside deviation and skewness can provide further insights into the characteristics of the managers, as illustrated in the following example. We have already shown that standard deviation can distort investment performance and lead to erroneous conclusions. This example illustrates this point as well: risk and return statistics for the five years 1991 through 1995 for two actual managers are shown in Table 5.4.

Traditional MPT analysis shows that the managers have identical Sharpe ratios, indicating that each has provided the same level of return per unit of volatility. PMPT analysis shows a very different picture, with Manager A's Sortino ratio more than 10 times that of Manager B. On this basis, A is clearly preferred to B. How can we explain these differences? The answer lies in the

Table 5.4 *Comparative statistics for MPT and PMPT performance analyses*

	Manager A	Manager B	Better manager
Return	19.3%	16.6%	A
MPT analysis			
Standard deviation	10.5%	9.0%	B
Sharpe ratio	1.84	1.84	Same
PMPT analysis (10% target)			
Downside risk	2.1%	17.4%	A
Sortino ratio	4.43	0.38	A
Volatility skewness	1.41	0.41	A
Upside volatility	58.4%	41.6%	A
Downside volatility	29.1%	70.9%	A

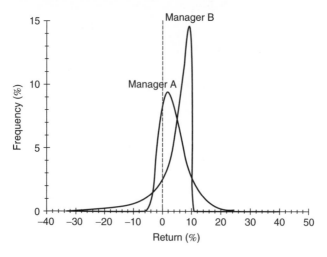

Figure 5.5 *Distribution of returns for Managers A and B*

shapes of the two distributions, which are shown in Figure 5.5. Manager B's distribution is negatively skewed. This is indicated by its tail extending more to the left than the right, illustrating a preponderance of downside (i.e. 'bad') volatility. In contrast, A's distribution is *positively* skewed, which is indicated by its tail extending more to the right than the left. This illustrates this manager's large upside (i.e. 'good') volatility. These two managers' performance records are clearly not similar, although they are indistinguishable from each other when viewed from a Sharpe ratio perspective!

The volatility skewness figures in Table 5.4 confirm this analysis: Manager A has significant positive skewness, while B has significant negative skewness, relative to a symmetrical distribution (1.00). Additional insights come from the upside and downside volatility values: Manager A has twice as much volatility from upside returns than downside returns; Manager B, on the other hand, has significantly more downside returns than upside returns.

This example shows how the PMPT analysis can be used to lift the veil of obscurity on each manager's true investment performance. In general, the Sharpe ratio can be safely used if the distributions are known to be close to normal *and* the goal is close to the risk-free rate. In all other circumstances the Sortino ratio will provide a more accurate result.

5.3 CRITICISMS AND MISCONCEPTIONS

5.3.1 Upside ignored

Some critics of downside risk claim that eliminating the upside returns from the risk calculation is incorrect since strongly positive returns somehow imply the inevitability of correspondingly strong negative returns. 'There is no free lunch in investing', and 'eventually, the Piper must be paid', are typical remarks in this vein. This criticism is anecdotal and is unsupported by any published research.

Since the mean of the distribution captures the upside returns, nothing is lost by concentrating on downside returns exclusively for the risk calculation. Any calculation of risk-adjusted returns, such as the Sortino ratio, will automatically consider the upside.

5.3.2   Difficulty in choosing a single target

The downside risk calculation requires a target return to be specified. But for those investors with multiple targets, which is the correct one? Sortino (1997) provides an eloquent response,

> *Investors should make a concerted effort to find out what they are trying to accomplish before they invest. Then, figure out what they have to earn at minimum in order to accomplish their goals. This will probably be different from what they can* expect *to earn (called the mean). This is just as true for 401(k) investors as it is for defined benefit pension sponsors.*
>
> *The goal is not to make money or earn a designated rate of return. Making money is* how *one accomplishes the goal, it is not the goal itself. If a 401(k) participant identifies the goal to be retirement at age 65, then a financial planner can determine the rate of return this investor must earn at minimum in order to accomplish this goal. If this same investor says, 'My goal is to beat inflation,' it might lead to investment in money market funds that could guarantee failure to earn a rate of return sufficient to retire at any age.*
>
> *Similarly, the goal to beat the S&P 500 may lead to asset allocations and manager selections that incur more risk than necessary to retire at age 65. In short, the greatest benefit of downside risk is that it is goal-oriented and unique to the target chosen.*

For investors with specific financial goals, a target chosen this way becomes a natural link between financial and investment policies. For a defined-benefit fund, for example, possible targets include the rate required to ensure that contributions do not exceed some specified dollar amount, or to maintain the funding ratio above a required level. Liability matching for defined benefit and insurance general accounts is another natural application of the downside risk approach. In these cases, the duration of the organization's liabilities is matched to a bond index with similar duration.[7]

Given the definition of the target return, it is incorrect to select a target less than the return that could be earned with certainty for the given time period. *This precludes the use of very low targets, such as zero*. As a practical matter, the yield-to maturity on zero-coupon or stripped Treasury bonds with maturity equivalent to the time period provides useful 'floors' to the target. These assets become the 'local' risk-free assets. Note that adjustments to the rates on zero coupon bonds should be made to account for default and credit risks. A better choice, however, are the stripped Treasury bond indexes offered by Ryan Labs. These maintain the same characteristics as T-bills which are used as the risk-free rate in traditional analysis.

5.3.2.1   *The small-sample problem*

Some critics claim that downside risk does not accurately capture the risk of assets when there are few observed returns below the target. Citing the performance of the 1980–89 Japanese stock market, in which there were no years with negative returns, they conclude that there was no downside risk.[8] This conclusion is based on a fundamental misunderstanding of how downside risk is calculated. The correct technique is to use the continuous form of the downside risk calculation, using the 120 *monthly* returns, not, as the authors did, merely observe that none of the ten annual returns was negative and then conclude that there was no downside risk.

When downside risk is calculated in the correct manner, it actually captures the risk of this market better than the traditional mean-standard deviation analysis. For example, the PMPT analysis shows that the downside risk for the Japanese stock market for the period 1980–89 was 4.8%, which is significantly different from zero. It also shows a higher downside frequency (11.8% using PMPT vs. 8.6% using MPT). Among the reasons for the difference in downside frequency values is the fact that Japanese stocks were negatively skewed for the period 1980–89.[9]

5.3.3   Focus on downside implies conservatism

In actual fact, the opposite is sometimes true. Cash, for example, is a risky investment for anyone with a target of, say, 10% – a fact that is recognized by downside risk.

5.3.4   Downside risk and standard deviation give the same results if the distributions are symmetrical

This is incorrect in those cases in which there is a symmetrical distribution, but the target used to calculate the downside risk is not equal to the mean. As the target moves further from the mean, the differences between the downside risk and one-half the standard deviation grow larger and larger. In understanding this characteristic of PMPT, it is important to bear in mind that downside deviation is itself an inherently asymmetrical risk measure, independent of the symmetry of the return distribution. Any asymmetry in the distribution merely serves to accentuate the differences attributable to the risk measure itself.

5.3.5   Downside risk forces the choice of a distribution

As previously stated, it is necessary to fit some distribution to the observed return-data points in order to accurately calculate downside risk and related statistics. However, this is no different from the traditional method used in MPT analysis in which the normal distribution is assumed in order to infer probabilities of loss, etc. from the observed data points.

5.4   CONCLUSION

Widely used for many years in portfolio optimization and asset allocation, PMPT is now being recognized for its applications to performance measurement. Investment practitioners can more accurately evaluate the true performance of investment managers, mutual funds, and other portfolios, without the restrictions imposed by MPT. The tools of PMPT are commercially available and can be easily incorporated into existing performance measurement programs. PMPT also widens the areas of use to incorporate asymmetric distributions such as futures, options, hedge funds and other derivative strategies.

NOTES

1. For a comprehensive survey of the early literature, see R. Libby and P. Fishburn (1979).
2. The semi-variance and target semi-variance terms in these quotes are what are more commonly known as downside risk.
3. Fishburn (1977). See also Harlow (1991).
4. The three-parameter lognormal distribution recommended for use in downside risk calculations permits both positive and negative skewness in return distributions. This is a more robust measure of portfolio returns than the normal distribution, which requires that the upside and downside tails of the distribution be identical.
5. Details of the full study are available in an unpublished report from the authors.
6. We are grateful to Madison Consulting Group, New York, NY for providing us with this information.
7. Often, standard bond indexes with known durations are used for this purpose. A refinement of this approach is to construct a custom liability index. These are available from firms such as Ryan Labs, New York, NY and investment

banks. Leibowitz, Kogelman and Bader of Salomon Brothers have written at length on shortfall and surplus optimization, which is a logical extension of these ideas.

8. This example first appeared in Kaplan and Siegel (1994).
9. These results are more fully discussed in Rom and Ferguson (1994).

REFERENCES

Balzer, L.A. (1994) Measuring investment risk: a review, *Journal of Investing*, Fall.

Fishburn, P.C. (1977) Mean-risk analysis with risk associated below target variance, *American Economic Review*, March.

Harlow, W.V. (1991) Asset allocation in a downside risk framework, *Financial Analysis Journal*, Sept–Oct.

Kaplan, P. and Siegel L. (1994) Portfolio theory is alive and well, *Journal of Investing*, Fall.

Leibowitz, M.L. and Kogelman, S. (1987) Asset allocation under shortfall constraints, *Salomon Brothers*.

Leibowitz, M.L. and Langeteig, T.C. (1989) Shortfall risks and the asset allocation decision, *Journal of Portfolio Management*, Fall.

Libby, R. and Fishburn, P. (1979) Behavioral models of risk taking in business decisions: a survey and evaluation, *Journal of Accounting Research*, Autumn. See also D. Kahneman and A. Tversky (1979) Prospect theory: an analysis of decision under risk, *Econometrica*, March.

Rom, B. and Ferguson, K. (1993) Post-Modern Portfolio Theory comes of age, *Journal of Investing*, Winter.

Rom, B. and Ferguson, K. (1994) Portfolio theory is alive and well: a response, *Journal of Investing*, Fall.

Rom, B. and Ferguson, K. (1995) New breed of tools available to assess risk, *Pensions and Investments*, 13 November.

Sharpe, W.F. (1964) Capital asset prices: a theory of market equilibrium under considerations of risk, *Journal of Finance*, XIX.

Sortino, F. (1997) Looking only at return is risky, obscuring real goal, *Pensions and Investments*, 25 November.

Sortino, F. and Forsey, H. (1996) On the use and misuse of downside risk, *Journal of Portfolio Management*, Winter.

Sortino, F. and Price, L. (1994) Performance measurement in a downside risk framework, *Journal of Investing*, Fall.

Sortino, F. and van der Meer, R. (1991) Downside risk: capturing what's at stake, *Journal of Portfolio Management*, Summer.

Source: This chapter was first published as 'Using Post-Modern Portfolio Theory to Improve Investment Performance Measurement' in the *Journal of Portfolio Management*, Winter 1997/1998, pp. 5–13, and is reproduced by permission of Spaulding Group Inc.

Chapter 6

An evaluation of value at risk and the information ratio (for investors concerned with downside risk)

JOSEPH MESSINA

SUMMARY

This chapter evaluates two popular alternatives to the use of down-side risk in portfolio management. Messina (1995) demonstrates that on both a theoretical basis and an empirical basis, VaR and the information ratio (*IR*) have serious weaknesses for investors who can identify some return that must be earned at minimum (MAR) in order to accomplish their goal. This affects asset allocation results as well as performance rankings. While both VaR and the *IR* fit nicely into the mean-variance framework, VaR is shown to be inappropriate for risk-averse investors and the information ratio is shown to be misleading for investors who define risk as failure to achieve a partic-ular MAR. In comparison to a downside risk approach, the dramatic difference in both performance measurement and asset allocation, provide powerful results that should give those using and promoting VaR an *IR* pause for thought.

6.1 VALUE AT RISK (VaR)

In this section we consider value at risk (VaR). This risk management tool has gained wide usage in many areas of the financial services industry. VaR is not without its critics. In a recent article in the *Financial Analysts Journal* Tanya Beder (1995) discusses many problems in the application of VaR. In this chapter we discuss VaR from a conceptual point of view and examine the question of whether VaR defines risk in a manner that is consistent with the risk preferences of investors.

The basis for describing and analysing risk in modern finance is the Von Neumann–Morgenstern Axioms (VN–M). The MPT model of Markowitz (1959), the single factor CAPM model of Sharpe (1964), Ross' APT model (1976), the multiple factor style models of Sharpe (1992) and Fama and French (1995), Sortino's mean MAR model (Sortino and van der Meer, 1991), and the mean-risk models of Fishburn (1977), are all consistent with VN–M risk aversion. Within this same framework we will analyse VaR risk.

6.1.1 VaR and mean-variance MPT

In this section we compare VaR to other common measures of risk used with the mean-variance MPT (MV–MPT) model.

6.1.1.1 Two asset example

Let us assume we are allocating funds between two asset classes which we will label stocks and bonds. Our economic group has provided us with the following data based on the monthly returns of the Vanguard intermediate term bond fund and the Vanguard S&P index fund from March 1979 to July 1999.

$$E(R_B) = 6\%, \quad \text{std. dev. } (R_B) = 17\%, \quad \text{CORR}(R_B, R_S) = 0.1$$
$$E(R_S) = 22\%, \quad \text{std. dev. } (R_S) = 47\%$$

We define portfolio returns in the usual manner:

$$R_p = x_B R_B + x_S R_S, \quad x_B + x_S = 1.0$$
$$x_B = \text{fraction of funds invested in bonds}$$
$$x_S = \text{fraction of funds invested in common stock}$$
$$E(R_p) = x_B E(R_p) + x_S E(R_S)$$
$$\sigma_p^2 = x_B^2 \sigma_B^2 + x_S^2 \sigma_S^2 + 2x_B x_S \sigma_{B,S}$$
$$\sigma_p = \sqrt{\sigma_p^2}$$

Using these equations we generate columns 1 through 4 in Figure 6.1. Columns 3 and 4 (the means and standard deviations) are plotted in Figure 6.2 titled Opportunity Set.

6.1.2 Representing risk by the standard deviation

We can see from Figure 6.1 that risk is minimized at approximately 90% of our money in bonds and 10% in common stock. It is important to note that this

Asset allocations for bonds and stocks

1	2	3	4	5	6	7
Fraction of bonds	Fraction of stock	Std. dev. (R_p)	$E(R_p)$	ZSCORE	BPROB	VaR
1.00	0.00	17.00	6.00	−0.1765	0.4300	22.05
0.90	0.10	16.45*	7.60	−0.2797	0.3899	19.54
0.80	0.20	17.29	9.20	−0.3586	0.3599	19.33**
0.70	0.30	19.34	10.80	−0.4033	0.3433	21.11
0.60	0.40	22.27	12.40	−0.4221	0.3365	24.34
0.50	0.50	25.78	14.00	−0.4267	0.3348***	28.53
0.40	0.60	29.66	15.60	−0.4248	0.3355	33.34
0.30	0.70	33.79	17.20	−0.4202	0.3372	38.56
0.20	0.80	38.09	18.80	−0.4148	0.3391	44.05
0.10	0.90	42.50	20.40	−0.4094	0.3411	49.73
0.00	1.00	47.00	22.00	−0.4043	0.3430	55.55

R_p = rate of return on the portfolio
$E(R_p)$ = expected rate of return on the portfolio
Std. dev. (R_p) = standard deviation of the rate of return on the portfolio
ZSCORE = $[MAR−E(R_p)]$/Std. dev. (R_p)
MAR = minimum acceptable rate of return
BPROB = below MAR probability
VaR = value at risk = $|E(R_p)−1.65$ Std. dev. $(R_p)|$, VaR assumes 5% chance of $R_p <$ VaR

*Minimum risk standard deviation portfolio
**Minimum risk VaR portfolio
***Minimum risk BPROB portfolio

Figure 6.1   *Asset allocations for bonds and stocks*

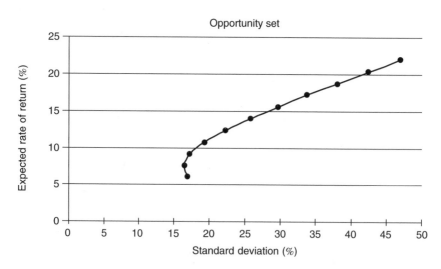

Figure 6.2   *Graph of 11 mean-standard deviation portfolios in Figure 6.1 (risk = standard deviation of R_p)*

is based on our definition of risk, which is defined as the standard deviation of portfolio returns. The standard deviation can be interpreted as the expected size of deviations from the mean return. This implies that on average over time the average return of this portfolio will be 6.7% per period, but the actual returns will vary about this average. In fact, the size of the deviations should average out to approximately 16.45% per period. Since most of this variation is due to price variability, the person who perceives risk in this manner must be concerned about the average size of fluctuations in the value of his/her portfolio regardless of whether the fluctuations are up or down. It also means that the individual believes security market returns can be well approximated by either normal or lognormal distributions. For some securities this is true, but for others it is a poor assumption.

6.1.3 Representing risk by the value at risk concept (VaR)

Another definition of risk is called VaR. VaR is defined as the value of R_p such that

Probability $(R_p < \text{VaR}) = \alpha = \text{alpha}$
$\alpha = $ a parameter determined by the investor's aversion to risk.

Since alpha is usually set in the range of 1–5%, this type of risk aversion is probably most appropriate for investors that are primarily concerned about near catastrophic events that will cause extremely bad portfolio returns. In our example we assumed normal distributions of returns and set alpha equal to 5%, a number commonly used in practice.

The assumption of normal distributions makes the VaR very easy to calculate. We first compute the standard normal deviate:

$$z = \frac{[\text{VaR} - E(R_p)]}{\sigma_\rho}$$

at $\alpha = 5\%$, $\quad z = 1.65 \quad \text{VaR} = E(R_p) - 1.65\sigma_\rho$

In our example we use the absolute value of VaR to make it easier to visually compare the VaR graph to the mean-standard deviation graph. The VaR graph is shown in Figure 6.3.

It is apparent from column 7 of Figure 6.1 that risk is minimized by the allocation of 80% in bonds and 20% in common stock which is different from the allocation that minimized portfolio fluctuations. This is because we define risk in a different manner.

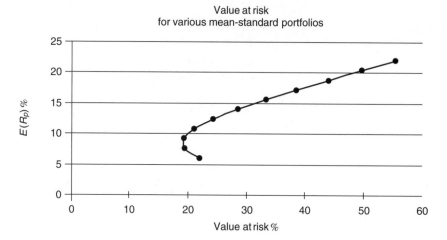

Figure 6.3   *Opportunity set: risk = VaR. VaR assumes probability $(R_p < VaR) = 5\%$*

6.1.4   Representing risk by the probability of failing to achieve a minimum acceptable rate of return (MAR)

Another interpretation of risk is concern about achieving a return on the portfolio that is especially important to the investor. Failure to achieve this MAR can usually be associated with various negative economic consequences. An example would be style managers who fail to meet or exceed the return of the style indices that serve as benchmarks for their style. Another example is the pension fund manager who fails to achieve the actuarial rate of return necessary to fully fund his defined benefit pension plan. Many retired investors are concerned about keeping up with the inflation rate. In each of these examples it would make sense to define risk as

$$\text{Risk} = \text{probability}(R_p < \text{MAR}) = \text{BPROB}$$

where the MAR might be the expected benchmark, the actuarial rate of return, or the expected inflation rate. In our example we chose an expected inflation rate of 3% as our MAR. It can be seen from the data in column 6 that the minimum risk portfolio is 50% in bonds and 50% in stock. This is a very different allocation from the others because we are basing our decision on a very different perception of risk. In the example we assumed normal distributions, but this is not necessary for MAR models. MAR models have the advantage that they can model some aspects of the volatility that concerns investors who use standard deviation to represent risk, and they can also model the type of catastrophic risk that concerns investors who use VaR to represent risk. The BPROB graph is shown in Figure 6.4.

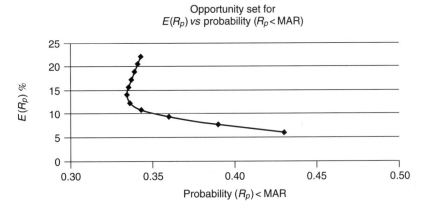

Figure 6.4 *Opportunity set: risk = probability(R_p < MAR). MAR = 3 % (expected inflation estimate)*

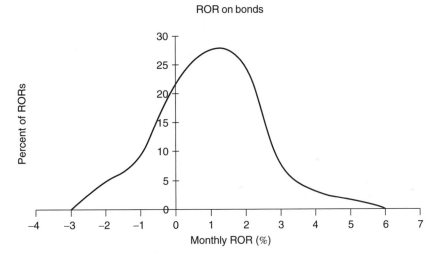

Figure 6.5 *Empirical distribution of bond returns*

6.1.5 When returns are not normal

Figures 6.5 and 6.6 show the empirical distributions for the bond and stock data used in the previous examples. Clearly the data is not normal. Mean-standard models cannot deal with this phenomenon because the standard deviation is not a good representative parameter for volatility when data is not normal or lognormal. VaR can still be used because one can empirically determine at what point in the data set

$$\text{probability}(R_p < \text{VaR}) = \alpha$$

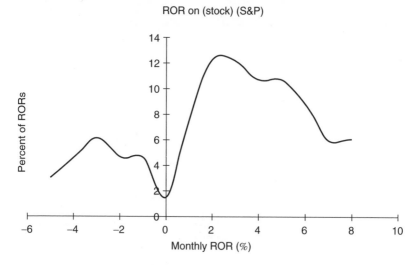

Figure 6.6 *Empirical distribution of common stock returns*

Unfortunately, VaR is still concerned primarily with catastrophic events so its ability to adequately represent risk preferences of investors is severely limited.

BPROB can also be used without relying on normality assumptions and has the added advantage that it represents risk preferences in a more general manner appropriate for many investment situations.

6.1.6 Conclusion

We have compared three measures of risk: VaR, variance and below MAR probability. Each measure of risk implies a portfolio strategy that is optimal for that measure of risk, but may not be optimal for other measures of risk. For instance, implementing a portfolio strategy to protect against VaR-type risk may do a good job against catastrophic risks, but may expose the portfolio to volatility risk or have a high probability of not meeting a particular MAR.

6.2 THE INFORMATION RATIO

This section concerns the information ratio (*IR*). Assuming a single factor linear return space for portfolio *P*, the *IR* for a portfolio *P* is defined as the excess return of the portfolio over the benchmark for portfolio *P* divided by the standard deviation of the excess return minus the benchmark. In equation terms it has the following form:

Single factor linear return space.

$$R_{Pt} = R_{Ft} + [R_{Bt} - R_{Ft}]\beta + \varepsilon_t$$
$$E(R_P) = R_F + [E(R_B) - E(R_F)]\beta$$

R_{Pt} = return on portfolio P at date t

R_{Ft} = return on hypothetical risk-free asset at date t

R_{Bt} = return on the benchmark portfolio B at date t

β = the beta for the factor represented by benchmark portfolio B

ε_t = specific risk for portfolio P

The Information Ratio (*IR*) for portfolio P is defined as

$$IR_P = \frac{[E(R_P) - E(R_B)]}{\text{std. dev. } [R_P - R_B]}$$

There is a considerable literature on the *IR* discussing it from the perspective of an ex ante portfolio and/or security selection measure and as an ex post portfolio performance (active management) evaluation measure. We will provide a brief, selected survey of this literature from both the ex ante and ex post points of view.

6.2.1 *IR* and expected utility (*EU*)

In his 1989 article, Grinold discusses the ex ante value of the *IR*. He points out that if an investor has mean-variance preferences of the form

$$EU(\overline{R}_P, \sigma_P^2) = \overline{R}_P - \text{RA}\sigma_P^2$$

$EU(\overline{R}_P, \sigma_P^2)$ = preference function

$\overline{R}_P$ = portfolio expected excess return

RA = risk aversion parameter

σ_P^2 = portfolio variance of excess return

then the investor will always prefer the portfolio with the highest possible *IR*. In other words, ranking portfolios by *IR*s is consistent with choosing the portfolio with the highest expected utility.

We will demonstrate Grinold's method of analysis with an example.

Definition of terms

$$R_{Pt} - R_{Ft} = \alpha + [R_{Bt} - R_{Ft}]\beta + \varepsilon_t$$

$$E(R_P) - R_F = E(\alpha) + [E(R_B) - E(R_F)]\beta$$

R_{Pt} = return on portfolio P at date t

R_{Ft} = return on hypotetical risk-free asset at date t

R_{Bt} = return on the benchmark portfolio B at date t

β = the beta for the factor represented by benchmark portfolio B

α = the excess return due to value added by active management

ε_t = specific risk for portfolio P

It is assumed the decision-maker is concerned with maximizing the added value from active management represented by the portfolio's alpha.

Preferences are expressed as

$$EU = E(\alpha) - RA\sigma_\alpha^2$$
E = expectation operator
RA = decision-maker's risk-aversion parameter
σ_α^2 = variance of the portfolio's alpha

The information ratio is defined as

$$IR = E(\alpha) \text{ std. dev. } (\alpha)$$

We can divide the analysis into two steps. First we group portfolios according to their information ratios. This is shown in Figure 6.7 by the three curves labelled *IR*1, *IR*2 and *IR*3. In this example every portfolio on curve *IR*1 has an information ratio of 0.2, every portfolio on curve *IR*2 has an information ratio of 0.4, and every portfolio on curve *IR*3 has an information ratio of 0.67. We see that as the *IR* gets larger the curves move up away from the origin.

The second step is to plot the decision-maker's preferences. We rearrange the *EU* function so it can be plotted on the same graph as the *IR* curves.

If $EU = E(\alpha) - RA\sigma_\alpha^2$ then rearranging the terms we obtain
$$E(\alpha) = EU + RA\sigma_\alpha^2$$

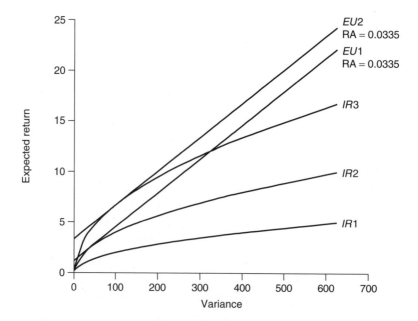

Figure 6.7   *Using IRs to optimize portfolios*

This is a straight line equation. *EU* is the intercept and RA, the risk-aversion parameter, is the slope.

To maximize *EU* we find the highest possible intercept. To do this we move the straight line representing the preference function upward in a parallel manner until it is tangent to one of the *IR* curves. The optimal portfolio will always be on the uppermost *IR* curve. This implies that higher *IR*s are always preferable to lower *IR*s. To complete our analysis let us assume a RA coefficient of 0.0335. This produces a tangent on the highest *IR* curve at $E(\alpha) = 6.67\%$ and a standard deviation of 10%.

To see what effect the decision-maker's risk aversion has on the optimal decision we will change the value of the risk-aversion coefficient from 0.0335 to 0.20. This lower value implies the decision-maker is less risk-averse. The revised optimal solution is graphed in Figure 6.8. The tangent point is now at $E(\alpha) = 11.22\%$ and a standard deviation of 16.75%, a higher risk, higher return portfolio which is consistent with less risk aversion.

6.2.2 *IR* and statistical significance of ex post performance

Grinold and Kahn (1992) discuss the relation between *IR*s and ex post performance. Using a simple active management strategy they demonstrate that the portfolios with the highest active management value added also have the highest

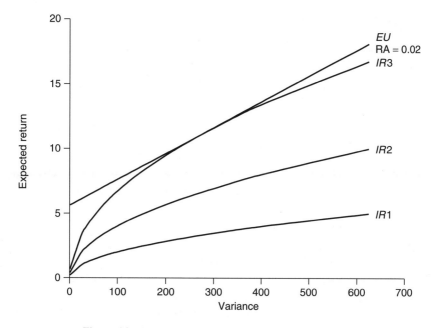

Figure 6.8   *Using IRs to optimize portfolios: revised solution*

*IR*s. They estimate the average active value added by the portfolio's alpha (α). This is summarized in equation form below.

Alpha is estimated as the intercept term and beta is estimated as the slope term in the simple linear regression

$$R_{Pt} - R_{Ft} = \alpha + \beta(R_{Bt} - R_{Ft})$$

Grinold and Kahn also explain the relationship among the average alpha, the *IR*, and the t statistic. The average alpha is the difference between the average active excess portfolio return ($\overline{R}_P - R_F$), and the passive excess return portfolio ($\overline{R}_B - R_F)\beta$. Testing for a non-zero alpha is a simple t-test for the difference in these two average returns. That is, we test the following hypothesis:

$$H_0: \alpha = 0$$
$$H_1: \alpha \neq 0$$

where we define μ_1 and μ_2 as

$$\mu_1 = E(R_P) - R_F$$
$$\mu_2 = [E(R_B) - R_F]\beta$$

The *IR* is defined as

$$\frac{(\mu_1 - \mu_2)}{\text{std. dev.}\,[(\mu_1 - \mu_2)]}$$

which is very similar to the statistical definition of the t-statistic. The exact relationship is

$$IR = \frac{t\text{-statistic}}{\sqrt{T}}$$

where T = number of periods of observations.

Therefore, testing for a high ex post *IR* is equivalent to performing a t-test to see if the active management return, the difference between the total return and the passive return, is significantly different from zero. In other words, the *IR* may be considered a sufficient statistic for determining if the active management return is statistically significant.

For example, assume we measure the performance an active portfolio manager over a 5-year period by regressing the manger's returns against the appropriate benchmark. Assume the regression produces a positive alpha and an ex post *IR* for this manager of 0.89. This *IR* of 0.89 is equivalent to a t-statistic of 2.0, i.e. $(2.0/\sqrt{5.0} = 0.89)$ This would imply there is a 95% probability that the positive alpha we measured was due to active management skill rather than luck.

6.2.3 Relationship between the *IR* and the Sharpe ratio

Sharpe (1994) examines the relation of the generalized Sharpe ratio (SR) to expected utility analysis and the *t*-statistic.

$$SR = \frac{E(R_P) - E(R_B)}{\text{std. dev. } [E(R_P) - E(R_B)]}$$

Defined in this manner, the generalized Sharpe ratio is identical to the *IR*.

Although Sharpe uses a different analytical approach than Grinold and Grinold and Kahn to get his results, he also demonstrated the extent to which the SR is consistent with maximizing expected utility and that the SR is equivalent to the $(t\text{-statistic})/\sqrt{T}$.

6.2.4 Conclusion

To conclude, the *IR* ratio is consistent with the Von Neumann–Morgenstern axioms for rational decision-making and the decision rule of maximizing expected utility. Investments with higher *IR*s are also the investments that are more preferred by investors with mean variance preferences. The *IR* is also consistent with classical statistical hypothesis testing. Ex post portfolios with the highest *IR*s are also the portfolios that have αs that are significantly different from zero.

6.3 MINIMUM ACCEPTABLE RETURN (MAR)

Although the *IR* has merit, it may not be useful as a decision-making criterion if it is measured in terms of the mean and standard deviation of returns.

Harry Markowitz, the 'father' of Modern Portfolio Theory, noted in his seminal work in the 1950s that semi-variance may be a better measure of risk than variance (Markowitz, 1959).

In a 1973 paper, psychologist John Payne noted that standard deviation accounts for very little of people's perception of risk. The most relevant factors were downside frequency and the magnitude of the possible loss.

There are situations in which an investor's primary concern is earning a return in excess of a particular minimum acceptable return (MAR). For instance, some investors want to protect their purchasing power so they have an MAR equal to the inflation rate. Other investors want to protect the value of their principal so they want to earn a positive rate of return which implies an MAR of zero. Pension fund mangers with defined benefit plans want to earn at least the actuarial rate of return required for their plan. These are examples where returns below the MAR are risky, but returns above the MAR are highly desirable, thus describing risk in terms of portfolio mean and variance would lead to sub-optimal decisions.

In the following sections we will discuss how to modify an analysis so it can be used to analyse the risks and returns of investors and other decision makers whose preferences are based on an MAR.

6.3.1   Defining risk and preferences in an MAR framework

6.3.1.1   *MAR risk*

The two most common forms of MAR preferences are mean-below MAR variance (M-BVAR) and mean-below MAR probability (M-BPROB).

MAR risk is defined in terms of below MAR variance (BVAR), below MAR standard deviation (BTSD) and below MAR probability (BPROB).

$$\mathrm{BVAR}_i = \int_{-\infty}^{\mathrm{MAR}} (R_i - \mathrm{MAR})^2 p(R_i) \, dR_i, \quad \text{if } R_i \le \mathrm{MAR}$$

$$\mathrm{BVAR}_i = 0, \quad \text{if } R_i > \mathrm{MAR}$$

$$\mathrm{BPROB}_i = \int_{-\infty}^{\mathrm{MAR}} p(R) \, dR$$

6.3.1.2   *MAR preferences*

Following Fishburn (1977), we assume preferences are of the form M-BVAR or M-BPROB and can be represented by the following preference functions consistent with the VN–M axioms of rational behaviour:

M-BVAR preferences:
$$EU = E(R) - \mathrm{RA} * \mathrm{BVAR}$$
$$EU = E(R) - \mathrm{RA} * \sigma_{\mathrm{BMAR}}^2$$

M-BPROB preferences:
$$EU = E(R) - \mathrm{RA} * \mathrm{BPROB}$$
RA = risk-aversion coefficient
$*$ indicates ordinary multiplication operator.

6.3.2   Making portfolio decisions in an MAR framework

Assume a pension fund sponsor has a portfolio with net asset value of \$A and the portfolio is managed by managers with styles like those defined in Sharpe (1992). The objective is to allocate funds among N managers based on preferences of the sponsor. To keep the analysis simple we will assume there are two asset classes, stock and bonds, and two money managers.

The sponsors preferences are represented by

M-VAR preferences:
$$EU = E(R) - \mathrm{RA}_{\mathrm{VaR}} * \mathrm{VaR}$$

M-BPROB preferences:

$EU = E(R) - \text{RA}_{\text{BPROB}} * \text{BPROB}$

RA = risk aversion coefficient.

* indicates ordinary multiplication operator.

We employ two different preference systems so we can demonstrate how different preferences lead to different optimal decisions. We use the same data employed for the example in section 6.1.

6.3.2.1 Two asset example

Let us assume we are allocating funds between two asset classes, which we will label stocks and bonds. Our economic group has provided us with the following data based on the monthly returns of the Vanguard intermediate term bond fund and the Vanguard S&P index fund from March 1979 to July 1999. We will use this historical data as a basis for our forecast of the future and assume the sponsor bases his MAR on the expected inflation rate. Risk is measured as the probability of not exceeding the inflation rate.

$$E(R_B) = 6\%, \quad \text{std. dev.}(R_B) = 17\%, \quad \text{CORR}(R_B, R_S) = 0.1$$
$$E(R_S) = 22\%, \quad \text{std. dev.}(R_S) = 47\%$$

We define portfolio returns in the usual manner:

$$R_p = x_B R_B + x_S R_S, x_B + x_S = 1.0$$
$$x_B = \text{ fraction of funds invested in bonds}$$
$$x_S = \text{ fraction of funds invested in common stock}$$
$$E(R_p) = x_B E(R_p) + x_S E(R_S)$$
$$\sigma_p^2 = x_B^2 \sigma_B^2 + x_S^2 \sigma_S^2 + 2x_B x_S \sigma_{B,S}$$
$$\sigma_p = \sqrt{\sigma_p^2}$$

The analysis of our asset allocation decision is shown in Figure 6.9. Columns 1 and 2 indicate the allocations of funds between stock and bonds. Column 3 shows the expected portfolio return that is expected from each allocation. Column 4 shows the risk level of each allocation if risk is measured by the standard deviation of returns. Columns 6, 8 and 10 show the risk of each allocation if risk is measured by the probability of failing to meet or exceed the appropriate MAR.

First we will assume the sponsor has mean-variance (mean-standard deviation) preferences. In order to minimize risk the sponsor should choose the portfolio with the smallest standard deviation. This implies allocating 90% of the funds to bonds and 10% to stock.

However, if we assume the sponsor has mean-BPROB preferences different allocations are required to minimize risk. We see from column 6 that an

1	2	3	4	5	6	7	8	9	10
Fraction of funds in bonds	Fraction of funds in stock	$E(R_p)$	Portfolio Std. Dev.	ZSCORE1	BTPROB1	ZSCORE2	BTPROB2	ZSCORE3	BTPROB3
1.00	0.00	6.00	17.00	-0.1765	0.4300	-0.1176	0.4532	-0.0588	0.4765
0.90	0.10	7.60	16.45	-0.2797	0.3899	-0.2189	0.4134	-0.1581	0.4372
0.80	0.20	9.20	17.29	-0.3586	0.3599	-0.3008	0.3818	-0.2429	0.4040
0.70	0.30	10.80	19.34	-0.4033	0.3433	-0.3516	0.3626	-0.2999	0.3821
0.60	0.40	12.40	22.27	-0.4221	0.3365	-0.3772	0.3530	-0.3323	0.3698
0.50	0.50	14.00	25.78	-0.4267	0.3348	-0.3879	0.3490	-0.3491	0.3635
0.40	0.60	15.60	29.66	-0.4248	0.3355	-0.3911	0.3479	-0.3574	0.3604
0.30	0.70	17.20	33.79	-0.4202	0.3372	-0.3906	0.3480	-0.3610	0.3590
0.20	0.80	18.80	38.09	-0.4148	0.3391	-0.3885	0.3488	-0.3623	0.3586
0.10	0.90	20.40	42.50	-0.4094	0.3411	-0.3858	0.3498	-0.3623	0.3586
0.00	1.00	22.00	47.00	-0.4043	0.3430	-0.3830	0.3509	-0.3617	0.3588

Figure 6.9

allocation of 50% in bonds and 50% in stock is required if the inflation forecast is 3%. Column 8 indicates that an allocation of 40% in bonds and 60% in stocks is necessary if the inflation forecast is 4% and column 10 indicates the sponsor should allocate 20% to bonds and 80% to stock if the expected inflation rate (i.e. MAR) is 5%. The sponsor's view of what constitutes risk has a very profound influence on the asset allocation decision.

Note that the mean-variance view of risk is not responsive to the expected inflation rate. Regardless of the MAR the same 10%, 90% allocation is implied. One implication of this example is that choosing managers based on a method like the *IR* that compares the managers return to a benchmark portfolio would be totally inappropriate for a fund that wanted to exceed a particular MAR.

6.3.3   Evaluating performance in an MAR framework

When decision-makers have MAR preferences, either M-BVAR or M-BPROB, the standard mean-variance methods may not be appropriate. Empirical evidence indicates this may be especially true for aggressive equity managers. In a paper presented to the national INFORMS meeting, Messina (1995) analysed the performance of approximately 2000 mutual funds using both a mean-variance methodology and a mean-BVAR methodology. Higher growth funds earned significantly higher rankings using M-BVAR methodology while lower growth funds earned significantly higher rankings using M-VAR methodology.

The data base for the study was MorningStar Mutual Funds OnDisc which contained approximately 6500 mutual funds with monthly data from 1976 to 1995. For the study we used 1998 funds with at least 5 years of monthly rates of return. We ranked the 1998 funds in descending order based on 5-year annualized rate of return. We then divided the funds into four groups.

Group 1: $Fund_1 - Fund_{500}$
Group 2: $Fund_{501} - Fund_{1000}$
Group 3: $Fund_{1001} - Fund_{1500}$
Group 4: $Fund_{1501} - Fund_{1998}$

$Fund_1$ had the highest and $Fund_{1998}$ had the lowest 5-year annualized rate of return.

We then did tests to compare excess returns on a fund by fund comparison.

6.3.3.1   *Performance method 1 (PM1): excess return using the information ratio (Sharpe ratio)*

IR for fund *i*

$$IR_i = \frac{A_i - R_F}{\sigma_i}$$

A_i = the average monthly return for fund i

$$A_i = \sum_{t=1}^{t=60} R_t/60$$

$$\sigma_i^2 = \sum_{t=1}^{t=60} (R_t - A_i)^2/59, \quad \sigma_i = \sqrt{\sigma_i^2}$$

6.3.3.2 *Performance method 2 (PM2): excess return using the M-BVAR index*

Index for fund i

$$\text{Index}_i = \frac{A_i - \text{MAR}}{\text{BSTD}_i}$$

A_i = the average monthly return for fund i

$$A_i = \sum_{t=1}^{t=60} R_t/60$$

$$\text{BVAR}_i^2 = \sum_{t=1}^{t=60} \{\text{Max}[0], (R_t - \text{MAR})\}^2/59,$$

$$\text{BSTD}_i = \sqrt{\text{BVAR}_i^2}$$

US Treasury Bond was used as the MAR in this study.

Results based on 5-year annualized rate of returns from 1990 to 1994 are summarized in Figure 6.10. The data show that the higher growth funds (funds 1–500) have significantly higher index scores on a risk-adjusted basis than the lower growth funds. We see that the comparative advantage of measuring performance using a below MAR method decreases as the growth rates decrease. One way to explain this result is that the higher growth funds have more volatility than the lower growth funds, but much of the volatility is above the MAR, not below the MAR. Using the standard deviation as a measure of volatility penalizes the higher growth funds more than the lower growth funds.

6.3.4 Conclusion

We see that from both an ex ante decision-making point of view and an ex post performance evaluation point of view the traditional *IR* index is not useful for individuals or institutions that define risk as the failure to achieve a particular MAR. This is true regardless of whether the preference system is based on below MAR probability or below MAR variance.

	Number of funds that had greater excess returns based on the M-BSTD index	Number of funds that had greater excess returns based on the IR (Sharpe) index
Funds 1–500	315***	185
Funds 501–1000	236 tie	264 tie
Funds 1001–1500	119	381***
Funds 1501–1998	85	413***

***Implies statistical significance at the 10% level.

Figure 6.10 *Comparison of excess rates of return: M-STD vs. M-BSTD*

REFERENCES

Beder, Tanya Styblo (1995) VAR: seductive but dangerous, *Financial Analysts Journal*, September–October.

Fama, Eugene R. and French, Kenneth R. (1995) Size and book to market factors in earnings and returns, *Journal of Finance*, March.

Fishburn, Peter C. (1977) Mean-risk analysis with risk associated with below target returns, *The American Economic Review*, March.

Grinold, Richard C. (1989) The fundamental law of active management, *Journal of Portfolio Management*, Spring.

Grinold, Richard C. and Kahn, Ronald N. (1992) Information analysis, *Journal of Portfolio Management*, Spring.

Markowitz, Harry (1959) *Portfolio Selection*, New York: John Wiley.

Messina, Joseph M. (1995) Mutual fund performance based on below target risk measures: a comparison of mean-variance and below target measures, Paper presented at the INFORMS National Meeting in New Orleans, LA, 29 October.

Morningstar Mutual Funds on Disc (1995) Chicago: Morningstar Inc., 1995.

Morningstar Principia Plus Mutual Funds on Disc (1999) Chicago: Morningstar Inc.

Payne, John (1973) *Journal of Psychology*.

Ross, Stephen (1976) The arbitrage theory of capital asset pricing, *Journal of Economic Theory*, V13.

Sharpe, William F. (1964) Capital asset prices: a theory of market equilibrium under conditions of risk, *Journal of Finance*, 19.

Sharpe, William F. (1992) Asset allocation: management style and performance measurement, *Journal of Portfolio Management*, Winter.

Sharpe, William F. (1994) The Sharpe Ratio, *Journal of Portfolio Management*, Fall.

Sortino, F. and van der Meer, R.A.H. (1991) Downside risk, *Journal of Portfolio Management*, Summer.

FURTHER READING

BARRA Newsletter, September/October 1992, May/June 1993, BARRA, Berkeley, CA.

Elton, Edwin J. and Gruber, Martin J. (1991) *Modern Portfolio Theory and Investment Analysis*, 4th edn, New York: John Wiley & Sons.

Ferguson, Robert (1975) Active portfolio management, *Financial Analysts Journal*, May/June.

Ferguson, Robert (1986) The trouble with performance measurement, *Journal of Portfolio Management*, Spring.

Fisher, Lawrence (1975) Using modern portfolio theory to maintain an efficiently diversified portfolio, *Financial Analysts Journal*, May/June.

Haugen, Robert A. (1993) *Modern Investment Theory*, 3rd edn, Englewood Cliffs, NJ: Prentice-Hall.

Joorion, Philippe (1997) *Value at Risk*, Homewood, IL: Irwin.

Olsen, Robert A. (1998) Behavioural finance and its implications for stock-price volatility, *Financial Analysts Journal*, March.

Pyle, David and Turnovsky, Stephen (1970) Safety first and expected utility maximization in mean-standard deviation portfolio analysis, *Review of Economics and Statistics*.

Rosenberg, Barr (1976) Security appraisal and unsystematic risk in institutional investment, *Proceedings of the Seminar on the Analysis of Security Prices*, University of Chicago, November.

Rudd, Andrew and Clasing, Henry K. (1982) *Modern Portfolio Theory: The Principles of Investment Management*, Homewood, IL: Dow Jones Irwin.

Sortino, Frank A. (1999) The price of astuteness, *Pensions and Investments*, 3 May.

Sortino, F.A., Miller, G. and Messina, J. (1997) Short term risk-adjusted performance: a style based analysis, *Journal of Investing*, Summer.

Treynor, Jack L. and Black, Fischer (1973) How to use security analysis to improve portfolio selection, *Journal of Business*, January.

Chapter 7

A portfolio manager's view of downside risk

NEIL RIDDLES

Risk is one of those subjects on which there is widespread agreement on the surface but little agreement on the details. I find clients agree that they do not like risk, but often disagree on just how much risk is involved in a particular investment.

The most widely used measure of investment risk, standard deviation, assumes all investors agree on the degree of risk in every investment. This 'one size fits all' view of risk does not capture the broad diversity of opinions I witness regularly among our clients. Not only do our clients have different goals but the difference in ages and amount of wealth also dictate different perceptions of the degree of risk in a given investment.

I believe downside risk can accommodate this diversity in risk perception. Downside risk, as the name implies, measures risk below some point. If an investor is only worried about losing money, then that point would be zero. In other words, the possibility of negative returns would be viewed as risky. If an investor needs to earn a 7% return in order to meet their goal, then any return under 7% would be unacceptable (risky). This investment return 'floor', which serves as the dividing line between good and bad outcomes, is called the minimum acceptable return or MAR.

While standard deviation interprets any difference from the average return, above or below, as bad, most investors' views of risk are towards the downside only. That is, investors only worry about their returns being below some point. In addition to a more intuitive definition of risk, the major advantage to downside risk over standard deviation is that it accommodates different views of risk.

Institutional investors often view investment risk as the possibility of under-performing the benchmark. Retail investors often view risk in absolute terms as the risk of not accomplishing their goal. By using downside risk, each investor can 'customize' the risk calculation using a unique MAR. In the above examples the institutional investor would use the benchmark rate as the minimum

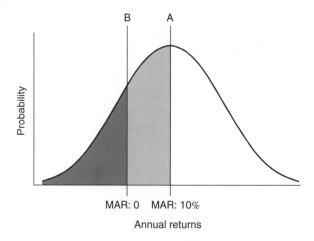

Figure 7.1 *Changing the minimum acceptable return*

acceptable return, while the retail investor would want to know the risk of falling below 7%. Since standard deviation can only measure how tightly distributed returns are around a mean it cannot be customized for the individual investor.

The following example will illustrate the importance of this unique ability of downside risk to accommodate a wide range of risk perceptions. Figure 7.1 shows the range of returns of an investment from minus 100% to plus 100%. It illustrates how two investors might view the same asset quite differently in terms of risk, due to different goals that require different MARs. Investor A needs an investment that returns 10% annually in order to maintain her standard of living as a retired person. Returns below 10% incur the risk of not being able to maintain her lifestyle. Investor B wants a good return but does not want to incur any losses. The additional area between lines A and B represent the additional risk perceived by investor A, as opposed to investor B.

Another limitation to standard deviation as a measurement of investment risk lies with the underlying data. Most investors will recall the 'normal distribution' from their introduction to statistics course. This nicely proportioned 'bell shaped' curve is what underlies all of the assumptions about standard deviation. If the underlying data is not normally distributed then the standard deviation is likely to give misleading results.

A number of studies have demonstrated that investment returns are not normally distributed. If the returns are not normally distributed then investors using standard deviation are likely to reach the wrong conclusions.

7.1 CALCULATION

As mentioned above, the distribution of investment returns is often non-normal. The most accepted way of calculating downside risk begins with a standard lognormal curve and adjusts it for three parameters. Basically, one starts with a lognormal curve and then stretches and compresses it for a closer fit to the actual distribution. This 'custom fit' gives a better indication of the true shape of the distribution.

A further enhancement to the calculation is available in systems that use bootstrapping routines. Bootstrapping is a technique that tries to increase the explanatory power of a limited amount of data. Bootstrapping in this case selects 12 months at random and links them together to form a one-year return. This process is repeated thousands of times resulting in a distribution with many observations instead of just a few.

An underlying assumption to bootstrapping is that the data is independent. That is, one period's return has no connection to another period's return. Empirical evidence suggests that sequential returns are not entirely independent, but the correlation between a return and that of a return two periods later is approximately zero. If the returns revert to the mean (tend to change direction) or trend (tend to stay in the same direction) then the returns are not independent and you cannot validly mix and match returns to form additional years.

For example, let's assume that markets always reversed direction or 'bounced back' after sharp moves. In that case, the bootstrapping procedure may string together 12 sharp downturns resulting in a one-year return which would never happen because returns always reverse direction. If returns follow a random walk then bootstrapping should capture that returns generating mechanism.

One must weigh the additional explanatory power gained by the increased number of observations against the error introduced because returns are not entirely independent. In spite of its possible drawbacks, many practitioners prefer to bootstrap data because they believe it is able to capture returns that could happen, but never did happen, therefore providing a more complete picture of the nature of uncertainty.

An often-cited example of bootstrapping's effectiveness is the Japanese market during the 1980s. From 1980 to 1990 there were no years in which the market was down. Based just on this limited amount of data it appears that the Japanese stock market had no risk during that period. However, bootstrapping the monthly data produced a distribution that clearly indicated the potential for negative annual returns. This riskiness showed itself in the early 1990s as the Japanese equity market suffered marked declines. Looking at the bootstrapped data might have alerted an investor that a sharp correction was possible.

7.2 THE DOWNSIDE RISK STATISTICS

Downside risk calculations provide the user with more information than just a downside deviation number. The additional statistics provide insight into the causes of the risk:

- *Downside frequency* tells the user how often the returns violated the MAR (minimum acceptable return). This is important because in order to assess the likelihood of a bad outcome you need to know how often one occurred.
- *Average downside deviation* indicates the average size of the unacceptable returns. This statistic helps an investor judge the severity of the average 'bad' return. An investment that lost money twice as often as a second investment may still be preferable if it tended to lose far less than the second investment.
- *Downside magnitude* is the return at the 99th percentile on the downside. This is a worst-case scenario. An investment may lose money only occasionally, may average small losses when they do occur, and yet may prove unacceptable if the potential exists for huge losses.
- All of these statistics are combined into the *downside risk statistic*. It includes the size and the frequency of unacceptable returns. Downside risk can be thought of as the equivalent to the standard deviation.
- One method of ranking investments is by their risk-adjusted returns. For downside risk, the accepted risk-adjusted return is the *Sortino ratio*, named after Frank Sortino at San Francisco's Pension Research Institute. It is the annualized return of the manager minus the MAR, divided by the downside risk. Similar to the Sharpe ratio (which uses standard deviation), the Sortino ratio measures how many units of return were received per unit of risk experienced.

Table 7.1 provides an example of some downside risk statistics calculated on a portfolio and benchmark. It is important to note that these statistics were calculated with an MAR of zero. That is, any negative return was seen as bad.

In this case the actively managed portfolio underperformed the benchmark by an annualized 70 basis points (15.6–14.9%). The portfolio and the benchmark look similar on a risk-adjusted basis when using standard deviation as the measure of risk. The efficiency ratio (return/standard deviation) of the portfolio is 1.1 compared to the benchmark's 0.9.

Table 7.1 *Downside risk statistics: [Sixteen years of monthly returns]*

	Int'l equity port.	MSCI EAFE index
Annualized return	14.9%	15.6%
Efficiency ratio (ROR/St. Dev.)	1.1×	0.9×
Standard deviation	13.3%	17.7%
Sortino ratio @ 0.0% goal (ROR/DD)	10.9×	2.2×
Downside deviation @ 0.0% goal	1.4%	7.2%
Downside frequency @ 0.0% goal	10.7%	19.6%
Average downside deviation @ 0.0% goal	3.3%	12.2%
Downside magnitude @ 99th p'ctile	7.1%	33.5%

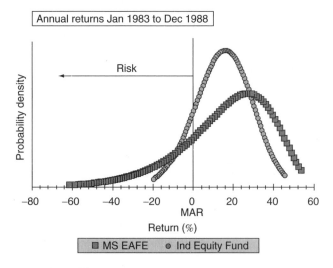

Figure 7.2 *Downside risk example: return distributions*

The Sortino ratio, which is the return divided by downside risk, is demonstrably higher for the portfolio than the benchmark. An inspection of the other statistics explains what happened. Downside frequency tells us that the portfolio lost money half as often as the benchmark (10.7% of the time vs. 19.6%). The average downside deviation indicates that when the portfolio did suffer a loss, the loss was much smaller than the average loss suffered by the index (3.3% vs. 12.2%).

An investor who is not willing to suffer losses would be better off in the active portfolio than with an index investment. On the other hand, a pension fund or other long-term investor might be more concerned with underperforming the benchmark than with the possibility of losses. In that case an investment in an index fund might be more acceptable.

Figure 7.2 graphically shows the return distributions of the active portfolio and the index. The index curve extends further into negative territory. The active portfolio's curve, while shifted a little lower than the index's curve, has much less of the curve in negative territory. It is also easy to imagine that if the MAR were shifted to about 10 then the risk of the portfolio would rise proportionately more than the index because the active portfolio's curve is so sharply peaked.

7.3 RISK RELATIVE TO A BENCHMARK

There are drawbacks to downside risk as it is often calculated. Many investors define risk as underperforming a benchmark. Most downside risk software handles this by allowing the investor to input the benchmark's return as the

MAR. This does not accurately reflect the investor's view of risk. By using the annualized index return as the minimum acceptable return one is assuming that the index went up by exactly that amount every year. In fact, the benchmark return may have been quite volatile during the period.

For example, if the index were up 10% over the period measured, then using that as the MAR would label any portfolio return of less than 10% as bad. In fact, an investor concerned with performance relative to the index would look upon an 8% return as quite good in a year when the benchmark was down −3% (see Figure 7.3).

Figure 7.3 shows a bootstrapped distribution of returns for an active portfolio. The minimum acceptable return is 7.8%, the benchmark's return over the period. The downside risk is calculated at 14.9% over this period.

During the period measured, the portfolio outperformed the index five out of the eight years. However, when the index's annualized return over the entire period is compared to the portfolio's return each year then the portfolio is seen as underperforming in five out of eight years. In one year the portfolio return is 0.4% and the benchmark lost −8.4%. Investors who are concerned with risk relative to the benchmark would consider this a successful year. Instead, using the index's annualized return as the MAR indicates the portfolio underperformed by −7.4% that year.

Figure 7.4 depicts the distribution of the active returns (portfolio return minus the benchmark return) for the same portfolio and time period. Any return below zero indicates the portfolio underperformed the benchmark. Calculating downside risk in this manner results in a downside risk statistic of 7.3%, considerably lower than the other method's 14.9% statistic. This calculation leads to a different conclusion that is a more realistic measure of risk for benchmark-sensitive investors.

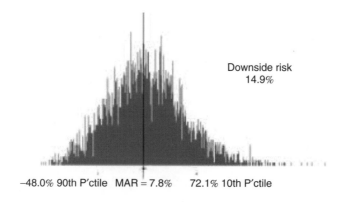

Downside risk
14.9%

−48.0% 90th P'ctile   MAR = 7.8%   72.1% 10th P'ctile

Figure 7.3   *Risk of portfolio with index return as MAR*

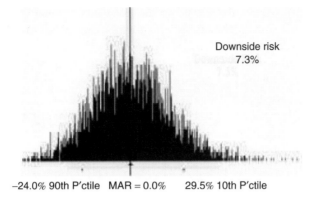

Downside risk
7.3%

−24.0% 90th P'ctile   MAR = 0.0%   29.5% 10th P'ctile

Figure 7.4 *Risk of active return portfolio ROR – index ROR*

While this is a non-standard way to calculate downside risk, I believe it is a superior method for those investors who are primarily concerned with underperforming a benchmark. For investors who have an actual set rate they need out of their investments or for investors who define risk as the possibility of loss, MAR adequately captures their risk preferences. For investors who are concerned with performance relative to a benchmark, then determining the downside risk of the active returns is preferable.

7.4 CONCLUSION

When discussing downside risk, the question of why it was not adopted earlier arises. Part of the reason may be the more complex calculation required. Today, computing power and memory are relatively cheap commodities. Desktop software is readily available, which will calculate downside risk. There is even freeware on the Internet at www.sortino.com.

If software is readily available and most investors agree that it more closely parallels actual risk preferences, why isn't this risk measurement more widely used? The likely answer is inertia. Investors do not accept new statistical methodologies rapidly. We tend to use that which we are comfortable with. Investors have a healthy scepticism for new statistics. For most investors downside risk is a new concept.

Another reason for the slow acceptance of downside risk is that investors are already using standard deviation. James Gleick, in his book *Faster*, quotes the old saw that 'A man with a watch knows what time it is, a man with two watches is never sure'. Investors may be reluctant to adopt another statistic that could give conflicting results. I believe investors should embrace any valid new statistic that can provide additional insight into the risk profile of potential investments.

Downside risk is gaining acceptance in the financial community. Among the reasons for this is that defining risk as a return below some point is consistent with many investor's view of risk. A methodology that determines the downside risk of the portfolio's active return has advantages for investments where success is determined relative to a benchmark.

A word of caution, however, to those who are inclined to adopt the statistic unquestioningly. As outlined above, there are a number of ways to calculate downside risk and they are likely to yield very different results. It is essential that those interpreting downside risk statistics understand the calculation methodology. Also, downside risk statistics calculated using different MARs are not comparable.

Part 2

Underlying Theory

Chapter 8

Investment risk: a unified approach to upside and downside returns

LESLIE A. BALZER

SUMMARY

The aim of this chapter is to increase the reader's understanding of the essential nature of investment risk and of the strengths and weaknesses of various risk measures.

The literature on investment risk is vast. The topic has attracted interest from academics and practitioners alike, and continues to do so – at an accelerating rate. This latter phenomenon is at least partially due to the increasing use of financial instruments with asymmetric pay-offs and to non-linear trading or portfolio management strategies. Such assets and strategies both encourage and produce essentially asymmetric investment return distributions, which in turn highlight the intrinsic shortcomings of using variance or standard deviation as the *only* measure of investment risk. Investors and their advisers further reinforce the trend by selecting and rewarding not only managers who produce high returns, but also those who produce asymmetric distributions of value-added above benchmark with enhanced upside and curtailed downside.

By the end of this chapter, it should have become clear that there is no single universally applicable risk measure and that, as Balzer (1990, 1994) pointed out, 'Risk, like beauty, is in the eye of the beholder.' Furthermore, the psychological literature indicates that not only do investors behave irrationally and inconsistently over time, but that they often form their own idiosyncratic risk measures *while* they are reviewing the data. No single predetermined measure can handle such a situation.

Continued on page 104

___ *Continued from page 103* _____

This chapter reviews most of the commonly used or proposed risk measures, points out their strengths and weaknesses, and eventually develops a unified theory of the utility of upside and downside returns relative to the investor's benchmark(s). The unified theory provides a coherent, powerful and elegant framework for real investment decisions in portfolio management.

8.1   NATURE OF INVESTMENT RISK

We begin by developing some properties of an ideal measure of investment risk. In the following sections, we then discuss probability based measures, the psychology of risk, methods of comparing probability distributions, moment based measures and the non-linearity of risk. From these discussions, it will become clear that any realistic measure of investment risk should be:

- Asymmetric
- Relative to one or more variable benchmark(s)
- Investor-specific
- Multidimensional
- Complete (in a specific sense)
- Numerically positive, and
- Non-linear

It will be seen that the underlying phenomena of risk perception demand that any ideal risk measure should capture all of these properties.

8.1.1   Asymmetry of risk

Consider an investment, 'A' which produces the hypothetical time series of returns shown graphically in Figure 8.1. The investment return is drawn from a normal distribution with a mean of 10% pa and a standard deviation of 5% pa. A small amount of serial correlation[1] is also present. Consider now, the higher volatility 'Investment B' shown in Figure 8.2, which is identical to 'A' except that the standard deviation is twice that of 'A', namely 10% pa. Which is the more risky? Intuitively, most investors would consider 'B' to be more 'risky' than 'A'. The key question, however, is 'Why?'

The comparison is made easier in Figure 8.3, which shows 'A' and 'B' on the one graph. Do the upside extremes of 'B' (above say 20%) feel 'risky'? Most people would not think so. Do the downside extremes of 'B' seem in someway related to 'risk' and contribute to the feeling that 'B' is more 'risky' than 'A'?

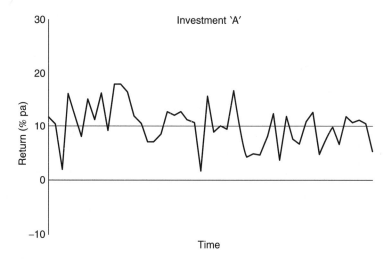

Figure 8.1

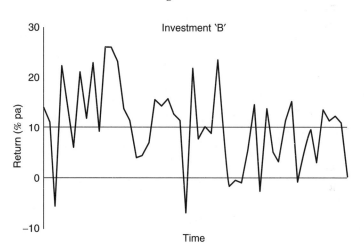

Figure 8.2

Most people would say 'Yes'. What can we conclude from this? Whilst the examples are simple and the discussion brief, it is clear that our intuition tells us that *risk is an asymmetric phenomenon* related to downside, and that an intuitive and realistic risk measure should also be *asymmetric* – it should treat upside and downside differently. This is the first feature of investment risk.

8.1.2 Relativity of risk

Consider again investments 'A' and 'B', but this time as shown in Figure 8.4. Note in particular the shaded areas. Intuitively, these shaded areas seem to be

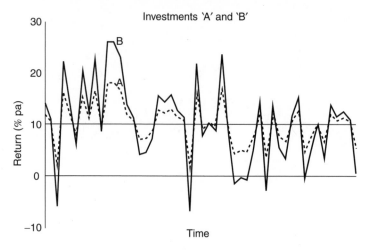

Figure 8.3

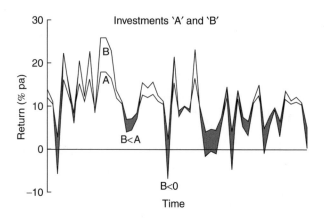

Figure 8.4

related to the portions of the performance histories which lead most people to form a qualitative judgement that 'B' is more risky than 'A'. The shaded areas correspond to those periods in which the return from 'B' is less than that from 'A'. Furthermore, the areas of most concern to many people are probably those where 'B' is less than zero – in other words, negative returns and the loss of capital. Again, the examples are simple and the argument brief, but it is clear that any intuitively satisfying measure of risk is related to *relative* and *not absolute* performance. Risk is related to doing worse than some alternative investment or reference standard – a benchmark.

Later in the chapter we shall compare investments by using the probability distributions of their returns. The conclusions there will also be seen to support the intuition that *risk is relative*. This then is our second feature of investment risk.

8.1.3 To what might risk be relative?

Balzer (1990) and others have proposed that investment risk might be measured by the probability of the investment return falling below a specified risk benchmark. That risk benchmark might itself be a random variable, such as the inflation rate or the return from an alternative investment.

Risk benchmarks are not unique. We now proceed to consider a number of possible risk benchmarks.

8.1.3.1 *Liabilities*
In the case of a defined benefit superannuation or pension fund, the importance of meeting the liabilities is obvious. Yet Arthur and Randall (1990), comment:

> ... *scant, if any, attention is paid to how assets relate to the liabilities that they are held to meet; yet these liabilities are the sole rationale for accumulating the assets in the first place.*

In these circumstances, an obvious choice for a risk benchmark is some value or variable which represents those liabilities. In the absence of such a figure or variable, a proxy must be found. The remainder of this section presents a non-exhaustive list of possible choices for a proxy, where the liabilities or objectives are not available in an appropriate quantitative form.

8.1.3.2 *Negative returns*
Those who have traded volatile leveraged instruments know the gut-wrenching feeling of being long in a falling market or short in a rising market. This is an example of risk at a very basic level. The possibility of losing capital, i.e. negative returns is all too vivid. Here, the risk benchmark could simply be zero return.

8.1.3.3 *Real returns*
Another investor in retirement might be concerned about not keeping pace with inflation and hence be concerned about negative *real* returns. In this case the risk benchmark becomes the inflation rate, or possibly inflation plus some safety margin.

8.1.3.4 *Risk free rate of return*
Alternatively, a fund manager might be concerned about falling below the risk free rate of return, which the investor could have achieved without hiring the manager.

8.1.3.5   Median or bottom quartile returns
The same manager might also be concerned about how often he or she falls into the bottom quartile in the performance surveys. On the other hand, the investor or fund advisor might be concerned if the manager frequently falls below the median manager.

8.1.3.6   Below budgeted return
In a bank treasury, senior management might be concerned when its dealing room profit falls more than say 15% below budgeted profit.

8.1.3.7   Sector index returns
For a sector fund, or its manager, the risk benchmark might relate to an appropriate sector index or some margin above it.

8.1.3.8   Return from an alternative investment
In yet another situation, members of a defined contribution fund might have a different view of risk. The risk of fund manager under-performance is passed straight through to their retirement or exit benefits. They are usually not impressed when their fund achieves a rate less than some readily available alternative investment, for example a building society deposit, cash management trust or money market fund.

8.1.3.9   Change in average weekly earnings
In the minds of the trustees of a defined benefit fund, however, the primary risk is that of the investment performance not being sufficient to meet the liabilities arising from the defined benefits. Actuaries often quote a rule of thumb that the investment returns should not fall below the change in average weekly earnings plus a margin of 1–2% pa. The later then becomes yet another risk benchmark for such funds.

8.1.3.10   A list
In summary then, a non-exhaustive list of possible benchmarks includes, or is implied by, the following undesirable events:

- Not meeting liabilities
- Not meeting objectives (if quantified)
- Negative returns
- Negative real returns
- Less than the risk-free rate of return
- Lower quartile or below median returns (relative to an appropriate universe of investment managers)
- Less than budgeted return, or a specified margin below budget

- Less than an appropriate market or cross-market index
- Returns below readily available alternative investments, such as cash management trusts, building societies, money market accounts, etc.
- Returns below the growth in average weekly earnings plus a margin.

8.1.3.11 *Risk benchmarks versus performance benchmarks*

Some of the risk benchmarks implied by these examples could also be viewed as performance benchmarks. Falling below them, however, is not simply disappointing, but is demonstrably undesirable. They relate to the genuine concerns of the fund sponsors, members, trustees and managers. Hence they are clearly and directly relevant to risk. Some risk benchmarks might make quite good performance benchmarks under appropriate conditions. There is absolutely no reason, however, for them not making equally good risk benchmarks. In fact there is some logical consistency in the performance and risk benchmarks being identical.

8.1.4 Risk is investor-specific

From the preceding discussion, it is clear that risk is related to doing worse than some risk benchmark. This supports the earlier claim that risk is a relative rather than an absolute concept. It is also clear that different investors have different risk benchmarks, since those risk benchmarks are related to, or are proxies for, the liabilities or objectives of the investor. Risk is *investor-specific*.

8.1.5 Multidimensionality of risk

Not only do different investors have different risk benchmarks, the same investor is likely to have multiple objectives and hence multiple risk benchmarks. Risk is thus clearly *multidimensional*.

8.1.6 Completeness, positivity and non-linearity

Having now justified the first four of the desirable features of an investment risk measure, we now turn to the last three, namely *completeness, positivity* and *non-linearity*. The easiest way to introduce and to establish the need for completeness and non-linearity is to show why various measures are unsatisfactory. Hence attention now turns to the examination of various measures. Positivity will be seen later to be only a convenient convention.

8.2 PROBABILITY-BASED RISK MEASURES

8.2.1 Probability of shortfall

Over the years, Balzer (1990) and others have proposed that investment risk might be measured by the probability of the return falling short of a specific risk benchmark. Markowitz (1959), Fishburn (1977), Sortino and Price (1994) and others, have argued that risk should be measured relative to some fixed target or minimal acceptable return (MAR). From the earlier discussion on risk benchmarks, however, it is clear that this concept needs to be extended. It should also be clear that the risk benchmark will usually be a random variable rather than a constant.

A probability of shortfall measure of investment risk is specified:

$$\text{Risk} = \text{Prob}\{R < B\} \qquad\qquad (8.1)$$

where

    $\text{Prob}\{\cdot\}$ = Probability of the event occurring;
    $R = R(t)$ = Return from the investment; and
    $B = B(t)$ = An appropriate risk benchmark.

Earlier, two investments, 'A' and 'B', which had the same mean but different standard deviations, were considered. Figure 8.4 showed the returns from those investments, with the addition of some areas which had been shaded grey. Intuitively, the shaded areas seemed to be related to the portions of the performance histories, which lead most people to form a qualitative judgement that 'B' is more risky than 'A'. Another way of comparing investments 'A' and 'B' is to look at their probability distributions. The probability density functions, from which the returns from 'A' and 'B' are drawn, are shown in Figure 8.5.

Clearly, investment 'B' has more downside than 'A', but note also the shaded area. Everywhere in the shaded area, investment 'B' has a higher probability of producing a lower return than investment 'A' does. Superficially, *probability of shortfall* looks like an interesting risk measure. While it is an interesting statistic associated with risk, it is not sufficient. It is not *complete*.

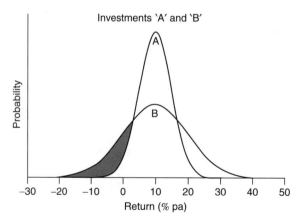

Figure 8.5

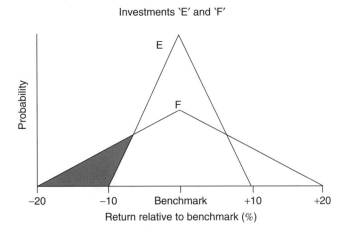

Figure 8.6

8.2.2   Incompleteness of probability of shortfall

Assume that an investor, who is concerned about losing capital relative to an important benchmark, is confronted with two hypothetical investment possibilities, 'E' and 'F', the stylized probability density functions of which are shown in Figure 8.6. Both have an expected return of zero relative to the benchmark, and both are symmetric about zero relative return. Both have a probability of shortfall of 50%, but are they equally risky?

The risk measure specified in equation (8.1) gives the probability that an undesirable event, a 'shortfall below benchmark' will occur. If the investor's only risk measure is the probability of shortfall, then he or she will be indifferent between the two alternatives 'E' and 'F'. From Figure 8.6, the shortfalls (i.e. negative returns relative to benchmark) for investment 'E' are limited to 10% below benchmark, whereas those for 'F' can range down to 20% below. Furthermore, everywhere in the area shaded grey in Figure 8.6 represents a point, where the probability of shortfall is greater for 'F' than it is for 'E'. Most investors would rate 'F' more risky than 'E'. The problem with using probability of shortfall as the only risk measure is that it does not address the issue of how severe the undesirable event might be. Hence, the probability of an adverse event, while of considerable interest and a useful piece of risk-related information, is insufficient and *incomplete* as a risk measure.

8.2.3   Maximum shortfall

We have just seen that the probability of falling short of the risk benchmark answered the question, 'How often?', but not the question, 'How badly?'.

One response to this problem might be to define risk as the magnitude of the maximum (worst) shortfall:

$$\text{Risk} = \text{Max} \left\{ \begin{array}{ll} |R - B|, & R < B \\ 0, & R \geq B \end{array} \right\} \qquad (8.2)$$

where

Max$\{\cdot\}$ = Maximum value of $\{\cdot\}$

$|\cdot|$ denotes absolute value.

An obvious shortcoming of this measure of risk is that it says nothing about the size of the *typical* shortfall. Two investments might have the same worst outcome, but one might have many large losses and the other have very few.

Consider another hypothetical investment 'G', which has a uniform distribution between benchmark relative returns of −20% and +20%. If an investor had to choose between 'F' and 'G', which would they choose? As shown in Figure 8.7, both investments have a 50% probability of a shortfall and equal maximum losses. Are they equally risky? Most people would consider that 'G' is more risky than 'F'. Everywhere within the area shaded grey, 'G' has a higher probability of having the larger shortfall.

Information about the end point of the lower tail of a more realistic probability distribution for an investment says little about the distribution overall. Furthermore, estimation of statistics relating to the tails of a distribution from empirical data is a very ill-conditioned problem. Hence, maximum shortfall is both an *incomplete* and a *numerically ill-conditioned* risk measure.

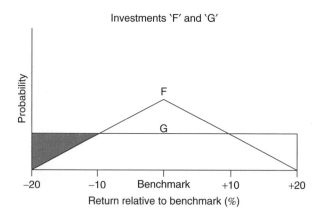

Figure 8.7

8.2.4 Completeness of a risk measure

The discussion involving the last two sections clearly demonstrates that *completeness* is an essential feature of any risk measure, especially if it is to be used as the only measure of risk.

8.2.5 Value at risk

Value at risk (VaR) has become popular in recent years. There is no doubt that it provides useful information. For example, an organization using it knows how much money is at risk in an open position held overnight. The problem, however, is that the 'value at risk' is only the amount which is at risk with a particular probability. It says nothing about how much is at risk at twice that probability or, possibly more importantly, at half that probability. It is clearly incomplete. It only tells part of the risk story. A far more useful set of information would be the complete cumulative probability distribution of how much is at risk at every level of probability.

8.2.6 Numerical positivity

Whilst properties of risk measures are under discussion, a clarification of a sign convention is useful. Maximum shortfall might be defined by replacing the *Max* function in equation (8.2) with *Min*, and by removing the absolute value operator. This would lead to negative numerical values for risk. Risk, however, is usually defined such that the definition results in a positive number. This is a convenient convention for portfolio construction, where portfolio return is maximized subject to a penalty on undesirable features such as risk. The convention is that penalties are measured as positive quantities and preceded by a negative sign. This situation has probably arisen for two reasons. First, in scientific optimization, quadratic penalties are very common. Hence if one starts with a negative numerical value, once it is squared, it becomes positive and has to be subtracted. Secondly, the most common 'risk measure' in investment practice, namely standard deviation, is positive.

As an aside, it should be noted that contrary to common (but incorrect) usage, variance itself is *not* a risk measure. Variance is used in portfolio construction because it results from applying a quadratic penalty to a particular choice of risk measure, namely standard deviation. (See later for a more detailed discussion.)

'Numerically positive' is a desirable, but not essential, feature of a risk measure.

8.2.7 Expected shortfall

Returning to probability-based risk measures, both probability of shortfall and maximum shortfall were seen to be incomplete. An obvious response to this is to consider expected (average) shortfall, since all shortfalls are included in its calculation.

Risk = Average shortfall

$$= E\{|R - B|, \text{ for all } R - B < 0\} \tag{8.3}$$

where

$E\{\cdot\}$ = Expected value of $\{\cdot\}$

The expected shortfalls for investments 'E', 'F' and 'G' are:

E   3.3%
F   6.7%
G   10.0%

These numerical values certainly rank investments 'E', 'F' and 'G' in the intuitively correct order of 'riskiness'. They capture the feeling that 'G' is more risky than 'F', and that 'F' is more risky than 'E'. Furthermore, the magnitudes are also intuitively reasonable.

Figure 8.8 shows the superimposed probability density functions for these three hypothetical investments. Geometrically, expected shortfall can be interpreted as the horizontal distance from the zero point on the horizontal (return minus risk benchmark) axis to the centroid of the downside (below-benchmark) areas.

As a risk measure, expected shortfall clearly captures the whole of the downside portion of the relative probability density function and *is* complete. Unfortunately, the major difficulty with expected shortfall is that it is a linear

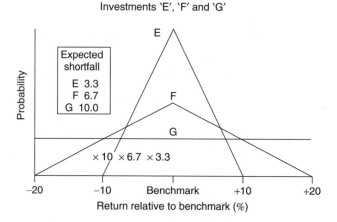

Figure 8.8

measure of downside risk. We shall see in the next section, however, that most investors do not have a linear response to risk.

8.2.8 Non-linearity of risk

How many of us insure our pets? How many of us insure our homes? Why? In asking these questions at investment conferences in Europe, North America and in Australia, only one person has admitted insuring their dog, and no one has admitted not insuring their home. Why is this so? Consider a dog, which cost $1000. It is an expert fence climber, has no road sense, loves chasing buses and trucks, and is the most stolen breed in the country. Its probability of loss is 50% and the expected loss is $500. Consider now a home, which cost $500 000. It is better behaved than the dog, but is not far from a bush fire area. Its probability of loss is 0.1% and hence the expected loss is $500. Both home and dog have the same expected loss, and are possibly equally loved. Yet almost everybody insures their home and hardly anybody insures their dog. Why?

Consider two investments, which both have the same expected shortfall. In one case, however, this arises from a high probability of many small shortfalls, and in the other, a low probability of a very large shortfall. An investor who employs expected shortfall as their only risk measure will be indifferent between the two investments. Such an attitude, however, is not common. Most investors perceive a low probability of a large loss to be far more risky than a high probability of a small loss, even when the expected losses are the same.

This is confirmed by the results of a survey by Olsen (1997) of 630 professional portfolio managers and 740 experienced individual investors. Forty per cent of the experienced individuals rated 'A large loss' as the most important characteristic of investment risk. The professional portfolio managers, being much more benchmark aware, were almost equally divided between 'Below target returns' and 'A large loss' as the most important characteristic.

Clearly we must conclude that risk is *non-linear*. Measures that capture this non-linear attitude to risk are covered later. The list of features of an ideal risk measure, which appeared earlier, is now complete (for current purposes[2]).

8.3 PSYCHOLOGY OF RISK

At this stage it is extremely important to appreciate one aspect of the psychological perception of risk.[3] For anyone searching for a single universally applicable risk measure, the most devastating perceptional phenomena are summarized succinctly by Tversky and Thaler (1990):

First, people do not possess a set of pre-defined preferences for every contingency. Rather, preferences are constructed in the process of making

*a choice or judgement. Second, the context and procedures involved in
making choices or judgements influence the preferences ... In practical
terms, this implies that behaviour is likely to vary across situations that
economists consider identical.*

This means that no single predetermined risk measure, no matter how intuitively
and apparently correct it is, will suffice in all situations.

How can we handle these psychological realities of investment risk, which
at first glance seem pathologically intractable? First, we must acknowledge that
risk, like beauty, is in the eye of the beholder. Hence risk must be measured relative to one or more risk benchmarks, which represent the investor's objectives
or liabilities. Secondly, where possible and practicable, the investor should be
presented with the complete probability distribution of expected returns relative
to the risk benchmark(s). Such distributions explicitly and implicitly provide *all*
of the relevant statistical information available about an individual investment.

For other aspects related to the psychology of investment risk, Begg (1992)
reviews the literature for an actuarial audience in a very readable manner.
Another interesting partial review relating to the irrationality of investors is
provided by Clark-Murphy (1997)

8.4 COMPARING PROBABILITY DISTRIBUTIONS

One solution to the psychological problems discussed above is to provide the
complete probability distribution to the decision-maker. Provision of the probability distribution of investment returns relative to the risk benchmark allows
the probability of any particular relative return (or group of relative returns),
any moment of the distribution, such as the mean, standard deviation, skewness,
kurtosis, any other statistics, like the median, mode, inter-quartile range, and
many other features to be determined.

Various probability-based measures of risk were described earlier and their
strengths and weaknesses discussed. In later sections, various moments will be
discussed. Are there, however, methods for comparing complete distributions of
two alternative investments? There are, but before discussing two of them, we
shall address the question of whether to compare probability density functions
or cumulative probability distribution functions.

8.4.1 Density or distribution?

Consider the histograms shown in Figure 8.9 for 500 samples from probability
density functions for the returns from two hypothetical investments 'X' and
'Y'. It is difficult to see by eye how the two differ and which is the more desirable investment. The same underlying data are shown as sample cumulative

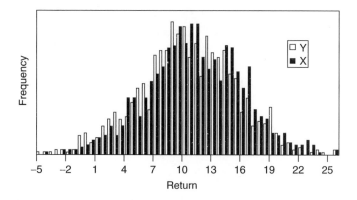

Figure 8.9 *Probability density function*

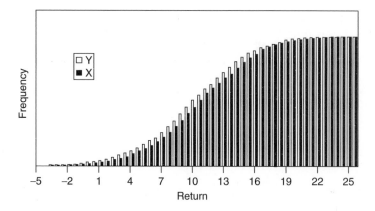

Figure 8.10 *Cumulative probability distribution*

probability distributions in Figure 8.10. It is now quite clear how the two investments differ. The following criteria for comparing distributions are presented in terms of cumulative probability distribution functions.

8.4.2 First order stochastic dominance

Consider the same two investments 'X' and 'Y', with cumulative probability distribution functions, $P_x(R)$ and $P_y(R)$, as shown in Figure 8.10. If, for any return, R_1,

$$P_x(R_1) \leq P_y(R_1), \text{ for all values of } R_1 \tag{8.4}$$

then 'X' is said to first order stochastically dominate 'Y'. Geometrically, this is equivalent to the cumulative distribution function $P_x(R)$ always lying below (or touching) that for $P_y(R)$ but never crossing it. Hence 'X' always has a lower probability of poor returns than 'Y'. Under the simple assumption that investors prefer more to less, then 'X' becomes the preferred investment.

Unfortunately, in many if not most practical situations of interest, the cumulative distribution functions cross and neither investment stochastically dominates the other using a first order criterion. A real example of such a situation, involving the median large diversified fund and the median capital guaranteed fund in Australia over a particular period, is given in Figure 8.11. In such cases, the approach fails to discriminate between the two investments.

While discussing first order stochastic dominance, Promislow (1989) states:

> *When choosing between two possible investments, where one has a higher expected return but also carries more* [intuitive] *'risk' ... it is usually the case that neither distribution dominates.*

8.4.3   Second order stochastic dominance

Second order stochastic dominance can be considered for situations like that shown in Figure 8.11. Starting at the lowest returns (left-hand side), calculate cumulatively

$$\text{Area under } P_y(R) - \text{Area under } P_x(R)$$

If it is always positive, or at least non-negative, for any level of return, then 'X' is said to second order stochastically dominate 'Y'. If investors both prefer more to less and are risk-averse, it can be shown (see for example Elton and Gruber, 1987) that rational investors will prefer an investment which second

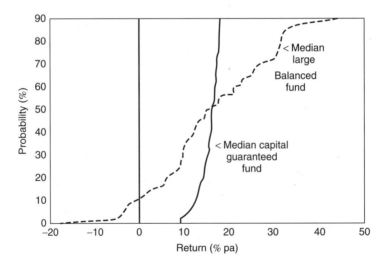

Figure 8.11   *Based on 12-monthly returns after tax and fees. (Source: Noble Lowndes Quarterly Superannuation IPM, Dec. 1981 to June 1992)*

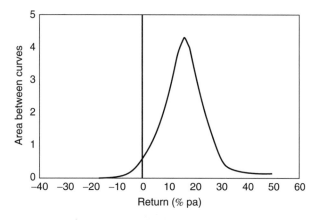

Figure 8.12

order stochastically dominates another. In this case, 'risk aversion' is defined to mean that each increment of higher return is less valuable to the investor than the last.

Whilst superficially promising, unfortunately this approach can also be less than helpful. Figure 8.12 shows the net area between the cumulative probability distribution functions shown in Figure 8.11. As the levels of return increase from their most negative values through to the crossover point near 15% pa in Figure 8.11, the second order stochastic dominance of the capital guaranteed fund over the market linked fund is pronounced. Once past the crossover point, however, the decline is equally steep, leading to only a minor level of dominance if the whole distribution is considered.

For a defined benefit fund with low reserves, which cannot stand any significant losses of capital, the enormous protection against downside risk inherent in the capital guaranteed fund is grossly underestimated by second order stochastic dominance. In fact, if the mean return for the capital guaranteed fund had been slightly lower, the guaranteed fund would have failed to dominate the fund without the guarantee.

Promislow (1989) comments:

> *the concept of dominance cannot help us to solve the problem that we are all too frequently faced with, namely, how to choose from two possibilities, when one has a higher return but also carries more risk.*

Furthermore, he adds:

> *It is possible to have a set* [of investment allocations] *that is theoretically efficient with respect to* [second order stochastic] *dominance but that contains risks that no reasonable decision-maker is likely to want.*

As can be seen from Figure 8.12, the net area concept involved in second order stochastic dominance sheds light on the comparative risk, but its successful use is not simple.

8.5 CONVENTIONAL MOMENT-BASED MEASURES OF INVESTMENT RISK

In many situations a single number, which represents the level of risk associated with a financial asset, is required. Given the shortcomings of the *probability-based* measures considered previously, attention now turns to *moment-based* measures.

8.5.1 Moments of a probability distribution

To avoid confusion in the ensuing discussion, it is important to clarify precisely what is meant by some commonly used, but not necessarily properly understood, statistical terms.

Statistical moments measure various features of the probability distribution of a random variable. These moments can be measured relative to *any* value, a, of the random variable. The two most common values are the *mean* and *zero*. Consider a random return, R. The kth moment, $\mu_a^k(R)$, of R about (relative to) a value a is defined as

$$\mu_a^k(R) = E\{(R - a)^k\} \tag{8.5}$$

where

$$a = \text{value about which the moment is taken,}$$
$$\text{(i.e. deviations are measured from } a\text{),}$$
$$E\{\cdot\} = \text{Expected value of } \{\cdot\}$$

For the later sections of this chapter, it is important to note that many of our moments will be taken about zero and not about the mean as is more common.

For convenience, we shall drop the '(R)' from the moment notation in equation (8.5), when is it clear which random variable is involved. When we deal with upside and downside separately, it will be reintroduced to avoid any possible ambiguity.

Moments can be related to the population or to a sample. Statistically speaking, the 'population' is the set of all possible values of the random variable, whereas a 'sample' refers to some selection of realized values from that population. Greek letters, such as the μ in equation (8.5), are often used to denote a parameter based on the population, with non-Greek equivalents, such as m, used for a statistic based on a sample.

The *first moment about zero*, μ_0^1, is the *mean*, often denoted simply by μ. The mean is the statistically expected value or, more simply, the average value of the random variable.

The *second moment about the mean*, μ_μ^2, is the *variance* and is usually denoted by σ^2, where the superscript '2' denotes the square of σ. The *standard deviation*, σ, is a measure of the width of the probability distribution (strictly the probability density function). As such it is a measure of *uncertainty* in the random variable – typically the uncertainty of the return in investment applications.

The *third moment about the mean*, μ_μ^3, is related to the *skewness* of the probability density function. A skewed probability density function is *not* symmetric about its mean value. For example, a positively skewed distribution has an extended tail on the right (the higher return side), whereas a negatively skewed distribution has a long tail on the left (the lower return side).

The *coefficient of skewness*, s, is a normalized version of μ_μ^3, defined as

$$s = \mu_\mu^3/\sigma^3 = \mathrm{E}\{[(R - \mu)/\sigma]^3\} \tag{8.6}$$

Other measures of skewness include

$$(\mu - \text{Mode})/\sigma$$

and the robust non-parametric measure

$$(Q_3 - 2 \times \text{Median} - Q_1)/(Q_3 - Q_1)$$

where Q_1 and Q_3 are the first and third quartile boundaries within the appropriate sample. For a normal (Gaussian) distribution, the coefficient of skewness is zero because the distribution is symmetric.

Even though many finance practitioners think of *kurtosis*, the *fourth moment about the mean*, μ_μ^4, as a measure of the thickness of the tails, it is primarily a *measure of the peakedness* of the probability density function near the mode, the most frequent value. The *coefficient of kurtosis*, k, is defined as a normalized and modified version of the fourth moment of the distribution:

$$k = \mathrm{E}\{[(R - \mu)/\sigma]^4\} - 3 \tag{8.7}$$

The coefficient of kurtosis is zero for a normal distribution,[4] which is termed *mesokurtic*. A distribution that is less peaked has a negative coefficient of kurtosis and is termed *platykurtic*. It also has 'thinner' tails. A distribution that is more peaked has a positive coefficient of kurtosis, is termed *leptokurtic* and has 'fatter' tails. Many financial distributions are fat tailed and leptokurtic.

The kth moment of the population about the *mean* is sometimes denoted by μ^k. The practice is not followed here, because too much ambiguity would result.

A normal (Gaussian) distribution is completely specified by its mean and variance, since the distribution has only two parameters, μ and σ, which specify its location on the horizontal axis and its breadth.

8.5.2   Standard deviation measures uncertainty not risk

Perhaps the greatest disservice done to standard deviation in the finance literature has been to call it *the* measure of investment *risk*. There is no doubt that it is *a* measure of *uncertainty*, but *uncertainty is not necessarily risk*. It is uncertain whether you might win $1 million in a lottery, but that uncertainty is hardly risk.

In the portfolio construction context, even the father of Modern Portfolio Theory, Markowitz (1959) has commented, 'Analyses based on S [semi-variance] tend to produce better portfolios than those based on V [variance]'. His main reason for proceeding with variance, however, seems to have been the lack of adequate computing power in the 1950s.

8.5.3   Problems with standard deviation as a risk measure

Standard deviation is a statistical measure of variability. When applied to investment returns, it is a measure of the volatility of those returns. Quite obviously, other things being equal, most investors will prefer less volatile returns to more volatile returns. Other things, however, are not usually equal and these are precisely the conditions under which the deficiencies of standard deviation as a risk measure begin to surface.

Consider again investment 'A' shown in Figure 8.1. If standard deviation of return is used as a measure of investment risk, then because the standard deviation of 'B' is higher than that of 'A', investment 'B' would be classed as more risky than 'A'. This conclusion coincides with our intuition.

In Figure 8.13, a third investment 'C', which has the same standard deviation as 'B' but a higher mean, is introduced. The standard deviation of 'C' is twice that of 'A'. Hence using standard deviation as the risk measure would lead to the conclusion that 'C' is more risky than 'A'. Intuitively, however, most investors would consider 'A' to be more risky than 'C' – exactly the opposite conclusion.

Another practical difficulty with standard deviation as a risk measure can be illustrated by considering investment 'D', as shown in Figure 8.14, which has the same standard deviation as both investments 'B' and 'C'. Since the standard deviations of 'C' and 'D' are equal, using standard deviation as the risk measure leads to the conclusion that 'C' and 'D' are equally risky. Most investors would be very uncomfortable with such an assertion. Most investors would feel very strongly that 'D' is far more risky than 'C'.

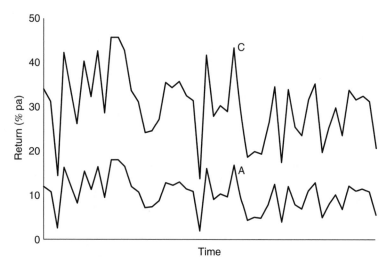

Figure 8.13

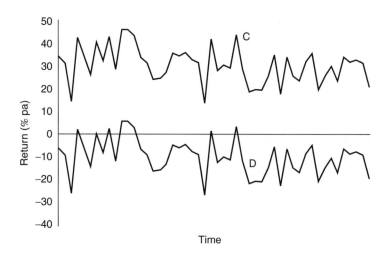

Figure 8.14

In summary, the preceding examples indicate that using standard deviation of return as a stand alone measure of investment risk *can* lead to:

- intuitively reasonable results when the means are equal, or close to equal;
- rankings of investment risks which are sometimes the reverse of investors' intuitive rankings; and
- equal numerical risk rankings for investments which have very different levels of intuitive risk.

8.5.4   Discussion of problems with standard deviation

8.5.4.1   *Equal influence of positive and negative deviations*
Calculation of the standard deviation of return begins with deviations from the mean return. Above-average returns lead to positive deviations and below-average returns to negative deviations. The deviations are then squared which produces all positive values. The average of the squared deviations is then determined. Finally, the square root is taken to restore the dimensions and units of the measure to those of the original time series. As a consequence of the squaring operation, positive and negative deviations from the mean contribute equally to standard deviation. Thus, if standard deviation is used as a risk measure, over-performance relative to the mean is penalized just as much as under-performance. Most investors find such a feature counter-intuitive in a risk measure.

8.5.4.2   *Options, non-linear trading strategies and non-normal distributions*
If a large number of factors influence the outcome of a random process in a linear manner, the probability distribution for that process will tend towards a normal (Gaussian) distribution.[5] We saw earlier that a normal distribution is completely described or specified by its first two moments, namely the mean and standard deviation. In the presence of non-linearities, such as options and non-linear trading and portfolio management strategies, however, investment return distributions can become markedly distorted away from a normal distribution. In such cases, higher order moments are required to describe and specify the distribution.

Bookstaber and Clarke (1985) present examples where:

> *If one used standard deviation or variance as a proxy for risk, it would appear that covered call writing is preferable* [for risk reduction] *to buying puts*

and where:

> *buying puts* [for risk reduction] *is inferior to the stock-only portfolio.*

Most investors would consider such propositions ludicrous. Bookstaber and Clarke then draw the obvious conclusion that:

> *Variance is not a suitable proxy for risk in these cases because option strategies reduce variance asymmetrically.*

Clearly, the presence of non-linear instruments or strategies, which distort the return distribution, render standard deviation an even less meaningful measure of investment risk than we might otherwise have concluded.

8.5.4.3 Non-stationarity

Stationarity simply means that the probability distribution does not change with time. Hence the mean, standard deviation and any other descriptive measures of the distribution are constant over time. If the investment return process is essentially non-stationary, which many market participants believe, then the process will not be ergodic. Its ensemble statistics at a point in time will not be the same as its time series statistics. Hence any standard deviation calculated along a sample time series in the conventional manner will not be the same as the true ensemble standard deviation at a fixed point in time. The sample standard deviation will then be unsatisfactory as a measure of uncertainty, let alone as a risk measure. It should also be realized that non-stationarity creates the same problem for all of the risk measures discussed in this chapter.

8.5.5 Utility function basis for variance as a risk measure

How did the use of variance or standard deviation as a risk measure come about? The theory of utility functions is often claimed to lead to variance, and hence standard deviation, as *the* natural measure of investment risk. It will be seen later, however, that utility theory can be used to arrive at an infinite set of downside risk and upside utility leakage measures, simply by formulating the problem differently.

Expected utility is a generalization of expected value and is thought to have been developed over 200 years ago by Nikolaus Bernoulli when working on the St Petersburg Paradox. Consider an unspecified function, $U(R)$, which purports to represent the usefulness or utility of the time-varying investment return $R(t)$ to some particular investor.[6] If the utility function is expanded about the mean value, μ, of the return using a Taylor series expansion

$$
\begin{aligned}
U(R) &= U(\mu) + U'(\mu)(R - \mu) \\
&\quad + U''(\mu)(R - \mu)^2/2 \\
&\quad + Higher\ order\ terms
\end{aligned}
\tag{8.8}
$$

where

U' denotes dU/dR, the first derivative U with respect to R, and

U'' the second derivative.

Taking expected values in equation (8.8) and using σ^2 to denote the variance of the return, R, leads to the expected value of the utility function

$$
\begin{aligned}
\mathrm{E}\{U(R)\} &= U(\mu) + U''(\mu)\sigma^2/2 \\
&\quad + \mathrm{E}\{Higher\ order\ terms\}
\end{aligned}
\tag{8.9}
$$

since $\mathrm{E}\{\mu\} = \mu$ and $\mathrm{E}\{R - \mu\} = 0$.

If the returns are normally distributed, then the odd *Higher order terms* are zero. Neglecting the even ones leads to

$$E\{U(R)\} \approx U(\mu) + U''(\mu)\sigma^2/2 \qquad (8.10)$$

If investors are concerned only about the expected (i.e. average) utility, then it is claimed that they need only be concerned with the mean and the variance of the investment return. Since variability of return can provide some discomfort for an investor (as seen for Investment 'B' earlier) and has some connection with intuitive risk, variance is said to be the natural risk measure. But we saw that variance or standard deviation can lead to intuitively unreasonable results. Wherein lies the problem?

8.5.5.1   *Accuracy in region of interest*
Most students of mathematics are fully aware that a truncated Taylor series expansion is only approximately true in the neighbourhood of the point about which the expansion is taken – the mean return μ in this case. It is not in the neighbourhood of the mean, however, where the risk-related concerns of most investors lie. Earlier, we saw that investors are most concerned about downside returns. Furthermore, they are more concerned about those downside returns that are most painful and hence well away from the mean. Thus investors are most concerned about a region of returns where the truncated expansion in equation (8.10) is known to be potentially – possibly highly – inaccurate. Interpreting equation (8.10) to imply that variance is the only, or even the best, measure of risk could be expected to lead to difficulties. To gain accuracy further into the downside region of interest requires retention of the higher order terms which have been discarded. Even for normal distributions, the even order terms are non-zero.

8.5.5.2   *Non-linear instruments and strategies*
In portfolios with non-linear instruments, such as options or non-linear trading strategies, return distributions are known to have highly non-normal distributions. In such situations, the discarded *higher order terms* are non-zero and their neglect could be expected to lead to potentially erroneous results. Using standard deviation as the only risk measure does just this.

8.5.5.3   *Decreasing marginal utility*
For increasing variance to reduce utility, equation (8.10) implies that $U''(R)$ must be strictly negative, i.e. the utility curve must be concave downwards. Decreasing marginal utility must prevail for all returns. Balzer (1994) claimed that requiring marginal utility to be strictly decreasing presents some difficulties. Balzer quotes Knott (1991), Alexander and Francis (1986) and others as pointing

out that it implies that 'wealthier investors prefer to take less financial risk (in absolute terms) than poorer investors'. Balzer (1994) adds that the corollary, that poorer investors are prepared to take higher risks than wealthier investors, is totally untenable.

There is an important *non sequitur* here. The decreasing marginal utility required for $U''(R)$ to be negative is along an individual's own utility curve. Decreasing marginal utility is not required *across* different individuals with different wealth levels. As we shall see later, decreasing marginal utility for an individual *is* a realistic assumption.

8.5.5.4 Jump discontinuities

In addition, equations (8.8), (8.9) and (8.10) all require that the utility function be at least twice differentiable. There is some uncertainty, however, that the first derivative even exists at all points, let alone the second or higher ones. Lipman (1989) argues, *inter alia*, that utility functions are both multivariate and discontinuous. He claims that utility functions suffer finite jumps at actual or perceived psychological benchmarks, such as zero returns or the minimum return required to meet a fund's liabilities. He argues that for many investors, a transition from positive to negative returns leads to a step reduction in utility rather than a smooth quadratic change. Similarly, failing to meet liabilities usually precipitates regulatory sanctions, which cause a similar sudden step reduction in utility of return. Finite values for the first, second and higher order derivatives do not exist at such points of discontinuity, rendering the Taylor series expansion in equation (8.8) not just unhelpful, but non-existent.

8.5.5.5 Benchmark relativity

A final difficulty with equation (8.10) is that it takes no account of the risk benchmarks which, as we saw earlier, act as important proxies for the liabilities or objectives of the investor.

8.5.5.6 Conclusion

It is clear that measures justified on the basis of the above use of the Taylor series expansion, which is only accurate for near average returns, and on utility functions, which are multiply differentiable, cannot be expected to be robust nor applicable over a wide range of returns, especially those on the far downside.

In a later section we shall see that by starting with benchmark relative returns, separating upside returns from downside, by using separate Maclaurin series expansions for the upside and downside, and by retaining more of the higher order terms, all of the above problems are overcome. This approach leads directly to a rich set of intuitively reasonable and mathematically justifiable measures of downside risk and upside utility leakage.

8.5.6   Skewness as a risk measure

Positive skewness in investment returns implies some curtailment of the downside. As such it is a feature that risk-averse investors would look favourably upon. The latter does not imply, however, that skewness makes a good investment risk measure. Equation (8.6) shows that the coefficient of skewness is affected by returns that are greater than the average return. Consequently, it is possible to have investments with similar skewness but quite different downside behaviour. Measures which only involve the downside are to be preferred.

8.5.7   Fourth moment – kurtosis

If two investments have similar means and are symmetric, then risk-averse investors will prefer negative kurtosis due to the less frequent occurrence of extremely negative results. When the mean returns are dissimilar, kurtosis as a risk measure suffers from the same problems as standard deviation.

8.5.8   Variance, skewness and kurtosis relative to benchmark

It was noted earlier that the kth moment of a distribution could be taken relative to *any* particular value, a, of the random variable – see equation (8.5). In financial applications, the second, third and fourth moments are typically calculated relative to the mean value. They could be taken, however, relative to some constant target return τ [per cent pa], related to the investor's liabilities or objectives. Sortino and Price (1994) and others have termed this value the minimum acceptable return, MAR. Thus τ would replace μ in equations (8.5), (8.6), (8.7) and in the calculation of standard deviation, σ. This would lead to a relative standard deviation, relative skewness and relative kurtosis.

If risk benchmarks similar to those discussed earlier, such as the inflation rate, etc. are introduced, then the constant parameter τ should be replaced by the random variable $B(t)$. The necessary calculations can then proceed in at least two ways. First, if the joint probability distribution $p(R, B)$ of R and B is known, or is to be assumed, then it can be used directly in forming the expectations in equations (8.5), (8.6) and (8.7). Alternatively, especially if empirical distributions are to be employed, the simplest approach is to construct a time series of benchmark-relative returns $r(t) = R(t) - B(t)$ and then to carry out the calculations using $p(r) = p(R - B)$ in a one-dimensional framework.[7]

While these relative measures explicitly acknowledge the existence of a benchmark representing the liabilities or objectives of the investor, they still suffer from the same problems as the original non-relative measures.

8.6   RELATIVE LOWER PARTIAL MOMENTS

8.6.1   Definition of RLPMs

From arguments similar to those regarding probability-based measures appearing earlier in this chapter, Balzer (1994) concluded:

> *It is clear that investors are primarily concerned with* downside risk *relative to one or more proxies for their liabilities and objectives, i.e. relative to their personally relevant risk benchmarks. Hence we should concentrate on moments related to the downside tails of the return distributions relative to potentially random, rather than simply static, benchmarks.*

Markowitz (1959) considered returns relative to a fixed target return. Bawa (1975), Fishburn (1977), Harlow (1991) and others considered a group of lower partial moments (LPMs) relative to such a fixed target return. Balzer (1994) then went on to make a conceptual extension of this work by generalizing the constant 'target return τ' to a random benchmark return, $B(t)$, which varies over time. To emphasize the difference, Balzer modified the formulation and defined a class of *benchmark relative* lower partial moments

$$\text{RLPM}^n = \text{E} \left\{ \begin{matrix} |(R - B)^n| \, ; & R - B < 0 \\ 0, & R - B \geq 0 \end{matrix} \right\} \tag{8.11}$$

The concept of a relative lower partial moment captures a number of intuitively appealing investment risk measures.

The resulting class of RLPMs provide an elegant set of interesting information regarding returns which fall short of the benchmark.

RLPM^0 is the *probability of shortfall*
RLPM^1 is the *expected shortfall*
RLPM^2 is the *relative lower partial variance*
RLPM^3 is related to the *relative lower partial skewness*
RLPM^4 is related to the *relative lower partial kurtosis*

8.6.2   Inclusion of zeros

In calculating the RLPMs, it is very important to replace positive relative returns with zeros as indicated in equation (8.11) and then to include them when calculating the average values. For example, in the case of RLPM^0, without the zeros, the probability of shortfall will always be 100%, which of course is totally misleading. Also, without the zeros, the upside and downside variances do not add up to the total variance. See later for further details.

8.6.3   Expected shortfall

There is an important difference between the expected shortfall calculated according to equation (8.3) and RLPM^1 obtained from equation (8.11) with $n = 1$. Equation (8.3) finds the average of only the shortfalls. Whereas the RLPM^1 based expected shortfall will be a smaller number because of the additional zeros included in the average. Both are of interest and are equally valid, but just different, ways of looking at the benchmark relative returns.

8.6.4   Relative semi-variance

RLPM^2 is particularly interesting. Several names can be given to it. In the RLPM framework it is the *relative lower partial variance* of the return relative to the risk benchmark. In Markowitz-like terminology, it is the *relative semi-variance*.

As an investment risk measure, relative semi-variance avoids the problems of all the probability- and moment-based measures considered thus far. It is clearly both an *asymmetric* and a *relative* measure, which penalizes returns below the risk benchmark, but avoids penalizing over-performance. Consequently, it will give meaningful results in portfolios with options and non-linear trading strategies. Because multiple benchmarks can be used, it is potentially *multidimensional*. Unlike all but one (expected shortfall) of the probability-based measures considered earlier, it is *complete*, since its calculation includes all shortfalls. Expected shortfall was shown to suffer from an implicit linear penalty on shortfalls. Relative semi-variance, by squaring the relative downside deviations, penalizes larger shortfalls (below the risk benchmark) more than smaller ones. This captures an essential *non-linear* feature of observed investor behaviour – that most investors perceive infrequent large losses or shortfalls far more risky than more frequent smaller losses or shortfalls.

The use of semi-variance and relative semi-variance for performance measurement and asset allocation are the subject of ongoing research. Suffice it here to remember Markowitz's (1959) comment noted earlier that semi-variance tends to produce better portfolios than those based on variance. Similar results favouring semi-variance in asset allocation have been obtained by many others. Dolan (1991), Harlow (1991) and Cariño and Fan (1993) get similarly good results in asset allocation after introducing a *constant* target rate of return relevant to the investor. The use of relative semi-variance goes one step further by introducing a *time varying* risk benchmark, which serves as a proxy for the investor's liabilities or objectives. By calculating semi-variance relative to the investor's own *investor-specific* risk benchmark, the results can only be improved.

8.6.5 RLPM^3

RLPM^3 is obviously related to *relative lower partial skewness* or *relative semi-skewness*, in a similar way to the relationship of the normal third moment to the normal coefficient of skewness – see equation (8.6). RLPM^3 does not suffer from the problem of returns above the risk benchmark being included. Being a one-sided measure, it differs from relative semi-variance only in the power to which the downside deviation is raised. In effect it puts a cubic penalty on deviations below the benchmark return, in place of the quadratic penalty in variance. Hence its behaviour should be similar to relative semi-variance, except that it will 'dislike' larger shortfalls even more strongly.

8.6.6 Relative lower partial kurtosis

RLPM^4 is related to *relative lower partial kurtosis* or *relative semi-kurtosis*. It penalizes large downside deviations even more strongly than the lower order moments by applying a quartic power to them.

8.6.7 RLPM conclusions

The RLPMs provide a powerful group of risk measures, which can be used for performance measurement and for portfolio construction. Although they are intuitively very appealing, they can be criticized for not having a theoretical basis for their use as the natural way of measuring investment risk. The following section addresses this shortcoming.

8.7 UTILITY AND PARTIAL MOMENTS

Balzer (1994) and others appeal to investors' intuition, investment experience and logic to justify the use of downside risk measures. In the following sections, a mathematical derivation, which leads naturally to downside risk measures, is developed. In the process of this development, a unified theory of measures of upside and downside utility is achieved.

8.7.1 Separation of upside and downside utility

We begin by considering returns relative to a benchmark, $B(t)$, which is a random variable. Define the benchmark relative return, $r(t)$

$$r(t) = R(t) - B(t) \qquad (8.12)$$

Because we are particularly interested in downside returns, we pursue the simple device of separating the time series of relative returns into two series, one for 'upside' and one for 'downside'

$$r(t) = u(t) + d(t) \tag{8.13}$$

where

$$u(t) = \left\{ \begin{array}{ll} r(t), & r(t) \geq 0 \\ 0, & r(t) < 0 \end{array} \right\} \tag{8.14}$$

and

$$d(t) = \left\{ \begin{array}{ll} 0, & r(t) > 0 \\ r(t), & r(t) \leq 0 \end{array} \right\} \tag{8.15}$$

The variable $u(t)$ obviously represents upside returns. It contains all of the positive values of the relative return, where the investment outperforms the benchmark, together with zeros for those instances where the investment return falls short of the benchmark. Similarly, the variable $d(t)$ represents the downside returns. It contains all of the negative values of the relative return, where the investment falls short of the benchmark, together with zeros for those returns where the investment outperforms the benchmark. Note that the downside series, $d(t)$, carries the actual negative values of the relative return and not just the magnitudes. The rare occasions upon which the investment return and the benchmark return are exactly equal produce zeros in both time series.

Consider an unspecified function, $U(r)$, which represents (to the limited extent that any simple univariate function can) the usefulness or utility[8] of the investment returns $r(t)$ relative to a particular investor's benchmark. Because the upside and downside time series are disjoint (with the exception of zero), linearly additive and orthogonal, the utility of the relative return time series is simply the sum of the utilities of the separate upside and downside time series. In this situation, utility is essentially a distributive operator and

$$U(r) = U(u) + U(d) \tag{8.16}$$

We next expand each of the upside and downside utility functions using separate Maclaurin series expansions about zero benchmark relative return. This is a particularly attractive point, about which to develop the expansions, as it marks the division between out-performing and under-performing the benchmark.

The upside utility about $u = 0$ becomes

$$U(u) = U(0) + U'(0)u + U''(0)u^2/2! + U'''(0)u^3/3! + \cdots \tag{8.17}$$

where U' denotes dU/du, the first derivative of U with respect to u, U'' the second derivative, U''' the third, etc.

We now turn to downside utility. It was noted earlier that, because of the psychological idiosyncrasies exhibited by investors, a small negative return is likely to be significantly more undesirable than a small positive return (of the same magnitude) is desirable. To allow for the possibility of a jump discontinuity at zero, we modify the problem formulation slightly, but very significantly, by expanding the downside utility function about a point infinitesimally below zero. This feature is very powerful. It allows *all* or *any* of the derivatives of the utility function to be discontinuous at zero. Hence the utility function can have a downward jump discontinuity at zero, or the slope can kink, or both, if desired. Furthermore, the curvature, the rate of change of curvature, etc. can all be discontinuous across zero.

Expanding the downside utility function about a point, 0^-, infinitesimally below zero,

$$U(d) = U(0^-) + U'(0^-)d + U''(0^-)d^2/2! + U'''(0^-)d^3/3! + \cdots \quad (8.18)$$

Taking the expected values of equations (8.17) and (8.18) leads to the expected (i.e. average) upside utility:

$$E\{U(u)\} = U(0) + U'(0)E\{u\} + U''(0)E\{u^2\}/2!$$
$$+ U'''(0)E\{u^3\}/3! + \cdots \quad (8.19)$$

and to the expected downside utility

$$E\{U(d)\} = U(0^-) + U'(0^-)E\{d\} + U''(0^-)E\{d^2\}/2!$$
$$+ U'''(0^-)E\{d^3\}/3! + \cdots \quad (8.20)$$

Combing the expected upside and downside utilities according to the expected values of equation (8.16) gives the complete expected utility of the benchmark relative return:

$$E\{U(r)\} = U(0) + U(0^-) + U'(0)E\{u\} + U'(0^-)E\{d\}$$
$$+ U''(0)E\{u^2\}/2! + U''(0^-)E\{d^2\}/2!$$
$$+ U'''(0)E\{u^3\}/3! + U'''(0^-)E\{d^3\}/3!$$
$$+ U^{iv}(0)E\{u^4\}/4! + U^{iv}(0^-)E\{d^4\}/4!$$
$$+ \textit{Higher order terms} \quad (8.21)$$

8.7.2 Zeroth order utility

The first term in equation (8.21), $U(0)$, is the utility of zero relative return – the utility of meeting but not exceeding the benchmark. Since this is essentially a neutral result, $U(0)$ can be set to zero, without any loss of generality for comparing investments or for portfolio construction

$$U(0) = 0 \quad (8.22)$$

The second term $U(0^-)$ represents the disutility of falling short of the benchmark by even a very small amount. It reflects the reality that, illogically or otherwise, many trustees, plan sponsors and individual investors dislike even the smallest amount of negative return. If $U(0)$ is zero, then $U(0^-)$ is the magnitude of the sudden drop in the utility function when the returns fall short of the benchmark and the relative return becomes negative. Clearly, it will not be positive.

$$U(0^-) = \text{Downward jump in utility at zero } r(t)$$

$$\leq 0 \tag{8.23}$$

If one believes that the effect is not present for the investor(s) of interest, then it can be set to zero, otherwise it will assume a negative value.

8.7.3   First order utility

The third and fourth terms in equation (8.21), namely $U'(0)E\{u\}$ and $U'(0^-)$ $E\{d\}$, capture the utility of the average upside $E\{u\}$ and average downside $E\{d\}$.

Mathematically, $U'(R)$ represents the marginal utility of return. Geometrically, it is the slope of the utility curve at a particular return, r. If the investor prefers more to less, then $U'(r)$ is positive and so are both $U'(0)$ and $U'(0^-)$. Furthermore, it is not unreasonable to assume that they are equal. Why? When optimizing the risk/return characteristics of a portfolio, it is normal to maximize the expected return subject to some penalty on risk. The expected return is simply the sum of the upside and downside returns

$$E\{r\} = E\{u\} + E\{d\} \tag{8.24}$$

In the optimization, the weighting placed on the return is unity and the investor's risk aversion is incorporated by the weighting placed on the risk term(s). Given these two observations, it is clearly reasonable to make the upside and downside marginal utilities equal to each other, and equal to unity

$$U'(0) = U'(0^-) = 1 \tag{8.25}$$

8.7.4   Second order upside utility

The fifth term in equation (8.21), $U''(0)E\{u^2\}$, represents the rate of change of upside marginal utility of return, weighted by the upside variance measured about zero.

The many practitioners and theoreticians who have argued for the replacement of variance with downside semi-variance in portfolio construction are implicitly arguing that this term is irrelevant to the investor. This is equivalent to arguing that $U''(0)\mathrm{E}\{u^2\} = 0$. Now, since $\mathrm{E}\{u^2\}$ is non-zero, $U''(0)$ must be zero. If $U''(0)$ is zero, so must all the higher derivatives of $U(0)$. Combining this with equations (8.17), (8.22) and (8.25), the upside utility function would collapse to an upwardly sloping straight line

$$U(u) = u$$

The use of downside semi-variance in place of variance is equivalent to assuming no decrease in the marginal utility of return as the upside return increases.

Balzer (1994) was well aware of this implication, but believed it to be a true description of actual investor behavior. Later in 1994, however, discussions with the late and eminent psychologist Amos Tversky, at Stanford University, indicated that the empirical evidence was, as Tversky put it, 'overwhelmingly in favour of decreasing marginal utility of [upside] return'. Whilst we might think that we do not behave this way, objective observation of our actual behaviour indicates that we do.

The mathematical consequences of decreasing marginal utility of upside return are that $U''(u)$ and hence $U''(0)$ are non-zero and negative. Mathematically

$$U''(0) < 0$$

We shall see in the following section that the marginal utility of downside returns is also decreasing. The rapidly decreasing steepness of the utility curve as we move away from larger negative returns compared with the far more gentle decrease in steepness of the curve as we move towards larger upside returns implies that

$$U''(d) < U''(u) < 0 \qquad (8.26)$$

Thus the rate of change of the marginal contribution to upside return is decreasing, but decreasing at a lesser rate than for downside returns. At zero benchmark relative return, the rates might be and probably will be equal, hence

$$U''(0^-) \leq U''(0) < 0 \qquad (8.27)$$

8.7.5 Second order downside utility

The sixth term in equation (8.21), $U''(0^-)\mathrm{E}\{d^2\}$, represents the rate of change of marginal utility of downside return, weighted by the downside variance measured about zero. Decreasing marginal utility also applies to downside returns. This is consistent with the utility curve being steeper at very large downside returns than it is at smaller ones. Hence the rate of change of marginal utility is negative

$$U''(0^-) < 0 \qquad (8.28)$$

Since $E\{d^2\}$ is always positive due to the squaring of negative values of d, the contribution to total utility is negative

$$U''(0^-)E\{d^2\} < 0 \qquad\qquad (8.29)$$

This term reduces utility by applying a quadratic penalty to downside returns and is clearly risk-related. Furthermore, $E\{d^2\}$ can be interpreted as relating to the *amount of risk* and $U''(0^-)$ as relating to the investor's *aversion to this particular measure of risk*. It is important to note that we have not said that $E\{d^2\}$ is the *only* measure of risk. Other measures will emerge.

Is $E\{d^2\}$ related to risk? Yes, clearly so! Is it a risk measure? No! There is a widespread misconception that, when variance is used in mean-variance portfolio construction, it is the measure of risk. It is not. The risk measure is in fact *standard deviation* and variance is the result of applying a quadratic penalty to it via the objective function used in the optimization process.

The application of quadratic penalties in optimization problems is widespread throughout science and engineering. It is done for several reasons, including the removal of negative signs so that positive and negative deviations from the optimal solution do not cancel each other out. Far more important, however, is the concept of applying penalties to features that are considered undesirable in the optimal solution. Large values of the undesirable features are usually considered to be far worse than smaller values. Hence a quadratic penalty which penalizes large values very much more than small ones is usually employed. Furthermore, in many optimization problems with quadratic penalties, analytical solutions can be found,[9] thus avoiding often massive, time-intensive and ill-conditioned numerical procedures.

It also makes sense for the measure of a feature of return, namely risk, to be dimensionally homogeneous with return itself. Return is measured as a proportion or percentage per unit time, expressed dimensionally as $[T^{-1}]$, whereas variance of return is measured in those units squared, i.e. (percentage per unit time)^2, which is dimensionally $[T^{-2}]$. Using variance as the risk measure is dimensionally inconsistent.

The utility function in equation (8.21) is essentially the investor's objective function and can be used to find the investor's optimal portfolio. Consequently, the conceptually correct interpretation of $E\{d^2\}$ is that it is a quadratic penalty applied to downside returns and that the correct risk measure is its square root, $\sqrt{E\{d^2\}}$. Various names and notation are possible for this quantity. Probably the most common scientific or engineering designation would be RMS (Root Mean Square) *downside*, designated d_{RMS}. Conventionally, the RMS value is taken to be the positive square root. Using the μ_a^k notation introduced in equation (8.5), the second order downside risk measure would be denoted $\sqrt{\mu_0^2(d)}$, which, while avoiding any possible ambiguity, is somewhat cumbersome. Attempting to use the relative lower partial moment notation becomes equally cumbersome, $\sqrt{\text{RLPM}_0^2}$, and is too unwieldy to verbalize.

Another possibility is to use $\sigma_0(d)$, where the zero subscript denotes measurement of deviations about zero. This is also unambiguous and reasonably compact. It could be verbalized as 'downside semi-standard deviation', but this verbal descriptor *is* ambiguous, because it might be interpreted incorrectly as being calculated about either the mean relative return, or even the mean downside return, and not about zero.

In the sequel, the term RMS *downside* and the symbol d_{RMS} will be used both for compactness and for the avoidance of any possible ambiguity. Using this notation, the term $U''(0^-)\text{E}\{d^2\}$ in equation (8.21) becomes $U''(0^-)d_{\text{RMS}}^2$, which clearly indicates a quadratic penalty with negative weighting, $U''(0^-)$, on the RMS downside risk measure, d_{RMS}.

8.7.6 Second order 'upside utility leakage'

Using the RMS notation, the second order upside utility term in equation (8.21), namely $U''(0)\text{E}\{u^2\}$, can be rewritten as $U''(0)u_{\text{RMS}}^2$. Since $U''(0)$ is negative, there is clearly a quadratic reduction in utility for very high upside returns. Should the RMS upside, u_{RMS}, then be thought of as 'upside risk'? No! The reduction in utility arises from our psychological devaluation of the contribution of very high returns to upside utility. It does not arise from a classification as something that is 'risky', or even 'unpleasant'. The phenomenon is better thought of as *upside utility leakage*, quantified by $U''(0)u_{\text{RMS}}^2$. One might even think of $U''(0)$ as a devaluation operator acting on the RMS upside squared. We shall simply refer to it as a *sensitivity* to upside utility leakage.

8.7.7 Third order upside utility

The third order upside utility term in equation (8.21) is $U'''(0)\text{E}\{u^3\}$. For consistency with the RMS notation, we define RMC *upside* to denote the cube-Root Mean Cube upside

$$u_{\text{RMC}} = \sqrt[3]{\text{E}\{u^3\}}$$

The third order upside utility term can then be written as $U'''(0)u_{\text{RMC}}^3$.

The nature and properties of the weighting, $U'''(0)$, placed on the RMC upside are interesting. $U'''(0)$ is obviously the rate of change of the marginal upside utility, but this interpretation sheds little light on its properties or on the values it might assume.

The term u_{RMC}^3, however, is identical to $\mu_0^3(u)$ and is hence directly related to upside skewness measured about zero. Since u_{RMC}^3 is positive, a positive value for $U'''(u)$ would lead to a positive third order contribution to upside utility. This is consistent with anecdotal evidence suggesting that most investors view positive skewness as a desirable feature in a return distribution. It seems reasonable to assume that $U'''(u)$ is positive.

$$U'''(u) > 0 \qquad (8.30)$$

8.7.8   Third order downside utility

The third order downside utility term in equation (8.21) is $U'''(0^-)\mathrm{E}\{d^3\}$. In a similar manner to the upside, we define RMC *downside* to denote the cube-Root Mean Cube downside

$$d_{\mathrm{RMC}} = \sqrt[3]{\mathrm{E}\{d^3\}} \qquad (8.31)$$

The third order downside utility term then becomes

$$U'''(0^-)d_{\mathrm{RMC}}{}^3$$

Again, the quantity $d_{\mathrm{RMC}}{}^3$ is identical to $\mu_0^3(d)$ and is directly related to downside skewness measured about zero. The research of Olsen (1997) and others has shown that investors particularly dislike very large downside returns, so a positive skewness in returns below benchmark should be desirable. Hence $U'''(0^-)$ should be positive

$$U'''(0^-) > 0 \qquad (8.32)$$

Since the downside returns are negative by definition, so is the expected value of the cubed downside returns. Its cube root is thus also negative. With $U'''(0^-)$ positive, the third order downside utility term is then clearly negative.

In the same way that the second order downside utility was seen to be a quadratic penalty on downside returns, the third order term is clearly a cubic penalty on returns that fall short of the benchmark. Thus RMC downside, d_{RMC}, is not only another risk measure, but one which satisfies all of the desirable features listed earlier, except for positivity. The latter is of no great consequence, as positivity was seen to be a matter of convention rather than substance. The weighting placed on the cubic penalty is $U'''(0^-)$.

Later, it will be shown that both $U'''(0)$ and $U'''(0^-)$ are positive for the logarithmic utility function, which is consistent with equations (8.30) and (8.32).

8.7.9   Fourth order upside utility

The fourth order upside utility term in equation (8.21) is $U^{iv}(0)\mathrm{E}\{u^4\}$. Again for consistency with the RMS notation, define RMQ *upside* to denote the positive fourth-Root Mean Quartic upside

$$u_{\mathrm{RMQ}} = \sqrt[4]{\mathrm{E}\{u^4\}} \qquad (8.33)$$

The fourth order upside utility term can then be written as $U^{iv}(0)u_{\mathrm{RMQ}}{}^4$.

The quantity u_{RMC}^4 is identical to $\mu_0^4(u)$ and is directly related to upside kurtosis measured about zero.

The nature and properties of the weighting, $U^{iv}(0)$, placed on the RMQ upside, are interesting. A positive weighting on u_{RMC}^4 in the utility function could produce unpleasant consequences. The fourth power would lead to very large returns contributing enormously to upside utility. In portfolio construction applications, this could easily lead to the selection of stocks with rare and perhaps very uncertain large returns. Most portfolio managers, however, prefer frequent small to moderate upside contributions. They typically dislike and actively avoid infrequent very large ones. The risks of not being overweight at exactly the right time are just too great.

Another important behavioural consideration arises from performance measurement. When unusually large returns drop out of rolling 12 and 36 month performance figures, the latter suffer quite dramatic falls. Large falls arising for whatever reason are usually disliked by superannuation and pension fund members and are not received well by fund administrators or their advisers. Fund managers, in turn, dislike such events because their clients do.

These attitudes imply that $U^{iv}(u)$ is negative for large returns.

It was noted above that u_{RMC}^4 is directly related to upside kurtosis. Positive upside kurtosis not only means fatter upside tails, but also a more pronounced peak near the mode – 'narrower shoulders'. This in turn means fewer small positive returns. But part of the fund manager aversion to infrequent very large returns is a liking, other things being equal, for frequent smaller returns. Hence the weighting factor $U^{iv}(u)$ is likely to be negative for smaller as well as larger returns.

All of these considerations imply that $U^{iv}(u)$ should be negative.

$$U^{iv}(0) < 0 \tag{8.34}$$

This is another instance of upside utility leakage, but at a higher order.

Later, the logarithmic utility function will be seen to have a negative fourth derivative.

8.7.10   Fourth order downside utility

The fourth order downside utility term in equation (8.21) is $U^{iv}(0^-)E\{d^4\}$. In the now familiar manner, we define RMQ *downside* to denote the positive fourth-Root Mean Quartic downside

$$d_{RMQ} = \sqrt[4]{E\{d^4\}} \tag{8.35}$$

The fourth order downside utility term then becomes

$$U^{iv}(0^-)d_{RMQ}^4$$

The quantity d_{RMQ}^4 is identical to $\mu_0^4(d)$ and is directly related to downside kurtosis measured about zero. As noted earlier, investors particularly dislike very large downside returns, so the fourth order downside contribution to utility will clearly be negative. Since $d_{RMQ}{}^4$ is positive, the fourth derivative of utility must be negative

$$U^{iv}(0^-) < 0 \tag{8.36}$$

The fourth order term is a quartic penalty on returns, which fall short of the benchmark. Thus RMQ downside, d_{RMQ}, is yet another risk measure, which satisfies all of the desirable properties listed earlier.

Later it will be shown that $U^{iv}(0^-)$ is negative for the logarithmic utility function and hence satisfies equations (8.34) and (8.36).

8.7.11   Higher order terms

The higher order terms in equation (8.21) involve quintic and higher powers on upside and downside returns relative to the benchmark.

On the upside, if the corresponding derivative is positive, this will lead *ceteris paribus* to portfolios skewed further and further towards the stocks with more returns in the upside tails of the relative return distribution. Portfolios could be expected to become more and more concentrated in fewer and fewer stocks. Given fund managers' negative attitude to returns highly dependent on a small number of very big winners, the higher derivatives are likely to be negative or close to zero.

On the downside, higher order penalties on returns below benchmark will express more extreme risk aversion. In addition, portfolios could be expected to become narrower and more concentrated in the stocks that have fewer returns in the downside tails of the relative return distribution. This is one of the results found by Nawrocki (1992) in his research into using individual lower partial moments in portfolio construction.

The higher order terms also become increasingly negligible quite rapidly for two reasons. First, within the range of convergence of the power series in equations (8.17)–(8.21), both u and d have magnitudes that are less than one, otherwise the power series do not converge. Raising u and d to higher and higher powers will lead to smaller and smaller quantities. Secondly, each term is divided by the factorial of same number as the power. These divisors increase very rapidly $-120, 720, 5040, \ldots$ for the quintic, etc. terms. Later, an analysis of approximating the logarithmic utility function will show the decreasing significance of the higher order terms.

8.7.12   Utility, downside risk and upside utility leakage

The utility of the return relative to benchmark can now be summarized in the RMS style notation developed in the preceding sections.

Equation (8.21), which gives the expected utility, can now be restated as

$$
\begin{aligned}
E\{U(r)\} = {} & E\{r\} \\
& + U(0^-) + U''(0^-)d_{\mathrm{RMS}}^2/2! + U'''(0^-)d_{\mathrm{RMC}}^3/3! + U^{iv}(0^-)d_{\mathrm{RMQ}}^4/4! \\
& + U''(0)u_{\mathrm{RMS}}^2/2! + U'''(0)u_{\mathrm{RMC}}^3/3! + U^{iv}(0)u_{\mathrm{RMQ}}^4/4! \\
& + \text{Higher Order Terms}
\end{aligned}
\tag{8.37}
$$

Equation (8.37) provides a powerful and fascinating insight into the nature of the trade-off between investment risk and return. The first line confirms that *expected return* is a major component of the *expected utility* of an investment. The second line, however, immediately reduces that utility by a number of penalties on *downside risk* measures. The third line then reduces it further by what is termed, in this work, *upside utility leakage*. The final line acknowledges that, strictly speaking, there are an infinite number of measures of downside risk and upside utility leakage, as indicated by the *higher order terms*. These higher order terms could reasonably be expected to be negligible in most applications.[10]

The *downside risk* terms are very intuitive. The first, $U(0^-)$, was seen in equation (8.23) to be negative and to represent the downward jump in utility encountered as soon as the investment return falls below the benchmark. It is essentially the *disutility of a negative sign* in the relative return. The second term, $U''(0^-)d_{\mathrm{RMS}}^2/2!$, is a *quadratic penalty* on the RMS *downside* risk measure, d_{RMS}. The weight, $U''(0^-)/2!$, placed on this penalty is the *second order risk aversion* parameter, which is negative. The third term, $U'''(0^-)d_{\mathrm{RMC}}^3/3!$, is a *cubic penalty* placed on the RMC *downside* risk measure, d_{RMC}. The weight, $U'''(0^-)/3!$, placed on it is the *third order risk aversion* parameter. Unlike the even order downside risk measures, d_{RMS} and d_{RMQ}, the odd order d_{RMC} is negative. Hence the weight on it was seen to be positive. The fourth risk term, $U^{iv}(0^-)d_{\mathrm{RMQ}}^4/4!$, is a *quartic penalty* placed on the RMQ *downside* risk measure, d_{RMQ}. The weight, $U^{iv}(0^-)/4!$, placed on it is the *fourth order risk aversion* parameter, which is negative.

The *upside utility leakage* terms capture investors' devaluation of upside returns. There are likely to be at least two psychological phenomena at work here. The first is probably a general steadily decreasing marginal utility of upside return – a sort of 'Why bother? Is the effort really worth it?' effect. The second is a more clear-cut unease about infrequent very large returns – an unease about depending on a few big wins to keep the average return up.

The first upside utility leakage term, $U''(0)u_{\mathrm{RMS}}^2/2!$, is a *quadratic penalty* on the RMS *upside* leakage measure, u_{RMS}. The weight, $U''(0)/2!$, placed on this is the *second order leakage sensitivity*, which is negative. Perhaps it captures most of the gentle and diffuse diminishing returns to upside utility. The second term, $U'''(0)u_{\mathrm{RMC}}^3/3!$, is a *cubic penalty* placed on the RMC *upside* utility leakage measure, u_{RMC}. The weight placed on it, $U'''(0)/3!$, is the *third order leakage sensitivity*, which is probably (anomalously) positive to reflect investor preference for mild positive skewness. The third term, $U^{iv}(0)u_{\text{RMQ}}^4/4!$, is a *quartic penalty* placed on the RMQ *upside* utility leakage measure, u_{RMQ}. The weight, $U^{iv}(0)/4!$, placed on it is the *fourth order leakage sensitivity*, which is almost certainly negative to capture investor unease about depending on a few infrequent very large returns to obtain adequate average returns.

These utility leakage effects could be expected to be much more gentle than the vigorously expressed dislike, bordering on fear at times, of large losses of capital. These statements are consistent with the Olsen (1997) behavioural research and also with the shape of the often used logarithmic utility function analysed later.

The sensitivities to upside and downside are not equal. Hence the use of double-sided moments incorporating both upside and downside in one measure are not a realistic representation of investor preferences and behaviour.

8.7.13   Special cases: mean–variance, mean–semi-variance and mean–RLPMs

Equation (8.37) is a particularly elegant summary of the risk/return behaviour of most investors. It is also a generalization of several of the most widely accepted theories and contains them as special cases. This is a highly desirable situation.

8.7.13.1   Relative mean–RLPM portfolio construction

If we assume that there is no special psychological aversion to a negative sign appearing in front of the benchmark relative return, i.e. there is no downward jump in utility at $r = 0$, then

$$U(0^-) = 0 \tag{8.38}$$

If, contrary to the psychological research, it is assumed that the marginal utility of upside return does not decrease (or increase), then

$$U''(0) = U'''(0) = U^{iv}(0) = \cdots = 0 \tag{8.39}$$

and if the terms of order higher than four are neglected

$$\text{Higher order terms} = 0 \tag{8.40}$$

then under all of these assumptions equation (8.37) reduces to

$$\boxed{\begin{aligned} E\{U(r)\} = E\{r\} + U''(0^-)d_{\text{RMS}}^2/2! + U'''(0^-)d_{\text{RMC}}^3/3! \\ + U^{iv}(0^-)d_{\text{RMQ}}^4/4! \end{aligned}} \tag{8.41}$$

If equation (8.41) is used as the objective function for portfolio optimization, the optimal portfolio will have *maximal return relative to the benchmark* after the *relative lower partial variance, skewness and kurtosis*, all calculated using deviations from zero benchmark relative return, have been *penalized*.

8.7.13.2 *Relative mean–relative semi-variance portfolio construction*

The behavioural research of Olsen (1997) and others indicates that investors are very averse to deep downside returns –very large shortfalls below benchmark. This risk aversion is probably not captured by a quadratic downside penalty alone, and needs both cubic and quartic penalties to capture it. (See later analysis of logarithmic utility function and its approximation by a power series.) If, however, one ignores this evidence and not only makes the above assumptions in equations (8.38), (8.39) and (8.40), but also assumes that the cubic and quartic penalties in equation (8.37) can be neglected

$$U'''(0^-) = U^{iv}(0^-) = 0 \qquad (8.42)$$

then equations (8.37) and (8.41) further reduce to

$$\boxed{E\{U(r)\} = E\{r\} + U''(0^-)d_{\mathrm{RMS}}^2/2!} \qquad (8.43)$$

This is a relative mean–relative semi-variance objective function, where the semi-variance is measured using deviations from zero benchmark relative return. Thus the optimal portfolio will have a *maximal return relative to the benchmark* after the *downside semi-variance* (measured about zero relative return) has been *penalized*.

8.7.13.3 *Mean–semi-variance portfolio construction*

In this chapter, the importance of measuring returns relative to a benchmark, which acts as a proxy for the investor's liabilities or objectives, has been emphasized. If, however, those liabilities or objectives are ignored entirely, the relative return collapses down to the total return. Ignoring the benchmark is mathematically equivalent to setting it identically equal to zero

$$B(t) \equiv 0 \qquad (8.44)$$

so that the benchmark relative return becomes the total return

$$r(t) = R(t) - B(t) = R(t) \qquad (8.45)$$

and the first term on the right-hand side of equation (8.43) becomes

$$E\{r\} = E\{R\} \qquad (8.46)$$

In the second term, the second order risk aversion parameter becomes

$$U''(r = 0^-) = U''(R = 0^-) \qquad (8.47)$$

and the variable $d(t)$ now contains the downside values of the total return $R(t)$ from the investment. The RMS downside squared then becomes

$$d_{RMS}{}^2 = E\{d^2\} = [\mu_0^2(d)]^2 = [\sigma_0(d)]^2 = \sigma_0(d)^2 \qquad (8.48)$$

where the σ notation has been used for greater transparency. In words, $\sigma_0(d)$ is the standard deviation, *measured about zero total return*, of the downside total return series, which, as in equation (8.15), is padded with zeros when the investment return $R(t)$ is positive.

With all of the preceding assumptions and the additional assumption of benchmark irrelevance, equations (8.37) and (8.43) reduce to

$$\boxed{E\{U(R)\} = E\{R\} - \lambda_d \sigma_0(d)^2} \qquad (8.49)$$

where the modified risk aversion parameter λ_d is

$$\lambda_d = -U''(R = 0^-)/2! \qquad (8.50)$$

This is a mean–semi-variance objective function, where the semi-variance of the downside total investment return is measured using deviations from zero total return. Thus the optimal portfolio will have a *maximal return* after the *downside semi-variance* (about zero total return) has been *penalized*.

8.7.13.4   *Mean–variance portfolio construction*

The array of simplifying assumptions made in the preceding subsections is substantial. Many features, which are either confirmed by behavioural or other research, or are believed strongly by intelligent and experienced practitioners to exist, have been assumed away. If one of these assumptions is reinstated, a mean–variance utility function will be seen to emerge as a special case of equation (8.37).

In equation (8.39), the sensitivity to second order upside utility leakage, $U''(0)$, was assumed to be zero. If this assumption is reversed and the phenomenon of diminishing marginal upside utility reinstated, but all of the other simplifying assumptions retained, then

$$E\{U(R)\} = E\{R\} + U''(R = 0^-)d_{RMS}{}^2/2! + U''(R = 0)u_{RMS}{}^2/2!$$

If it is further assumed that the second derivative of the utility function is continuous and smooth at zero total investment return, then

$$U''(R = 0^-) = U''(R = 0) = U''(0) \text{ [say]} \qquad (8.51)$$

and

$$E\{U(R)\} = E\{R\} + U''(0)(d_{RMS}{}^2 + u_{RMS}{}^2)/2! \qquad (8.52)$$

From equations (8.13), (8.14) and (8.15), it is fairly simple to show algebraically that

$$r_{\mathrm{RMS}}^2 = u_{\mathrm{RMS}}^2 + d_{\mathrm{RMS}}^2 \tag{8.53a}$$

or

$$\sigma_0(r)^2 = \sigma_0(u)^2 + \sigma_0(d)^2 \tag{8.53b}$$

or

$$Var_0(r) = Var_0(u) + Var_0(d) \tag{8.53c}$$

where $Var_0(\cdot)$ denotes the variance measured about zero and not about the mean.

Under these circumstances, equation (8.52) reduces to

$$E\{U(R)\} = E\{R\} + U''(0)r_{\mathrm{RMS}}^2/2!$$

But since the benchmark has been ignored

$$r_{\mathrm{RMS}} = R_{\mathrm{RMS}} \tag{8.54}$$

and

$$\boxed{E\{U(R)\} = E\{R\} - \lambda\sigma_0(R)^2} \tag{8.55}$$

where the risk aversion parameter is

$$\lambda = -U''(0)/2! \tag{8.56}$$

and where $\sigma_0(R)$ denotes the standard deviation of the total return $R(t)$ *measured about zero*. It is *not* equal to the normal standard deviation $\sigma(R)$, which is measured about the mean value of $R(t)$.

$$\sigma_0(R) \neq \sigma(R) \tag{8.57}$$

This is a very interesting result. Maximizing the utility function in equation (8.55) is a mean–variance optimization – but not quite the traditional one. It will result in a portfolio with *maximal total return* after a *quadratic penalty* has been applied to the *double-sided variance measured about zero*. It is a form which Markowitz investigated (see Levy and Markowitz, 1979), but it is not the one which has subsequently become popular. Originally, Markowitz concluded that taking the Taylor series expansion about the mean total return was a better approximation of several utility functions than taking it about zero total return. This is not surprising since more of the returns will be in this region than near any other point. Equation (8.37), however, deals with benchmark relative returns. If Markowitz had been working with benchmark relative returns, he might very well have found that an expansion about zero benchmark relative return was the more accurate.

8.7.14   Conclusion

The unified theory of the utility of upside and downside benchmark relative returns expressed in equation (8.37) is both powerful and elegantly simple. It captures many features of investor preferences, which are not captured by previous models and paradigms.

8.8   LOGARITHMIC UTILITY

8.8.1   Asymmetric treatment of upside and downside returns

There is an interesting asymmetry between positive and negative percentage returns, whereby a $+x\%$ return is not equal and opposite in its effect on terminal wealth to a $-x\%$ return. For example, assume that an investor has \$100 and that over two consecutive periods, the returns are -50% and $+50\%$. At the end of the two periods, the investor has only \$75. If the chronological order of the returns is reversed, the result is unchanged. Clearly a $+50\%$ return does not cancel out a -50% return. It takes $+100\%$ to do so. The natural log of the return relative, $\ln(1 + r)$, however, does behave symmetrically:

$$-50\% \Rightarrow \ln(1 - 0.5) = -0.693$$

$$+100\% \Rightarrow \ln(1 + 1.0) = +0.693$$

Using a logarithmic utility function, $\ln(1 + r)$, -50% and $+100\%$ are seen to be equivalent in terms of their effect on terminal wealth.[11] Thus the logarithmic utility function treats upside and downside returns differently, but treats their effects on terminal wealth equally.

8.8.2   Motivation

We shall use the logarithmic utility function to explore two issues. The first is to gain a feel for realistic magnitudes for the downside risk aversion parameters and upside utility leakage sensitivities in equation (8.37). The second is to explore how quickly, or otherwise, the higher order terms become negligible.

8.8.3   Indicative magnitudes for parameters

Consider the logarithmic utility function

$$U(r) = \ln(1 + r), \quad \text{for } -1 < r \tag{8.58}$$

Note that this choice of $U(r)$ is not defined for relative returns less than or equal to -100%. Hence $(1 + r)$ will always be positive here.

The first four derivatives of the utility function are

$$U'(r) = \frac{1}{1 + r} = +\text{ve} \tag{8.59}$$

$$U''(r) = -1(1 + r)^{-2} = \frac{-1}{(1 + r)^2} = -\text{ve} \tag{8.60}$$

$$U'''(r) = 2(1 + r)^{-3} = \frac{2}{(1 + r)^3} = +\text{ve} \tag{8.61}$$

$$U^{iv}(r) = -6(1 + r)^{-4} = \frac{-6}{(1 + r)^4} = -\text{ve} \tag{8.62}$$

Values for the risk aversion parameters and the utility leakage sensitivities are shown in Table 8.1.

First, let us consider the parameter values for zero benchmark relative return, $r = 0$. Since the utility curve is continuous at zero, there is no downward jump at zero and the 'disutility of a negative sign' is zero.

$$U(0^-) = 0 \tag{8.63}$$

which is consistent with equation (8.23).

From equations (8.59)–(8.62), it is clear that all derivatives are continuous at zero and that

$$U^i(0^-) = U^i(0), \quad \text{for all } i$$

The marginal utility of zero relative return (i.e. benchmark return) is unity

$$U'(0^-) = U'(0) = 1 \tag{8.64}$$

which is consistent with equation (8.25).

The second order risk aversion parameter and utility leakage sensitivity are negative

$$U''(0^-)/2! = U''(0)/2! = -0.5 \tag{8.65}$$

which is consistent with equation (8.27).

Table 8.1 *Parameter values for logarithmic utility function*

Relative return	-50%	-25%	0%	$+25\%$	$+50\%$
r	-0.50	-0.25	**0**	$+0.25$	$+0.50$
$U(r)$	-0.69	-0.29	**0**	0.22	0.41
$U'(r)$	2.00	1.33	**1.00**	0.80	0.67
$U''(r)/2!$	-2.00	-0.89	**−0.50**	-0.32	-0.22
$U'''(r)/3!$	2.67	0.79	**0.33**	0.17	0.10
$U^{iv}(r)/4!$	-4.00	-0.79	**−0.25**	-0.10	-0.05

The third order risk aversion and utility leakage sensitivity are equal and positive

$$U'''(0^-)/3! = U'''(0)/3! = +0.33 \qquad (8.66)$$

which is consistent with equations (8.30) and (8.32).

The fourth order risk aversion and leakage sensitivity are negative

$$U^{iv}(0^-)/4! = U^{iv}(0)/4! = -0.25 \qquad (8.67)$$

which is consistent with equations (8.34) and (8.36).

Hence the signs of the parameters are consistent with earlier arguments. The magnitudes of these coefficients decrease as their order increases, which is consistent with the higher order terms contributing less to the total utility. It is also consistent with the convergence of the series expansions used in equations (8.17) and (8.18).

The behaviour of the magnitudes as one moves across the rows is also interesting. In Table 8.1, the row for the first derivative indicates that the utility curve is steepest for deep downside returns, which is entirely consistent intuition and the behavioural research. It becomes less steep as relative returns become less negative and flatter as they move positive. The row for the second derivative shows a progression from larger negative to a smaller negative values is consistent with decreasing marginal utility and equation (8.26).

The progression of the second, third and fourth derivatives (from left to right across the bottom three rows in Table 8.1) from larger to smaller magnitudes is consistent with *downside risk aversion being a more powerful phenomenon and upside utility leakage being a much weaker phenomenon.*

8.8.4 Importance of higher order terms

The above results can also be used to test how many terms in equation (8.37) are required to obtain a reasonable approximation to a known and realistic utility function, namely the logarithmic utility function currently under analysis. We begin by substituting the numerical values from equations (8.63)–(8.67) into equation (8.37).

In Figure 8.15, the actual logarithmic utility function is shown by the thick black line. The crudest possible approximation to it involves only the first term on the right-hand side of equation (8.37)

$$E\{U(r)\} \approx E\{r\} \qquad (8.68)$$

In Figure 8.15, this is shown by the thin dotted straight line. This is the base case with no downside risk aversion or upside utility leakage.

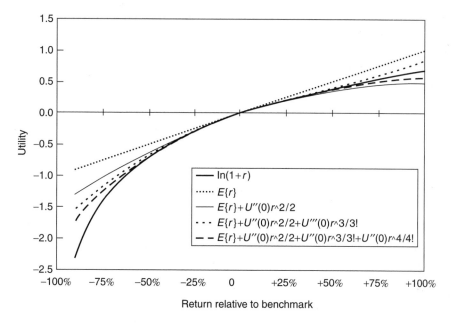

Figure 8.15 *Logarithmic utility function*

The next level of approximation is gained by adding the second order terms, which leads to

$$E\{U(r)\} \approx E\{r\}$$
$$+ U(0^-) + U''(0^-)d_{\text{RMS}}^2/2! + U''(0)u_{\text{RMS}}^2/2! \qquad (8.69)$$

This is shown in Figure 8.15 by the thin solid line. For negative relative returns, the gap between the dotted line of equation (8.68) and this line is due entirely to the second order downside risk aversion arising from the quadratic penalty on the RMS downside, d_{RMS}. This is what downside semi-variance would capture, provided that the deviations were measured about zero relative return and not about the mean total, or relative, return. For deep downside returns, it is clear that this risk measure and penalty only capture about *half* of what is specified by the logarithmic utility function! For returns closer to benchmark, there is little difference on the scale of this graph.

For large positive relative returns, the second order upside leakage penalty very significantly overestimates the decrease in marginal utility as returns rise. This indicates that precisely the same thing will happen if simple variance is used as the risk measure.

The next level of approximation is gained by adding in the third order terms, which leads to

$$E\{U(r)\} = E\{r\}$$

$$+ U(0^-) + U''(0^-)d_{\text{RMS}}^2/2! + U'''(0^-)d_{\text{RMC}}^3/3!$$

$$+ U''(0)u_{\text{RMS}}^2/2! + U'''(0)u_{\text{RMC}}^3/3! \tag{8.70}$$

which is portrayed by the thick dotted line in Figure 8.15. This captures more of the aversion to downside returns inherent in the logarithmic utility function, but is still well short of the very significant logarithmic aversion to deep downside returns. On the upside, however, the cubic penalty on RMC upside causes an underestimate of the upside utility leakage, driving it from the level of equation (8.69) closer to but above the logarithmic utility line.

The final level of approximation to be considered here is to add the fourth order terms which leads to

$$E\{U(r)\} = E\{r\}$$

$$+ U(0^-) + U''(0^-)d_{\text{RMS}}^2/2! + U'''(0^-)d_{\text{RMC}}^3/3! + U^{iv}(0^-)d_{\text{RMQ}}^4/4!$$

$$+ U''(0)u_{\text{RMS}}^2/2! + U'''(0)u_{\text{RMC}}^3/3! + U^{iv}(0)u_{\text{RMQ}}^4/4! \tag{8.71}$$

and the thick dashed line in Figure 8.15. On the deep downside, there is again a noticeable improvement in capturing the extreme aversion to deep downside returns – returns far below the benchmark returns. But it still falls short of the logarithmic disutility of such returns. On the upside, utility leakage is again over-estimated at high returns, but less so than for the simpler approximations.

On the downside, the convergence associated with increasing the number of terms is monotonic. On the upside, however, the convergence is oscillatory.

From this indicative analysis, we can conclude that the higher order terms are important in capturing realistic levels of downside risk aversion and upside utility leakage at returns well away from benchmark returns.

For returns closer to benchmark, it might be concluded that the higher order terms are not so important. There are, however, three obvious dangers in this line of thinking. First, the scale of Figure 8.15 does not highlight the discrepancies, which are present at smaller returns. Secondly, small changes in utility might not necessarily be associated with small differences in the composition of the optimal portfolio. This is certainly true of mean-variance optimized portfolios. Thirdly, in the region of zero benchmark relative return, Figure 8.15 appears to suggest that the higher order terms are irrelevant.

The same visual feature also appears to suggest that none of the risk measures is relevant near the benchmark. Why? The simplest approximation, which is the thin dotted line representing equation (8.68), involves only the expected return and no risk measures whatsoever. Yet the difference between the thin dotted line and the original logarithmic utility function also appears to be negligible near zero. Such simplistic logic, based on the appearance of Figure 8.15 alone, would lead us to assume that we could proceed to construct an optimal portfolio without using any risk measure. Without any externally imposed constraints, however, this would result in a totally undiversified portfolio holding only one stock, namely the stock with the highest expected return. Few would find such a 'portfolio' acceptable. The simplistic visual logic is flawed.

It is prudent to assume that risk measures of order higher than two do add worthwhile information to portfolio construction, even with returns closer to benchmark.

8.9   PORTFOLIO CONSTRUCTION

It is not the purpose of this chapter to explore the effects of downside risk aversion and upside utility leakage on the results of the portfolio construction process. Much work has been done on using downside risk measures of various orders. See for example Nawrocki (1992), where the separate effects of individual downside risk measures of various order, integral and fractional, are examined. What is of greater interest, however, is the effect of using all of the downside risk measures in concert with each other, and in combination with the various upside utility leakage measures. This is a potentially rich field for investigation.

Numerical algorithms for portfolio construction are beyond the scope of this chapter. One interesting piece of work, however, is worth mentioning. Jackson (1996) successfully used genetic algorithms to construct portfolios using downside risk measures. Balzer (1993) implies that genetic algorithms are particularly useful for dealing with difficult non-linear optimization problems with a mixture of higher order soft penalties and hard constraints, as are likely to occur in the type of portfolio construction arising out of this chapter. Provided that sufficient genetic diversity is present in the initial population, global rather than local optima are virtually assured.

8.10   EFFICIENT ESTIMATION

The estimation of separate downside and upside moments is non-trivial. The matter is too extensive to address here, except to remark on one aspect. A recurring criticism of downside risk measures is that the estimation of downside statistics is usually based on a relatively small number of downside observations (relative to the number of upside plus downside observations combined). Hence it is less efficient and less accurate than the estimation of double-sided statistics. One way of avoiding this problem is to fit an analytical distribution to the whole data set and then to calculate the upside and downside statistics from the full distribution.

The question then becomes, 'Which distribution?' The author was fortunate enough to be invited to attend the Econometric and Financial Times Series Workshop, which formed part of the six month Nonlinear and Nonstationary Signal Processing Research Programme at the Isaac Newton Institute of Mathematical Sciences in Cambridge, UK (1998).[12] There was a surprising consensus among the leading academics present that the type of fat-tailed distributions found in financial markets are best modelled by a normal (Gaussian) distribution for the bulk of the sample, plus a generalized Pareto distribution for the additional fatness in the tails. Such a parametric approach, if well executed, should increase the efficiency of estimating the required upper and lower partial moments significantly.

8.11 META-RISKS

There are many risks which investors, fund managers, fund trustees, plan sponsors and other financial market participants face. This chapter only attempts to deal with one aspect of investment risk. Gray (2000), however, tackles a wider range of less quantifiable risk in an erudite and interesting manner. He defines meta-risks as risks 'born out of the complex interactions between the behaviour patterns of individuals and those of organizations'. He looks, *inter alia*, at the risks of moral hazard, hubris, insufficient quantitative analysis, inappropriate quantitative analysis, excessive quantitative analysis, liquidity risk, data mining, unchallenged or insufficiently challenged views, complexity, agency risk, and the managing of meta-risks. He concludes that 'a dialectic of risk may be the ultimate form of risk management'. Such a dialectic of the utility of upside and downside benchmark relative returns would be equally valuable.

8.12 CONCLUSION

In this chapter we have attempted to provide a wide-ranging review of the most commonly used or proposed measures of portfolio investment risk.

Realistic risk measures should be asymmetric and be measured relative to one or more benchmarks, which are investor-specific. Risk is multidimensional, and risk measures should be both complete and non-linear. Probability of shortfall and maximum shortfall are incomplete. Expected shortfall is complete, but is only linear and hence inadequate. Consideration of the psychological aspects of investment risk reveals that real investors are economically irrational and, worse still, they often construct the bases for their preferences while making their judgement. One solution is to provide the decision-maker with as much information as possible, preferably the complete cumulative probability distribution function of returns relative to the investor's benchmark(s). First and second order stochastic dominance purport to help in comparing such distributions, but both are of rather limited usefulness.

Conventional double-sided moments of the benchmark relative returns are better than those of total returns, but still not adequate. The major problem with using variance as a risk measure is that it penalizes upside as well as downside returns. It is a measure of uncertainty, but upside uncertainty is not usually classed as risky. Relative lower partial moments are each individually important and informative, but the development of a unified theory of the utility of upside and downside returns relative to benchmark indicates that all upside and downside moments are theoretically involved in measuring utility. RMS (Root Mean Square), RMC (cube-Root Mean Cube) and RMQ (fourth-Root Mean Quartic) downside and upside all meet the requirements for valid measures of downside risk and upside utility leakage, respectively. Quadratic, cubic and quartic penalties on each of these measures all contribute to defining utility by penalizing aspects of investment performance which are important to real investors.

Several methods of portfolio construction are simply special cases of the unified theory encapsulated in the rich and elegant formulation of expected upside and downside utility summarized in equation (8.37).

Analysis of the logarithmic utility function shows that the effects of upside utility leakage can be expected to be much smaller than those of downside risk. Furthermore, third and fourth order measures are likely to be needed to fully capture investor preferences adequately. Quintic and higher order terms are probably negligible.

There is much research to be done – a dialectic of upside and downside utility would be very valuable.

NOTES

1. The process used is lagged white noise with an autocorrelation of 0.2 at lag one and zero for higher order lags.
2. No doubt there are many other properties, features and phenomena associated with risk, but those developed here are sufficient for current purposes.
3. The author would like to express his gratitude to the late and eminent Amos Tversky, Professor of Psychology at Stanford University, for the time which he so graciously made available from a very busy schedule to discuss the importance of psychological perception to the measurement of investment risk.
4. Even though the coefficient of kurtosis is zero for a normal distribution, the fourth moment, μ_μ^4, is not.
5. This is a consequence of the Central Limit Theorem of statistics and is easily verified by numerical examples.

6. The psychological research referred to earlier casts doubt on the extent to which *any pre*-specification of risk, and hence utility, can be achieved, especially with a univariate function.
7. The 'half' surface for $R < B$ in the three dimensional $[R, B, p(R, B)]$ space is thus reduced to a 'half' curve for $X - R < 0$ in the two dimensional $[R - B, p(R - B)]$ plane.
8. We assume that the investor's situation is such that the returns, with which we are concerned here, do not change the investor's total wealth to the point where any wealth effect becomes significant.
9. For example, in the so-called 'LQG problem' of modern control theory, the dynamical system to be controlled is modelled by a set of linear differential or difference equations describing its state, quadratic penalties are applied to deviations from the desired state, and the disturbances to the system and the noise in measurements made on it are modelled as Gaussian processes. Perhaps surprisingly to many readers, and in spite of the need to solve time-varying non-linear matrix differential or difference equations, an optimal control strategy can be found analytically with 'relative' ease.
10. As with all power series expansions, the Maclaurin series expansion is only convergent within a certain range of values of the variable. In the present case, it is convergent for returns relative to benchmark within the range $-1 < r < +1$, where the decimal return '1' represents 100%. In the unlikely event that this restriction proves to be limiting, the problem can be rescaled.
11. A related way of handling the situation is to use continuously compounding returns. Here the equivalent continuously compounding returns are -69.3% and $+69.3\%$.
12. See References for details.

REFERENCES

Alexander, G.J. and Francis, J.C. (1986) *Portfolio Analysis*, Englewood Cliffs, NJ: Prentice-Hall.

Arthur, T.G. and Randall, P.A. (1990) Actuaries, pension funds and investments, *Journal of the Institute Actuaries*, London.

Balzer, L.A. (1990) How to Measure risk, Conference on investment performance, AIC Conferences, Sydney, Australia, 1990.

Balzer, L.A. (1993) Genetic algorithms: a mating game for fund managers, JASSA, Securities Institute of Australia, March.

Balzer, L.A. (1994) Measuring Investment risk: a review, *Journal of Investing*, 3(3), Fall.

Bawa, V.S. (1975) Optimal rules for ordering uncertain prospects, *Journal of Financial and Quantitative Analysis*, 14(2).

Begg, D.A. (1992) Psychology of risk, *Quarterly Journal of the Institute of Actuaries* (Sydney), October.

Bookstaber, R. and Clarke, R. (1985) Problems in evaluating the performance of portfolios with options, *Financial Analysts Journal*, Jan–Feb.

Cariño, D.R., and Fan, Y.-A. (1993) Performance of alternative risk measures, Draft research report, Frank Russell Company, Tacoma, WA, Feb.

Clark-Murphy, M. (1997) The irrational human condition: why some investors avoid logical choice, JASSA, Securities Institute of Australia, Spring.

Dolan, P. (1991) Private communication, Macquarie Bank, Sydney.

Elton, E.J. and Gruber, M.J. (1987) *Modern Portfolio Theory and Investment Analysis*, 3rd edn, Chichester: John Wiley & Sons.

Fishburn, P.C. (1977) Mean-risk analysis with risk associated with below-target returns, *American Economic Review*, 67(2), March.

Gray, J. (2000) Meta-risks: beyond the scope of explicit financial risks, *Journal of Portfolio Management*, 26(3), Spring.

Harlow, W.V. (1991) Asset allocation in a downside risk framework, Salomon Brothers, Equity Portfolio Analysis series, New York, March.

Isaac Newton Institute of Mathematical Sciences (1998) *Nonlinear and Nonstationary Signal Processing Programme*, Cambridge, UK, July–September, 1998. Details at www.newton.ac.uk

Jackson, A.R. (1996) Private communication regarding Honours thesis, Macquarie University, Sydney.

Knott, D. (1991) Semi-variance: an alternative measure of risk, *Relative Value and Credit*, CS First Boston Australia, September.

Levy, H. and Markowitz, H.M. (1979) Approximating expected utility by a function of mean and variance, *American Economic Review*, 69(3), June.

Lipman, R.A. (1989) Utility, benchmarks and investment objectives, *Transactions of the Institute of Actuaries*, Australia.

Markowitz, H.M. (1959) *Portfolio Selection*, CT: Yale University Press, New Haven.

Nawrocki, D.N. (1992) The characteristics of portfolios selected by n-degree lower partial moments, *International Review of Financial Analysis*, 1(3).

Olsen, R.A. (1997) Investment risk: the experts' perspective, *Financial Analysts Journal*, March/April.

Promislow, S.D. (1989) Discussion of preceding paper *An Empirical Method of Comparing Risks Using Stochastic Dominance, Transactions of the Society of Actuaries*, XLI.

Sortino, F.A. and Price, L.N. (1994) Performance measurement in a downside risk framework, *Journal of Investing*, 3(3), Fall.

Tversky, A. and Thaler, R.T. (1990) Anomalies: preference reversals, *Journal of Economic Perspectives*, 4(2).

Source: The first half of this chapter is a revised and extended version of a paper that appeared in *The Journal of Investing* in 1994 and was reprinted in 1995 after it won the journal's 'Paper of the Year' award.

Chapter 9

Lower partial-moment capital asset pricing models: a re-examination

STEPHEN E. SATCHELL

9.1 INTRODUCTION

The use of downside risk in asset pricing models has been available as a tool for financial economists since the papers of Markowitz (1959), Bawa and Lindenberg (1977) and Hogan and Warren (1974). These models have become known as lower partial-moment capital asset pricing models (LMCAPM) as opposed to mean-variance capital asset pricing models (MVCAPM). Specification of such models requires a choice of target rate, below which 'risk' is involved, the above-mentioned authors choosing the riskless rate. Later work by Harlow and Rao (HR) (1989) extended these models to an arbitrary target rate. Further ad hoc extensions not based on equilibrium considerations were advocated by Homaifar and Graddy (HM) (1990). The HM models were criticized by Chow and Denning (CD) (1994) for providing excess returns for the riskless asset. Further criticisms by CD centre on the belief that there were strong distributional assumptions implicit in the work of BL and MR. It is true that HR and BL only proved distribution-free results for $n = 1$, i.e. mean-based models. Proofs for $n > 1$ require making additional convexity assumptions for efficient sets or making distributional assumptions. The distributional assumption made was that the return distributions belong to the location-scale (LS) family which was assumed in proofs by HR. CD correctly point out that under the LS family the LMCAPM beta is equal to the MVCAPM beta or, to be precise, the mean-scale capital asset pricing beta. They also assert, on the basis of this, that the LMCAPM theory is redundant since, in the cases where it is valid, it gives the same (population) beta as the MVCAPM and hence we should use the MVCAPM. If this argument is correct, the whole idea of carrying out econometric work to see if there is a difference between the two models seems utterly misguided. Recent work, see Eftekhari and Satchell (1996), has attempted to measure the difference on the betas empirically in emerging markets where the data are probably not generated by the LS family.

The purpose of this chapter is to challenge this view of equivalence. We do this by applying some theoretical results of Fishburn (1977). This gives us an expected utility function which is consistent with a LMCAPM and does away with the need for distributional assumptions. We show, as a consequence, the validity of the BL and HR models, for all distributions such that the appropriate expectations exist, thereby extending results out of the LS family. This is necessary for establishing models which theoretically can produce different LMCAPM betas from MVCAPM betas. It may be argued that all we have done is replace a dubious assumption about the convexity of an efficient set by an equally dubious assumption about the existence of a representative agent. We present results in this chapter that establish two fund money separation which is a prerequisite for the construction of a representative agent. We use these to present a representative agent. Examination of the representative agent's portfolio suggests that target rates should lie between zero and the riskless rate. This finding strengthens the claims of the HR model rather than the BL model. We present the models and notation in section 9.2 and the theory in section 9.3, conclusions follow in section 9.4.

9.2   MODELS AND NOTATION

In this section we shall concentrate on defining the multitude of models discussed in section 9.1. We assume there are N risky assets, the market, and a riskless asset. We assume throughout that the rates of return of a typical risky asset is $\tilde{y}$, the market is $\tilde{x}$, and the riskless asset is r. For most of the chapter we can consider bivariate relationships involving $\tilde{x}$ and $\tilde{y}$. We define the means and the covariance matrix of $(\tilde{x}, \tilde{y})'$ as

$$E(\tilde{x}) = \mu_x, \quad E(\tilde{y}) = \mu_y, \tag{9.1}$$

and

$$\text{cov}\begin{pmatrix} \tilde{x} \\ \tilde{y} \end{pmatrix} = \begin{bmatrix} \sigma_x^2, & \rho\sigma_x\sigma_y \\ & \sigma_y^2 \end{bmatrix} = \Sigma$$

The CAPM relationships discussed in section 9.1 are of the form

$$(\mu_y - r) = \beta(\mu_x - r) \tag{9.2}$$

where β varies depending upon the theory. Under the Sharpe-Lintner MVCAPM,

$$\beta_{MV} = \frac{\text{cov}(\tilde{x}, \tilde{y})}{\text{var}(\tilde{x})} = \frac{\rho\sigma_y}{\sigma_x} \tag{9.3}$$

The BL and HW LMCAPM model for target rate $\tau = r$ has β defined as

$$\beta_{LM} = \frac{E[(r - \tilde{y})(r - \tilde{x})^{n-1}\Delta]}{E[(r - \tilde{x})^n\Delta]}, \quad n = 1, 2 \tag{9.4}$$

where

$$\Delta = 1 \quad \text{if } \tilde{x} < \tau \ (\tau = r \text{ in this case})$$

$$= 0 \quad \text{otherwise.}$$

We note here that to establish equation (9.4) for $n = 2$ requires some auxiliary assumptions about the convexity of certain sets (see Bawa and Lindenberg, 1977, n. 6). The HR extension for arbitrary τ has

$$\beta_{LM} = \frac{E[(r - y)(\tau - \tilde{x})^{n-1}\Delta]}{E[(r - \tilde{x})(\tau - \tilde{x})^{n-1}\Delta]}, \quad n = 1, 2 \tag{9.5}$$

Also, Proposition 1 of Harlow and Rao (1989) *explicitly* assumes that distributions belong to the LS family, thus equation (9.5) is only established in the special case that $\beta_{LM} = \beta_{MV}$; we also remark that Chow and Denning (1994) make this point very well.

Finally, the HG non-equilibrium based extension has, for arbitrary τ,

$$\beta_{LM} = \frac{E[(\tau - \tilde{y})(\tau - \tilde{x})^{n-1}\Delta]}{E[(\tau - \tilde{x})^n\Delta]}, \quad n = 1, 2 \tag{9.6}$$

Again, Chow and Denning (1994) have shown that this implies a risk premium for the riskless asset! For this reason, we shall not consider equation (9.6) again. The conclusion of this section is that legitimate questions can be raised as to the scope and validity of proofs establishing equations (9.4) and (9.5) under conditions more general than $n = 1$, and $\tau = r$ or where β_{LM} does not automatically equal β_{MV}.

9.3   THEORY

We shall now present our assumptions with discussion.

(1)   There exists a representative agent whose decision rule $(\mu(f), \phi(f))$ is such that she prefers, for given $\phi(f)$, a portfolio with higher $\mu(f)$ and for given $\mu(f)$ she prefers a portfolio with lower $\phi(f)$, where $\mu(f)$ is the expected value of the portfolio with probability density function (pdf), f and $\phi(f)$ is the value $E(\phi(\eta - \widetilde{W}))$ where ϕ is some differentiable convex function, $\widetilde{W}$ is the risky future wealth and E is taken with respect to f, the pdf of $\widetilde{W}$.

(2)   We assume that the class of risky investments are those such that $\mu(f)$ and $\phi(f)$ are finite for all f.

(3)   We assume that the preferences of the representative agent are consistent with expected utility.

We present our generalized CAPM model for such a representative agent investor. That such a representative agent exists is certainly true in the case where there are N identical agents. General assumptions under which we can prove existence are a separate matter that awaits later discussion. We note that we want our representative agent to have preferences that depend only on the aggregate wealth and not on, say, the distribution of wealth.

Proposition 1

If we assume (1), (2) and (3) then the generalized CAPM will be

$$\mu_y - r = \frac{\text{cov}(\bar{y}_i, \phi'(\eta - \widetilde{W})\Delta)}{\text{cov}(\widetilde{W}, \phi'(\eta - \widetilde{W})\Delta)}(\mu_x - r)$$

and Δ is an indicator variable, $\quad \Delta = 1$ if $\widetilde{W} \leq \eta$

and $\quad\quad\quad\quad\quad\quad\quad\quad\quad\quad \Delta = 0$ if $\widetilde{W} > \eta$

(where $\widetilde{W}$ is final period wealth).

Proof   From Fishburn (theorem 2, 1977), and (1), the representative agent must have an expected utility function of the form.

$$U(\widetilde{W}) = \widetilde{W} \text{ if } \widetilde{W} > \eta \quad\quad\quad\quad\quad\quad\quad (9.7)$$
$$= \widetilde{W} - \lambda\phi(\eta - \widetilde{W}) \text{ if } \widetilde{W} \leq \eta$$

if she also satisfies (3).

If we know the utility function of the representative agent we can apply standard equilibrium arguments, see e.g. Huang and Litzenburger (1988), Chapter 6, to show that

$$\mu_y - r = \frac{\text{cov}(\bar{y}_i, U'(\widetilde{W}))}{\text{cov}(\widetilde{W}, U'(\widetilde{W}))}(\mu_x - r)$$

It is assumed by Huang and Litzenburger that U is increasing, strictly concave and differentiable everywhere. These conditions are not necessary and sufficient however as they can be relaxed in certain cases; for example, if there are restrictions on the $\widetilde{W}$ distribution.

We shall rewrite $U(\widetilde{W})$ as

$$U(\widetilde{W}) = \widetilde{W} - \lambda\phi(\tau - \widetilde{W})\Delta$$

which is valid for all $\widetilde{W}$.

Then

$$U'(\widetilde{W}) = 1 + \lambda\phi'(\eta - \widetilde{W})\Delta$$

then

$$\text{cov}(\tilde{y}_i, 1 + \lambda\phi'(\eta - \widetilde{W})\Delta) = \lambda \, \text{cov}(\tilde{y}_i, \phi'(\eta - \widetilde{W})\Delta)$$

and

$$\text{cov}(\widetilde{W}_i, 1 + \lambda\phi'(\eta - \widetilde{W})\Delta) = \lambda\,\text{cov}(\widetilde{W}_i, \phi'(\eta - \widetilde{W})\Delta)$$

so result follows.

What we have proven so far is valid for all differentiable convex functions ϕ, we now specialize to consider the special use of Fishburn's (s, t) functions, i.e. $\phi(\eta - \widetilde{W}) = (\eta - \widetilde{W})^n$ for n a positive number.

Corollary 1.1
If $\phi(\eta - \widetilde{W}) = (\eta - \widetilde{W})^n$ and n a positive number then

$$\mu_y - r = \frac{\text{cov}(\tilde{y}_i, (\eta - \widetilde{W})^{n-1}\Delta)}{\text{cov}(\widetilde{W}_i, (\eta - \widetilde{W})^{n-1}\Delta)}(\mu_x - r)$$

Proof   This follows immediately since $\phi'(\tau - \widetilde{W}) = n(\eta - \widetilde{W})^{n-1}$ and the $-n$'s cancel.

If we wish to work with the market portfolio $\tilde{x}$, then noting that $\widetilde{W} = W_0(1 + \tilde{x})$, and define Δ' to be the same binary variable defined for $\tilde{x}$, setting $W_0 = 1$, without loss of generality, we can replace $(\eta - \widetilde{W})$ by $((\eta - 1) - \tilde{x})$. We define $\tau = \eta - 1$, then the relationship between Δ and Δ' is that $\text{prob}(\tilde{x} < \tau) = \text{prob}(1 + \tilde{x} < \eta)$, so that Δ and Δ' are equivalent binary variables.

We have Corollary 1.2 which converts wealth into returns.

Corollary 1.2
If we wish to measure our CAPM in returns and if we set W_0 (initial wealth) to 1, then

$$(\mu_y - r) = \frac{\text{cov}(\tilde{y}_i, (\tau - \tilde{x})^{n-1}\Delta)}{\text{cov}(\tilde{x}_i, (\tau - \tilde{x})^{n-1}\Delta)}(\mu_x - r) \tag{9.8}$$

The immediate question we wish to ask is whether we can use Proposition 1 to validate the LMCAPMs of BL and HR.

This will follow immediately; we set out the arguments in Proposition 2.

Proposition 2
If $\phi(\eta - \widetilde{W}) = (\eta - \widetilde{W})^n$ for $n = 1$ and $n = 2$ and $W_0 = 1$ and (1), (2) and (3) hold, then the models of HR and BL are valid for the representative agent economy given by (1) and (3) and the class of distributions given by (2).

Proof   For $n = 1$ and arbitrary τ, we need to show that

$$\mu_y - r = \left(\frac{E[(r - \tilde{y})\Delta]}{E[(r - \tilde{x})\Delta]}\right)(\mu_x - r) \tag{9.9}$$

and for $n = 2$ and arbitrary τ, we need to show that

$$\mu_y - r = \left(\frac{E[(r - \tilde{y})(\tau - \tilde{x})\Delta]}{E[(r - \tilde{x})(\tau - \tilde{x})\Delta]} \right) (\mu_x - r) \tag{9.10}$$

where we assume by Proposition 1, for $n = 1$,

$$\mu_y - r = \frac{\text{cov}(r - \tilde{y}, \Delta)}{\text{cov}(r - \tilde{x}, \Delta)} (\mu_x - r) \tag{9.11}$$

and

$$(\mu_y - r) = \frac{\text{cov}(r - \tilde{x}, (\tau - \tilde{x})\Delta)}{\text{cov}(r - \tilde{x}, (\tau - \tilde{x})\Delta)} (\mu_x - r) \quad \text{for } n = 2$$

Now, by definition,

$$\text{cov}(r - \tilde{y}, \Delta) = E((r - \tilde{y})\Delta) - E(r - \tilde{y})E(\Delta) \tag{9.12}$$

and

$$\text{cov}(r - \tilde{x}, \Delta) = E((r - \tilde{x})\Delta) - E(r - \tilde{x})E(\Delta)$$

then equation (9.9) will be implied by equation (9.12) since

$$(\mu_y - r) = \left(\frac{a + b}{c + d} \right) (\mu_x - r)$$

then

$$(\mu_y - r)(c + d) = (a + b)(\mu_x - r)$$

and

$$(\mu_y - r) = \left(\frac{a}{c} \right) (\mu_x - r)$$

if

$$(\mu_y - r)d = b(\mu_x - r)$$

We see that the above gives us,

$$-(\mu - r)E(r - \tilde{x})E(\Delta) = -E(r - y)E(\Delta)(\mu_x - r) \tag{9.13}$$

and the above holds. An identical argument follows for $n = 2$ the LHS of equation (9.13) being now

$$- (\mu_y - r)E[(r - \tilde{x})]E[(r - \tilde{x})\Delta] \qquad \text{Q.E.D.}$$

We can trivially extend Proposition 2 to cover all positive n. This validates the unproven formula for HR when n is any value other than $n = 1$ or 2.

Corollary 2.1

Under the assumption of Proposition 2, the HR model where

$$B_{LM} = \frac{E[(r - \tilde{y})(\tau - \tilde{x})^{n-1}\Delta]}{E[(r - \tilde{x})(\tau - \tilde{x})^{n-1}\Delta]}$$

is valid for all positive n.

We now address the issue as to circumstances when a representative agent exists. To do this we shall attempt to find situations under which two-fund money separation occurs.

We define our utility function for investor k as

$$U_k(z) = \lambda_k z - \frac{1}{n+1}(\eta_k - z)^{n+1} \text{ for } z \leq \eta_k \tag{9.14}$$

$$= \lambda_k z \qquad\qquad\qquad \text{for } z > \eta_k$$

where there are N risky assets and K investors, and where $\lambda_k = \theta(1 - \tau_k/r)^n$.

In preparation for our next proposition, we define the following terms,

$$\text{let } P_{k,\tau k} = \text{Prob} \left(\sum_{i=0}^{N} w_{ik}\tilde{z}_i > \tau_k \right)$$

where w_{ik} is the weight of the ith asset in the portfolio of the kth investor. We present our proposition for two-fund money separation. In Proposition 3, we initially make the overly restrictive assumption that initial wealth is equal. However, in Proposition 4 we relax this.

Proposition 3

Two-fund money separation occurs if the kth investor's utility function satisfies equation (9.14) and all investors have equal wealth and long positions in the risky fund.

Proof   In our proof, we adapt an argument in Ingersoll (1987). The optimal portfolio weights of investor k satisfy

$$E\left(U_k'\left(\sum_{i=0}^{N} w_{ik}\tilde{z}_k\right)(\tilde{z} - r)\right) = k \quad k = 1, \ldots, K \tag{9.15}$$

Since the riskless asset is one fund, the other fund needs to be a linear combination of the z_i's such that w_{ik}/w_{jk} $(i,j \# 0)$ is the same for all k. From equation (9.15) and the form of U_k given by (9.14), converted into returns, we see that, for $\tau_k = \eta_k - 1$,

$$\lambda_k E(z_i - r) + (1 - P_{k_j \tau_k})E$$

$$\times \left[\left(\tau_k - \sum_{i=0}^{N} w_{ik}\tilde{z}_i \right)^n (z_i - r) \middle| \sum_{i=0}^{N} w_{ik}\tilde{z}_i < \tau_k \right] = 0,$$

$$i = 1, N$$

$$k = 1, K \qquad (9.16)$$

Initially, we shall assume that $\tau_k = 0 \forall k$. Then the above equation becomes,

$$\lambda_k E(z_i - r) + (1 - P_{k_j 0})E$$

$$\times \left[\left(-\sum_{i=0}^{N} w_{ik}\tilde{z}_i \right)^n (z_i - r) \middle| \sum_{i=0}^{N} w_{ik}\tilde{z}_i < \tau_k \right] = 0,$$

$$k = 1, K$$

$$1, k = 1, N \qquad (9.17)$$

and where $\lambda_k = \theta(1 - 0/r)^n = \theta$.

We see that the solution of (9.17), w^*, is independent of k since λ_k does not depend on k, nor does $P_{k,0}$. We now turn to the general case where $\tau_k \neq 0$. We suppose that the investor places $1 - \beta_k$ of her wealth in the riskless asset and β_k in an optimal portfolio which includes the riskless asset. We define the weights of the new portfolio as $\tilde{\alpha}_k$ where $\tilde{\alpha}_k = (\alpha_0, \alpha_1, \dots, \alpha_{N_k})$ and $e'\tilde{\alpha} = 1$, the optimal portfolio is just the optimal solution of the previous problem, w_i^* where $w_{ik} = w_i \forall k$ as shown. We see that

$$\alpha_{0k} = (1 - \beta_k) + \beta_k w_0 \qquad (9.18)$$

and

$$\alpha_{ik} = \beta_k w_i, \quad i = 1, \dots, N$$

We now set $\beta_k = 1 - \tau_k/r$. If we substitute into equation (9.16), we see that, $\tilde{W}_k = 1 + \sum \alpha_{ik}\tilde{z}_i$,

$$\Rightarrow \lambda_k E(\tilde{z}_i - r) + (1 - P_{k,\tau_k}) \left(1 - \frac{\tau_k}{r} \right)^n$$

$$\times E\left(\left(-\sum w_i \tilde{z}_i \right)^n (\tilde{z}_i - r)/(\tilde{W}_k < \eta_k) \right) = 0$$

where we have substituted $\beta_k = \left(1 - \frac{\tau_k}{r} \right)$, but

$$\sum_{i=1}^{N} w_{ik}\tilde{z}_i < \tau_k \Rightarrow (1 - \beta_k)r + \beta_k \sum_{i=0}^{N} w_i \tilde{z}_i < \tau_k$$

$$\Rightarrow \tau_k + \beta_k \sum_{i=0}^{N} w_i \tilde{z} < \tau_k$$

or

$$\beta_k \sum_{i=0}^{N} w_i \tilde{z} < 0$$

Thus, we see that (9.16) becomes, since $\beta_k > 0$ by assumption.

$$E(z_i - r) + (1 - P_{k0})E\left(-\left(\sum w_{ik}\tilde{z}_i\right)^n (\tilde{z}_i - r)/\Sigma w_{ik}\tilde{z}_i < 0\right) = 0$$

Since this solution is independent of k as before, two-fund separation is proved

Q.E.D.

We next present a corollary to Proposition 3. Let W_{0k} be the initial wealth of investor k.

Corollary 3.1

If we allow W_{0k} to vary over k, so that initial wealth differs, we see that the result still holds except that we use η_k, the wealth trigger level, where $\eta_k = W_{0k}(1 + \tau_k)$ and

$$\lambda_k = W_{0k}\left(1 - \frac{\tau_k}{r}\right)^n \tag{9.19}$$

Proof   The proof is identical to Proposition 3 and is omitted.

Thus, we can find TFMS for investors with different wealth levels and different triggers, i.e. with the same n and different λ_k. We can now calculate total demand for asset i, d_i, where

$$d_i = \sum_{k=1}^{k} W_{0k} w_i \left(1 - \frac{\tau_k}{r}\right)$$

$$= w_i W_m - \frac{w_i}{r} \sum_{k=1}^{k} W_{0k} \tau_k \tag{9.20}$$

using the results in Corollary 3.1, and $W_m = \sum_{k=1}^{k} W_{0k}$.

From equations (9.19) and (9.20)

$$d_0 = \sum W_{0k}(1 - \beta_k) + \sum W_{0k}\beta_k w_0$$

$$= (1 - w_0) \sum \frac{W_{0k}\tau_k}{r} + w_0 W_m \tag{9.21}$$

For an equilibrium to require that $d_0 = 0$ so that cash is in zero net supply,

$$w_0 = \frac{\sum W_{0k}\tau_k}{\sum W_{0k} - r W_m} \quad \text{and} \quad \sum W_{0k}\tau_k \neq r W_m$$

If $\eta_k = (1 + r)W_{0k}$, for all k, a commonly chosen threshold, so that all investors guarantee themselves at least the cash rate, then, from (9.21), $d_0 = W_m$ and all investors invest all their wealth in bonds, no one holds the other fund; this is hardly an equilibrium situation seen in modern equity markets.

In general, individual behaviour is determined by the relationship between η_k and r. We outline two cases below, for $W_{0k} = 1$,

(1) $\eta_k = 1 + r, \beta_k = 0$ and the investor holds all her wealth in the riskless asset. In this case the condition for the validity of Corollary 3.1 implies that $\lambda_k = 0$ and the investor decision rule depends only on risk, not on expected return.

(2) $0 < \eta_k < (1 + r), \beta_k > 0$ and the investor is long both funds. This has the reasonable property that the 'riskless' asset is assigned zero risk by the representative agent and indeed all agents, see equation (9.7).

If we were to set η_k equal to 1 plus the expected return of the market, it would, in this context, not be compatible with holding the market long which is what asset managers typically do.

We are now in a position to describe the representative agent. As is standard in this literature, we shall assume that bonds are in zero net supply. Aggregate (market) demand for a wealth distribution $[W_{0k}, k = 1, \ldots, K]$ will be given by (9.17).

We have thus far identified the aggregate demand and the presence of TFMS. We shall complete our argument by showing that the aggregate demand is the solution of a Fishburn Utility function as in (9.7). Have we lost anything in our formulation? It is clear that a securities market equilibrium, such as ours, need not be Pareto-optimal when markets are incomplete. It is also true, that if the equilibrium is Pareto-optimal, then we can construct a representative agent although not one, in general whose demands are independent of the wealth distribution. It is not known to the author, if given a representative agent, we must have a Pareto-optimal allocation. It does not seem reasonable to make the extra assumption that markets are complete as that imposes restrictions on the asset distributions, something we are trying to avoid. We could assume pareto-optimality but again that might be rather restrictive. We shall simply construct our representative agent without endowing the equilibrium with any normative properties.

Proposition 4

Our representative agent with initial wealth W_m, has the following Fishburn Utility Function given by (9.7), where $W_m > \frac{\Sigma W_{0k} \tau_k}{r}$ the total wealth of society is greater than the sum of the discounted target returns and the social target rate is $\tau_m = \frac{W_m - \Sigma W_{0k} \tau_k}{W_m r}$ so our demands place $(1 - \tau_m)$ in (w^*) and τ_m in bonds so that net demand for bonds is zero, the portfolio w^* is the portfolio defined by (9.17).

Proof   Most of the proof has already been derived. We have shown that

$$w_0 = \frac{\sum W_{0k}\tau_k}{\sum W_{0k}\tau_k - rW_m}$$

$$\rightarrow W_m = \sum_{i=1}^{m} d_i$$

$$d_i = w_i \left(W_m - \frac{\sum W_{0k}\tau_k}{r} \right), \quad i = 1, N$$

$$d_0 = (1 - w_0)\left(\frac{\sum W_{0k}\tau_k}{r} \right) + w_0 W_m$$

Define our portfolio weights as

$$d_i^* = w_i(1 - \tau_m)$$
$$d_0^* = w_0 + (1 - w_0)\tau_m$$

$$= w^*(1 - \tau_m) + \tau_m \begin{pmatrix} 1 \\ 0 \\ \vdots \\ 0 \end{pmatrix}$$

The result follows because w^* is the solution of a utility function of the Fishburn form as in Proposition 3.

Remark 1
It is clear from Proposition 4 that in terms of a representative agent, a target rate set at r, as in the BL equilibrium, implies that in aggregate all wealth is held in the riskless asset and equity is in zero net supply. The appropriate target rate to use for both asset classes to be in positive net supply is for a rate lying between 0 and r.

Remark 2
Proposition 4 retains the property that the representative agent has a utility function independent of the wealth distribution except for the societal target rate which will be influenced by distributional changes. In particular, a shift of

wealth from low target rate (low risk) investors to high target rate (high risk) investors will raise the social target and make society more risk-averse.

9.4 CONCLUSION

It is well known that the MVCAPM is valid under various distributional assumptions (see Ingersoll, 1987) or, alternatively, under quadratic utility for the representative agent. Our results can be seen in a similar light and show that the LMCAPM is valid for any representative agent whose decision rules are based on means of expected utility and for all distributions with finite expectations of the parameters mentioned above. We also address the issue as to whether it is possible to have such a representative agent. Aggregation can be achieved within the class of Fishburn (1977) utility functions. What we have shown is that TFMS applies, under rather restrictive circumstances, and thus, if a representative investor exists, she will hold the two funds, i.e. cash and the market. We also demonstrate the existence of the representative investor. We find that equilibrium target rates should be below the riskless rate and above zero if all asset classes are in positive net supply. If we take the societal target rate to be a proxy for society's overall attitude to risk, where a higher rate implies higher sensitivity to risk, we find that transfers of wealth from low target to high target investors raises the social target, indeed, this is the only impact of wealth redistribution within our model. This TFMS result can be seen as an extension of Cass and Stiglitz's (1970) famous result on the validity of two-fund separation within the HARA class of utility functions, except that now our utility functions are not necessarily in U_2, the class of twice-differentiable utility function with first derivatives positive and second derivatives negative. Furthermore, since our condition for aggregation requires that λ_k depend on W_{0k}, they are rather unusual utility functions (for other examples of these see Ingersoll, 1987: equation 15b). Finally, our aggregation result holds for the class of Fishburn power utility functions, except for the impacting of the wealth distribution on the social target.

Overall, the result certainly 'frees up' the LMCAPM and allows us to set up meaningful statistical tests that will determine if downside moments measure investor risk more accurately than variance. Such tests already exist (see Harlow and Rao, 1989 and Eftekhari and Satchell, 1996), and this chapter gives a theoretical rationale for carrying out these procedures.

ACKNOWLEDGEMENTS

The author would like to thank B. Eftekhari and C. Pedersen for constructive comments and Inquire (UK) for financial support.

REFERENCES

Bawa, V. and Lindenberg, B. (1977) Capital market equilibrium in a mean, lower partial moment framework, *Journal of Financial Economics*, 5.

Cass, D. and Stiglitz, J. (1970) The structure of investor preferences and asset returns, and separability in portfolio theory: a contribution to the pure theory of mutual funds, *Journal of Economic Theory*, 2.

Chow, K.V. and Denning, K.L. (1994) On variance and lower partial moment betas and the equivalence of systematic risk measures, *Journal of Business Finance and Accounting*, pp. 231–241.

Eftekhari, B. and Satchell, S. (1996) Non-normality of returns in emerging markets, *Research in International Business and Finance*, Supplement 1, JAI Press.

Fishburn, P.C. (1977) Mean-risk analysis with risk associated with below-target returns, *American Economic Review*, 66.

Harlow, W.V. and Rao, K.S. (1989) Asset pricing in a generalised mean-lower partial moment framework: theory and evidence, *Journal of Financial and Quantitative Analysis*, 24.

Hogan, W. and Warren, J. (1974) Toward the development of an equilibrium capital market model based on semivariance, *Journal of Financial and Quantitative Analysis*, 9.

Homaifar, G. and Graddy, D.B. (1990) Variance and lower partial moment betas as alternative risk measures in cost of capital estimation: a defense of the CAPM beta, *Journal of Business Finance and Accounting*, 17.

Huang, C. and Litzenburger, R.H. (1988) *Foundations for Financial Economics*, Englewood Cliffs, NJ: Prentice Hall.

Ingersoll, J. (1987) *Theory of Financial Decision Making*, Totowa, NJ: Rowman and Littlefield.

Markowitz, H. (1959) *Portfolio Selection*, New York: J. Wiley and Sons.

Chapter 10

Preference functions and risk-adjusted performance measures

AUKE PLANTINGA AND SEBASTIAAN DE GROOT

SUMMARY

Both private and institutional investors delegate a considerable part of the management of their asset portfolios to external fund managers. Consequently, investors face the problem of selecting the best from a large set of potential portfolio managers. This selection process involves the evaluation of the return distribution generated by the portfolio manager. An important aspect of this evaluation is the risk attitude of the investor. There are at least two general approaches for the evaluation of the attractiveness of return distribution. The first approach is to choose a preference model, such as a utility function, and use the expected value of this preference model as the decision criterion. This approach allows the user to model explicitly the risk preferences of the investor. The second approach is to use a risk-adjusted performance measure to select the portfolio manager with the highest score. Usually, with this approach it is not possible to explicitly model the risk preferences of the investor.

The objective of this chapter is to study the relation between risk preference functions and risk-adjusted performance measures. More specifically, we want to determine the preference functions that best correspond to the risk-adjusted performance measures included in our study. Preference functions and risk-adjusted performance measures can be parameterized in an infinite number of ways. In order to prevent the need to investigate an endless number of combinations, we limit our study to three functional specifications

Continued on page 170

___ *Continued from page 169* ___

of preference functions and to five risk-adjusted performance measures.

We consider the quadratic utility function, since this function is often used to motivate the use of mean-variance analysis. Furthermore, we investigate the Fishburn utility function and the prospect theory value function, which both use the concept of a reference point. These preference functions motivate the choice of performance measures in this study. The first measure is the Sharpe ratio, which is a performance measure associated with mean-variance analysis. The other measures are the Sortino ratio, the Fouse index and the upside potential ratio. Like Fishburn's utility function and the prospect theory value function, the measures are based on a reference rate.

The objective of this chapter can be of great interest for practical applications of performance measures. For instance, it is reasonable to expect that risk-adjusted performance measures based on a reference rate correspond to the preference functions using a reference rate. However, our analysis does not confirm this expectation. We show that the accuracy of a risk-adjusted performance measure in representing the risk preferences of an individual depends on a general notion of risk aversion and less on the form of the preference function. For example, a ranking of risky investment opportunities based on the Sharpe ratio can be represented quite well with a quadratic utility function, a Fishburn utility function, or a prospect theory value function as long as the level of risk aversion of the investor is sufficiently low.

In particular we conclude that the Sharpe ratio and the Sortino ratio correspond to the behaviour of investors with a relatively low level of risk aversion. On the other hand, the Fouse index and the upside potential ratio correspond to the behaviour of investors with a high level of risk aversion.

The outline of our study is the following. First we discuss the different functional specifications of the preference function. Secondly, we introduce the risk-adjusted performance measures considered in our study. Thirdly, we discuss the data used in our study, which consists of a sample of returns from 105 Dutch mutual funds for the period 1993–99. Finally, we analyse the relationship between the preference functions and the risk-adjusted performance measures, followed by our conclusions.

10.1 PREFERENCE FUNCTIONS

The classical way to model preferences in financial theory is by means of a utility function. A utility function generally represents the relation between the utility or value attached by an individual to the level of wealth. The shape of the utility function reveals the risk attitude of the individual. Concave utility functions are representative for individuals with risk aversion, linear utility functions are representative for a risk-neutral attitude, and convex utility functions are representative for a risk-seeking attitude.

Consider three individuals with different attitudes towards risk. Individual I is risk-averse, individual II is risk-neutral and individual III is risk-seeking. Each individual has to choose between two investment opportunities, a risky investment opportunity and a riskless investment opportunity (see Table 10.1).

The expected value of the risky alternative is equal to the expected value of the riskless alternative. Therefore, from the perspective of individual II, both alternatives are equally attractive since they have the same expected value and risk does not matter to this individual. Individual I will choose the riskless alternative since both alternatives have the same expected value and risk is valued negatively by a risk-averse individual. Individual I is only willing to participate in the risky alternative if its expected value sufficiently exceeds the expected value of the riskless alternative. Individual III will choose the risky alternative since both alternatives have the same expected value and risk is valued positively by a risk-seeking individual. Individual III is only willing to participate in the riskless alternative if the expected value of the risky alternative is sufficiently below the expected value of the riskless alternative.

The preferences of individuals I, II and III might be represented by the utility functions as in Figure 10.1 below.

Due to the popularity of modern portfolio theory as developed by Markowitz (1952), it is often assumed that investors' preferences can be represented by a quadratic utility function of the following form:

$$U(x) = x - kx^2 \tag{10.1}$$

where x is wealth level and $k > 0$.

There is considerable doubt that a quadratic utility function really describes the preferences of investors, the main reason being that this function implies

Table 10.1

	Risky alternative	Riskless alternative
Probability	Outcome	Outcome
50%	0.5	2.5
50%	4.5	2.5

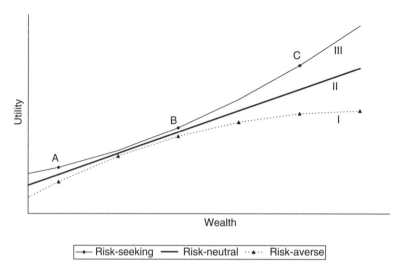

Figure 10.1   *Three different utility functions*

that the marginal utility of an extra unit of wealth actually decreases utility at a sufficiently high level of wealth. Although diminishing utility may be a reasonable assumption for some consumption goods, in general it is believed that this is not a realistic assumption for wealth. The quadratic utility function also implies increasing absolute and relative risk aversion.[1] This means that with increasing wealth, an investor tends to invest less in risky assets, both in absolute and in relative terms. This contradicts empirical studies by Blume and Friend (1975) and Cohn *et al.* (1975). While Blume and Friend find evidence that investors' behaviour displays constant relative risk aversion, Cohn *et al.* find evidence that investors show decreasing relative risk aversion. However, despite critique, quadratic utility functions remain popular as their use results in analytically tractable solutions to mean-variance optimization problems.

Another drawback of the quadratic utility function is that there is evidence that the preferences of individuals cannot be characterized by one global degree of risk aversion.[2] For example, Kahneman and Tversky (1979) showed that the degree of risk aversion of an individual might depend on the level of future wealth relative to the level of current wealth or another reference point. For values of future wealth below the current level, investors are likely to show risk-seeking behaviour and for values above the current level investors are likely to show risk aversion.

If, depending on the level of an outcome relative to a certain reference point, risk attitudes change from risk-averse to risk-seeking and back, then the preference function displays the property of sign dependence. The following model proposed by Fishburn (1977) has this property, with as reference point a target

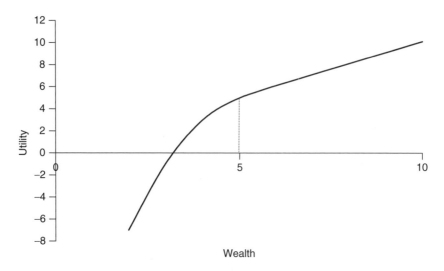

Figure 10.2 *Fishburn utility function*

level of wealth:

$$u(x) = \begin{cases} x & x \geq t \\ x - k(t-x)^a & x < t \end{cases} \tag{10.2}$$

where x is the end of period wealth level, t is the target wealth level, k is a positive constant >1 displaying empirically observed loss aversion,[3] and a is a positive constant displaying the degree of risk aversion (if $a > 1$). In Figure 10.2 we present an example of a Fishburn utility function, with $k = 1$, $a = 2$ and $t = 5$.

The prospect theory value function, as developed by Kahneman and Tversky (1979) and Tversky and Kahneman (1992), also uses the idea of sign dependence. However, for the prospect theory value function, the reference point, i.e. the wealth level at which the risk attitude changes, is the current wealth level. Tversky and Kahneman's three-parameter expression for their preference function is:

$$v(\Delta x) = \begin{cases} \Delta x^\alpha & \Delta x \geq 0 \\ -k(-\Delta x)^\beta & \Delta x < 0 \end{cases} \tag{10.3}$$

where Δx is the change in wealth level relative to the current wealth level, the parameter k captures loss aversion $\alpha > 0$ is a constant displaying risk attitudes in the so-called domain of gains, and $\beta > 0$ is a constant displaying risk attitudes in the so-called domain of losses.[4] Based on an empirical study, Tversky and Kahneman (1992) estimated the parameters as follows: $\alpha = \beta = 0.88$ and $k = 2.25$. Figure 10.3 presents the prospect theory value function with Tversky and Kahneman's parameter estimates.

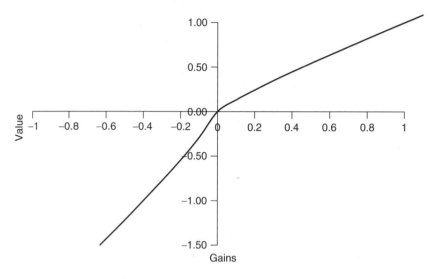

Figure 10.3   *Prospect theory value function*

The main difference between the prospect theory value function of Tversky and Kahneman (1992) and the utility function of Fishburn (1977) is that Fishburn assumes risk neutrality above the reference point, where Tversky and Kahneman's parameter estimate $\alpha = 0.88$ implies assumed risk aversion. Below the reference point, Fishburn assumes that investors are risk-averse (i.e. $\alpha > 1$), whereas Tversky and Kahneman assume risk-seeking behaviour in the domain of losses (i.e. $0 < \beta < 1$). This is consistent with the parameter estimate $\beta = 0.88$.

The prospect theory value function of Tversky and Kahneman allows different risk attitudes in different domains of the function. If an investor has to choose between two alternatives with only negative outcomes, the investor will choose the alternative with the highest risk – given that the expected value of the outcomes is the same. As an example, Table 10.2 presents two alternatives, both with exclusively negative outcomes. Both alternatives have an expected value of −70% and the alternatives only differ with respect to the volatility of the outcomes. Alternative 2 shows a larger spread between the maximum and the minimum outcome, which implies that this alternative has the highest volatility. Using the parameters provided by Tversky and Kahneman the expected prospect theory (PT) value of both alternatives can be calculated, which results in a value of −1.642 for Alternative 1 and −1.637 for Alternative 2. This implies that Alternative 2 is preferred over Alternative 1, which is consistent with risk-seeking behaviour.

In the domain of gains, a prospect theory investor displays risk aversion. This implies that such an investor who has to choose between two alternatives with

Table 10.2 *Two alternatives with negative outcomes*

	Outcome	Probability	PT value
Alternative 1			
$E[R] = -70\%$	$R = -80\%$	50%	-1.849
$\sigma[R] = 10\%$	$R = -60\%$	50%	-1.435
Alternative 2			
$E[R] = -70\%$	$R = -90\%$	50%	-2.051
$\sigma[R] = 10\%$	$R = -50\%$	50%	-1.223

exclusively positive outcomes and same expected value of the outcomes will prefer the alternative with the lowest volatility among its outcomes.

The interesting question remains what will happen to prospect theory investors if they have to choose between alternatives with outcomes both in the domain of gains and the domain of losses. The answer is that it depends on the shape of the distribution of outcomes. However, for most distributions with a positive expected value of the outcomes, the behaviour of a prospect theory investor is likely to be consistent with the behaviour of a purely risk-averse investor. For example, consider the two alternatives in Table 10.3. Both alternatives have an expected return equal to 0%. However, Alternative 3 has a smaller standard deviation than Alternative 4. The expected prospect theory value of Alternative 3 equals −0.340 and the expected prospect theory value of Alternative 4 equals −0.399, which means that a prospect theory investor prefers Alternative 3 above Alternative 4. So even though the alternatives are evaluated with a function that allows both risk-averse and risk-seeking behaviour, the overall result is consistent with preferences based on a traditional utility function displaying risk aversion. This result can be attributed to the loss-aversion condition $k > 1$, i.e. losses loom larger than gains or the negative value contribution of a loss exceeds the positive value of an equivalent gain.

Table 10.3 *Two alternatives with both positive and negative outcomes*

	Outcome	Probability	PT value
Alternative 3			
$E[R] = 0\%$	$R = -50\%$	50%	-1.223
$\sigma[R] = 50\%$	$R = +50\%$	50%	$+0.543$
Alternative 4			
$E[R] = 0\%$	$R = -60\%$	50%	-1.435
$\sigma[R] = 60\%$	$R = +60\%$	50%	$+0.638$

10.2   RISK-ADJUSTED PERFORMANCE MEASURES

In this section we discuss several risk-adjusted performance measures. Both risk-adjusted performance measures and preference functions can be used to rank risky investment alternatives. While preference functions explicitly model the risk attitudes of individuals, performance measures are calculated without detailed knowledge of risk attitudes. Consequently, a ranking of investment opportunities based on a preference function of one individual may differ completely from the ranking of the same investment opportunities by another individual with a different risk attitude. In other words, the concept of a preference function implies subjective rankings. In contrast, a ranking based on a performance measure is often calculated without any knowledge of the preference functions of the individuals that intend to use this ranking. Risk-adjusted performance measures combine a return and a risk measure into one overall measure. Usually, the adjustment for risk is achieved by either a division of the return measure by the risk measure or by subtracting the risk measure from the return measure.

The most popular risk-adjusted performance measures have been derived from the Capital Asset Pricing Model (CAPM). Within the context of the CAPM, the subjective balance between risk and return for an individual is reflected in the mix between the portfolio of risky assets and the riskless asset, while the portfolio of risky assets is the same for all individuals. This is the so-called two-fund separation theorem.

The Capital Asset Pricing Model can be considered as the equilibrium version of the modern portfolio of Markowitz (1991). Equivalent to Markowitz's portfolio theory, investors make decisions based on the means and variances of securities. In the simple version of CAPM, it is also assumed that investors can invest and borrow at a constant riskless interest rate. There are two assumptions that can independently justify the use of the mean-variance model. Either one has to assume that returns are normally distributed, which implies that the return distribution can be characterized solely in terms of mean and variance or one has to assume that investors have quadratic utility functions (see for example Huang and Litzenberger, 1988).

A well-known performance measure is the Sharpe (1966) ratio. The Sharpe ratio is related to the CAPM, as it can be used to construct the optimal portfolio of risky assets. If riskless lending and borrowing is possible and allowed, then the portfolio of risky assets can be obtained as the solution of a maximization problem, where the objective is to maximize the Sharpe ratio.[5]

The Sharpe ratio of portfolio p is calculated as follows:

$$S_p = \frac{E[r_p] - r_f}{\sigma_p} \qquad (10.4)$$

Table 10.4

Fund	$E[R] - r_f$	σ	S
A	6%	10%	+0.6
B	6%	20%	+0.3
C	−2%	−20%	−0.1
D	−2%	10%	−0.2

where E is the expectation operator, R_p is the return on portfolio p, r_f is the return on the riskless asset and σ_p is the standard deviation of portfolio p. An important motivation for the use of the Sharpe ratio is the claimed consistency of this ratio with the preference function of a mean-variance investor.

An interesting property of investors that maximize the Sharpe ratio is that their risk attitude shifts from risk aversion for investments with an expected return exceeding the riskless rate to risk preference for investments with an expected return below the riskless rate. Table 10.4 gives a clear illustration of this property.

While portfolios A and B have the same expected return, portfolio A has less risk than portfolio B. Therefore, an investor characterized by risk aversion will prefer portfolio A with the lower variance over portfolio B. The same must be true for portfolios C and D. Both portfolios have the same expected return, but portfolio D has less risk than portfolio C. So a risk-averse investor will prefer portfolio D over C. However, the Sharpe ratio of portfolio C is larger than the Sharpe ratio of portfolio D. Therefore, an investor using the Sharpe ratio as a decision criterion shows risk-seeking behaviour for portfolios with $E[R_p] < r_f$. Overall, the behaviour of this investor is similar to the prospect theory value function investor.

This result seems to be inconsistent with the CAPM assumption of risk-averse investors. Apparently, using the objective of maximizing the Sharpe ratio is not equivalent to using the objective of maximizing the expected value of a quadratic utility function as implied by the CAPM. Of course, it is possible to argue that the investor will choose only the best fund and that in general the best fund will have an expected return that is larger than the riskless rate. In addition to this ad hoc explanation, we discuss two alternative explanations for the apparent inconsistency.

The first explanation is that CAPM implies that investors only buy efficient portfolios. The funds presented in our example are not efficient portfolios. The investor maximizes the Sharpe ratio of his entire portfolio, which does not mean that each individual's securities should have a positive or high Sharpe ratios. If the interpretation of CAPM as equilibrium model holds, then investors should hold a positive fraction of all the securities in the universe, even if some securities have small or negative Sharpe ratios. So the funds C and D in our example are most likely to be individual funds or undiversified investment portfolios.

A second explanation is that we mixed up the economic interpretation of expected return with the calculation of the average return. It is common to use a historical time series of return as a proxy for a future return distribution. In order to do this it is necessary to assume that the return distribution is stationary. Apart from the possibility that the assumption of stationary returns is incorrect, it is possible that due to the small sample size a portfolio with an expected return above the risk-free has an average sample return below the risk-free rate.

In the spirit of the second explanation the Shape ratio can be interpreted as a *t*-statistic to test the hypothesis that return of the portfolio is larger than zero. If an investor considers to invest in a particular portfolio of risky asset as an alternative for a riskless asset, then the Sharpe ratio gives an indication of the likelihood that the portfolio will out-perform the riskless asset. This would justify the choice for the portfolio with the highest Sharpe ratio as it provides the biggest probability of outperforming the riskless asset. It would also justify the ranking of portfolio C over D as portfolio C, owing to its larger standard deviation, has a bigger probability of obtaining a return above the riskless asset.

Although these explanations may resolve the inconsistencies, the fact still remains that in practical applications, an investor using the Sharpe ratio can exhibit risk-seeking behaviour if confronted exclusively with portfolios that have an expected return exceeding the riskless return. The Sharpe ratio shares this property with other risk-adjusted performance measures that are based on the ratio of a return measure and a risk measure, such as the Treynor ratio and the information ratio. Therefore, we conclude that a maximization of a risk-adjusted performance measure is not necessarily equivalent to a maximization of a preference function. In general, evaluating a return distribution based on a preference function yields a different ranking than a one-parameter performance measure.

In addition to the Sharpe ratio, a large number of other performance measures have been developed from the CAPM and modern portfolio theory. Most of these alternative measures involve the specification of a benchmark portfolio to calculate the outcome of the performance measure. The most well known examples are the information ratio, Jensen's alpha and the Treynor ratio. These measures evaluate the performance of an investment portfolio relative to a benchmark and, therefore, evaluate only a part of the wealth accumulation of the investor. Since the preference functions are expressed in term of final wealth and absolute performance, we excluded measures based on relative performance from this chapter.

The primary focus of this chapter is on performance measures that are based on downside deviation, an alternative risk measure that focuses on potential losses as opposed to a general variability measure, such as standard deviation. Like the Fishburn utility function and the prospect theory value function, downside deviation is calculated relative to a reference rate. Downside deviation is defined as:[6]

$$\delta = \sqrt{\frac{1}{T} \sum_{t=1}^{T} \iota^-(R_{p,t} - R_{\text{mar}})^2} \tag{10.5}$$

where $R_{p,t}$ refers to return of the portfolio in period t, T is the total number of periods, R_{mar} is the minimal acceptable rate of return and ι^- is a dummy variable, with $\iota^- = 1$ if $R_{p,t} \leq R_{\text{mar}}$ and $\iota^- = 0$ if $R_{p,t} > R_{\text{mar}}$. Downside deviation is different from standard deviation in two ways. First, standard deviation is measured relative to the endogenous mean of the return distribution while downside risk is measured relative to an exogenous reference point, the minimal acceptable rate of return. This reference point can be interpreted in many ways. For example, the minimal acceptable rate of return could be the lowest return possible before any losses will show up in the accounting system, or the minimal return required to avoid bankruptcy. Secondly, standard deviation measures all deviations from the mean return, while downside deviation only measures deviations below the reference point.

Downside deviation is applied in several risk-adjusted performance measures, such as the Sortino ratio, the Fouse index and the upside potential ratio. The best known of these measures is the Sortino ratio, which is defined as:

$$\text{Sort} = \frac{R_p - R_{\text{mar}}}{\delta} \tag{10.6}$$

The Sortino ratio is the equivalent of the Sharpe ratio in mean-downside deviation space. Like the Sharpe ratio, it inherits the property of reversing risk attitudes from risk aversion to risk preference if the mean return of the portfolio falls below the minimal acceptable rate of return.

A second risk-adjusted performance measure based on downside deviation is the Fouse index. The Fouse index is calculated as follows:

$$FI = E[R_p] - A\delta^2 \tag{10.7}$$

where A is a measure of risk aversion. The Fouse index is not a ratio, and therefore it does not display the reversal of risk attitude. The Fouse index differs from other risk-adjusted performance measures as it incorporates a parameter that reflects the risk attitudes of the investor.

Sortino, van der Meer and Plantinga (1999) proposed the so-called 'upside potential ratio' (UPR). The upside potential ratio measures the upside potential relative to the downside variance. As the numerator of this ratio is always larger than or equal to zero, the upside potential ratio does not share the property of reversing the risk attitude. The upside potential ratio is defined as follows.

$$\text{UPR} = \frac{\sum_{t=1}^{T} \iota^+ p_t (R_t - R_{\text{mar}})}{\sum_{t=1}^{T} \iota^- p_t (R_t - R_{\text{mar}})^2} \tag{10.8}$$

with $\iota^- = 1$ if $R_{p,t} \leq R_{\text{mar}}$, $\iota^- = 0$ if $R_{p,t} > R_{\text{mar}}$, $\iota^+ = 1$ if $R_t > R_{\text{mar}}$ and $\iota^+ = 0$ if $R_t \leq R_{\text{mar}}$.

The upside potential ratio is strongly related to the Fishburn utility function. Like the Fishburn utility function, the UPR measures deviations relative to a target return. Furthermore, returns below the target return are weighted quadratically, whereas returns above the target return are weighted linearly. However, there are differences between the two performance measures as well. The upside potential ratio does not involve a risk-aversion parameter and it is calculated as a ratio.

10.3   DATA

In order to study the relationship between risk-adjusted performance measures and different choice models, we used a sample of 105 Dutch mutual funds. The data are obtained from Standard & Poor's Micropal database for the Netherlands. We derived monthly returns from the database, including both price changes and dividend payments. The data refers to the period starting at March 1993 and ending at March 1999. In Table 10.5 we present some general characteristics of the sample of mutual funds.

Our sample contains a variety of funds, ranging from money market funds to internationally diversified equity and mix funds. From Table 10.5 it can be observed that the interest-bearing funds such as money market and bond funds have on average the lowest standard deviation of returns. As can be expected, regional equity funds that specialize in a particular geographical region have

Table 10.5   *Characteristics of mutual funds in the sample*

Fund category	Number of funds	Market value of funds (million Euro)	$E[r]$	$\sigma[r]$
Asset allocation	18	5 028	0.92%	3.57%
International equity	9	7 023	1.63%	4.74%
Regional equity	27	7 736	1.41%	6.59%
Interest bearing	39	16 601	0.49%	1.24%
Real estate	12	1 681	1.33%	5.93%
Total	105	38 069	0.99%	3.85%

the highest standard deviation, as they do not profit from diversification over regions or asset categories. The next riskiest category is real estate, followed by internationally diversified funds and asset allocation funds.

The advantage of using a wide range of different mutual funds is that it allows us to elaborate on the different risk attitudes of investors. Highly risk-averse investors are expected to focus more on interest-bearing funds and diversified equity funds, whereas less risk-averse investors might focus on specialized funds such as regional equity and real estate. A different risk attitude will most likely result in a different ranking of the funds.

10.4 CONSISTENCY OF RISK-ADJUSTED PERFORMANCE MEASURES AND PREFERENCE FUNCTIONS

The objective of this study is to compare two approaches for evaluating the attractiveness of an investment opportunity to an individual investor. The first approach is based on the use of preference functions and the second approach is based on the use of risk-adjusted performance measures. In our discussion of risk-adjusted performance measures, we noticed that some of these measures are inconsistent with global risk aversion.

We compare the rankings based on risk-adjusted performance measures with the rankings based on the three different preference functions. However, first we want to show that a single functional form of a preference function can facilitate very different rankings due to differences in the risk-aversion parameter.

For our sample of 105 mutual funds, we calculated the ranking of the mutual funds based on the quadratic utility function specified in equation (10.1) using different values of the risk-aversion parameter k.[7] We calculated the rank correlation coefficient between the rankings of the mutual fund based on all combinations of the different risk-aversion parameters. The outcomes of this analysis are presented in Table 10.6. This table shows that for big differences between the risk-aversion coefficient, the correlation between the rankings can even become negative.

Table 10.6 *Cross-correlation between the rankings of investor with quadratic utility functions based on different levels of risk aversion*

a\a	0.5	1	5	25
0.5	1	0.966	0.489	−0.361
1		1	0.622	−0.201
5			1	0.423
25				1

10.4.1   Consistency between quadratic utility functions and performance measures

In order to see whether a ranking based on the Sharpe ratio corresponds with a ranking based on a quadratic utility function, we calculate rank correlation coefficients. From Table 10.6 we concluded that risk aversion of the investor has an important impact on the rank correlation. Therefore, we calculated the correlation between the ranking based on the Sharpe ratio and quadratic utility functions with different coefficients of risk aversion. The results can be found in Figure 10.4. The risk-free rate used to calculate the Sharpe ratio is equal to the monthly interbank offered rate for deposits with a maturity of 1 month. The maximum correlation between the rankings is obtained for a utility function with a risk aversion coefficient equal to 4, resulting in a rank-correlation coefficient equal to 0.845. It is interesting to note that the maximum correlation is part of an interval starting at a risk-aversion coefficient equal to 1 and ending at 4.5, for which the correlation coefficient exceeds 0.80. Surprisingly, the ranking based on the Sharpe ratio cannot be replicated with the ranking based on any of the quadratic utility functions. Nevertheless, the conclusion seems justified that the Sharpe ratio is a valid criterion for investors maximizing a utility function with a risk-aversion coefficient in the specified interval.

Figure 10.4 also presents the rank-correlation coefficient between the quadratic utility function and the other performance measures, as well as a ranking solely based on the mean return of the mutual funds. We choose the minimal acceptable rate of return for the Sortino ratio, the Fouse index and the upside

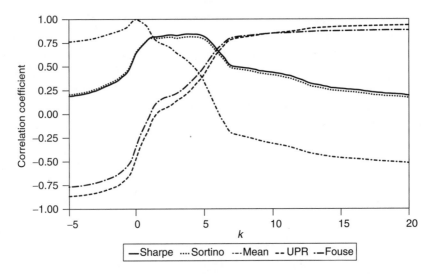

Figure 10.4   *Correlation between rankings based on quadratic utility functions and performance measures*

potential ratio equal to the riskless rate, in order to get results comparable with the outcomes for the Sharpe ratio.

The Sortino ratio (0.2 initial correlation) displays a pattern of behaviour that is similar to that of the Sharpe ratio, even though it is based on a different risk measure. For low levels of the risk-aversion parameter k, the correlation is low but positive, for intermediate values of k (between 0 and 5) the correlation is approximately 80% and for high levels of risk aversion the correlation is falling slowly. Apparently, an investor maximizing quadratic utility who would be willing to use the Sharpe ratio could also use the Sortino ratio.

By definition the ranking based on mean return only has a perfect correlation with a 'quadratic' utility function at a level of risk aversion equal to zero, since a quadratic utility function becomes linear when the risk aversion parameter equals zero. At a negative level of risk aversion (i.e. $k < 0$), correlation is very high. At a sufficiently high level of risk aversion the correlation becomes negative. This should not be surprising if one is willing to assume that high return levels are associated with high risk levels.

The upside potential ratio and the Fouse index behave in a similar fashion. At negative levels of risk aversion, the ranking based on the quadratic utility function selects the high risk funds whereas the rankings based on the upside potential ratio (UPR) and the Fouse index tend to select funds with low risk. Consequently, the rank correlation is negative for negative levels of risk aversion. At high levels of risk aversion ($k > 6$), the UPR and the Fouse index tend to correlate better with the utility function than the Sharpe and the Sortino ratio.

10.4.2 Consistency between the prospect theory value function and risk-adjusted performance measures

In the next experiment we calculated the rank correlation coefficients between the risk-adjusted performance measures and different prospect theory value functions. The prospect theory value function is characterized by three parameters. We choose to vary with the parameter k, which is the parameter that balances the relative value of gains against losses. In general, the higher the value of k, the more risk averse the investor is in terms of losses. We varied k from a value of 0 to a value of 5. The results of our experiments are presented in Figure 10.5.

In general, the results are similar to the results of the experiments based on the utility function. At low levels of risk aversion, the rankings based on the Sharpe and Sortino ratio have a better correspondence with the value function and at higher levels of risk aversion the UP ratio and the Fouse index perform better. For $k = 2.25$, the value Kahneman and Tversky found in their experimental study, the rankings based on Sharpe and Sortino ratios perform slightly better than the UP ratio and the Fouse index. If the parameters found

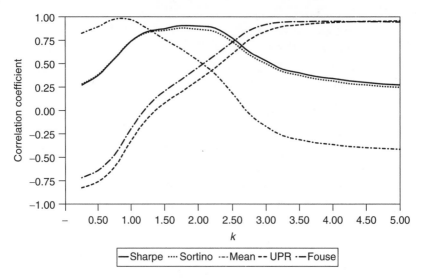

Figure 10.5   *Correlation between rankings based on prospect theory value functions and risk-adjusted performance measures*

by Kahneman and Tversky are considered to be representative for the average investor, then the conclusion is that the investor with more than average risk aversion should consult a ranking based on the UP ratio or the Fouse index. Vice versa, the investor with less than average risk aversion should consult the Sharpe or Sortino ratios.

The last experiments consider the relation with the Fishburn utility function. Again, we varied the coefficient k, one of the main determinants of the risk aversion of the individual. In order to be consistent with the quadratic utility function, the coefficient a was set at a value equal to 2. The outcomes of the analysis are presented in Figure 10.6.

As can be seen, the general impact on the performance of the risk-adjusted measures is similar as with the two kinds of preference functions. In comparison with the quadratic utility function with similar characteristics, the UP ratio and the Fouse index start to dominate the Sharpe and Sortino ratios at lower levels of the coefficient k.

10.5   CONCLUSION

The main objective of this study was to investigate how well the preferences of investors with different kinds of preference functions could be replicated with risk-adjusted performance measures. We used three different kinds of preference functions; namely the quadratic utility function, the Fishburn utility function and the prospect theory value function. For a universe of Dutch mutual funds, we

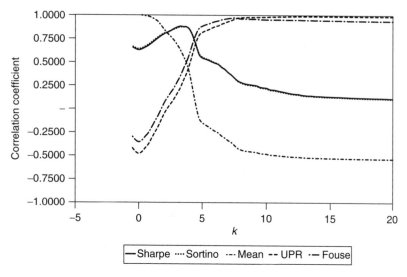

Figure 10.6   *Correlation between rankings based on Fishburn utility function and risk-adjusted performance measures*

calculated the rank correlation coefficients between the outcomes of the preference functions and a selected set of performance measures. Our main conclusion
is that the degree of correspondence in ranking between the preference function and the performance measure depends on the level of risk aversion of the
investor. None of the risk-adjusted performance measures resulted in a ranking
identical to any of the rankings generated by the preference functions. However,
independent of the type of preference function, we conclude that for lower levels
of risk aversion the Sharpe and Sortino ratio can be used as a good approximation of the preferences of an individual. For higher levels of risk aversion, the
UP ratio and the Fouse index are more appropriate.

ACKNOWLEDGEMENTS

The authors acknowledge the helpful comments of Nanne Brunia, Bo Hong,
Jan Jacobs, Robert van der Meer, Casper Oosterhof and Frank Sortino.

NOTES

1. See Arrow (1965) and Pratt (1964).
2. Actually, this is a drawback for many utility functions, not just the quadratic
    utility function.
3. Loss aversion is the notion that losses loom larger than gains (see Tversky and
    Kahneman, 1991).

4. In this specification of the value function, it is assumed that the reference point is equal to the current wealth level. A generalization of the prospect theory value function is (De Groot, 1998):

$$v(x;t) = \begin{cases} (x - t)^{\alpha} \ , \\ -k(t - x)^{\beta} \end{cases}$$

where t is the reference point and k is the loss aversion parameter.

5. See for example, Benninga (1997).
6. See Sortino and van der Meer (1991).
7. The rankings of the mutual funds based on different levels of risk aversion for the quadratic utility function are presented in Appendix 10.1.

REFERENCES

Arrow, K.J. (1965) Aspects of the theory of risk-bearing, reprinted in: *Essays in the Theory of Risk-Bearing*, Markham Publishing Co. (1971).

Benninga, Simon Z. (1997) *Financial Modeling*, Cambridge, MA: MIT Press.

Blume, Marshall and Friend, Irwin (1975) The asset structure of individual portfolios and some implications for utility functions, *Journal of Finance*, 10(2).

Cohn, Richard, Lewellen, Wilbur, Lease, Ronald and Schlarbaum, Gary (1975) Individual investor risk aversion and investment portfolio composition, *Journal of Finance*, 10(2).

De Groot, Sebastiaan (1998) *Behavioural Aspects of Decision Models in Asset Management*, The Netherlands: Labyrint Publication.

Fishburn, Peter C. (1977) Mean-risk analysis with risk associated with below-target returns, *American Economic Review*, 67(2).

Huang, Chi-fu and Litzenberger, Robert H. (1988) *Foundations for Financial Economics*, New York: North-Holland.

Kahneman, D. and Tversky, A. (1979) Prospect theory: an analysis of decision under risk, *Econometrica*, pp. 167–73.

Markowitz, H. (1952) Portfolio selection, *Journal of Finance*, 7(1).

Markowitz, H. (1991) *Portfolio Selection: Efficient Diversification of Investments*, 2nd edn, Oxford: Blackwell.

Pratt, J. (1964) Risk aversion in the small and in the large, *Econometrica*, Jan.–April.

Sharpe, William F. (1966) Mutual fund performance, *Journal of Business*, 1(2).

Sortino, Frank A. and van der Meer, Robert (1991) Downside risk, *Journal of Portfolio Management*, Summer.

Sortino, Frank A., van der Meer, Robert and Plantinga, Auke (1999) The Dutch Triangle, *Journal of Portfolio Management*, 26(1), Fall.

Tversky, A. and Kahneman, D. (1991) Loss aversion in riskless choice: a reference-dependent model, *Quarterly Journal of Economics*, pp. 1039–61.

Tversky, A. and Kahneman, D. (1992) Advances in prospect theory: cumulative representation of uncertainty, *Journal of Risk and Uncertainty*, pp. 297–323.

APPENDIX 10.1   COMPLETE RANKING OF MUTUAL FUNDS BASED
ON QUADRATIC UTILITY FUNCTIONS WITH DIFFERENT RISK
AVERSION PARAMETERS

Fund name	$a = 0.5$		$a = 1$		$a = 5$		$a = 25$	
ABN AMRO Aandelen Fonds	0.0148	(21)	0.0137	(18)	0.0048	(37)	−0.0396	(59)
ABN AMRO All In Fund	0.0087	(45)	0.0085	(40)	0.0068	(8)	−0.0017	(36)
ABN AMRO America Fund	0.017	(10)	0.0158	(9)	0.006	(19)	−0.0432	(68)
ABN AMRO Europe Fund	0.0169	(11)	0.0156	(10)	0.0054	(29)	−0.0457	(73)
ABN AMRO Far East Fund	0.0065	(58)	0.0048	(67)	−0.0087	(88)	−0.0766	(89)
ABN AMRO Liquid Groeifonds	0.002	(93)	0.002	(90)	0.002	(73)	0.0019	(15)
ABN AMRO Netherlands Fund	0.0188	(4)	0.0174	(4)	0.0057	(24)	−0.0529	(81)
ABN AMRO Oblig Groeifonds	0.0041	(78)	0.0041	(73)	0.0036	(58)	0.0014	(24)
ABN AMRO Obligatie Fonds	0.0065	(58)	0.0064	(54)	0.0059	(21)	0.0031	(3)
ABN AMRO Rente Dividend Fonds	0.0042	(76)	0.0042	(72)	0.004	(49)	0.0033	(2)
ABN AMRO Trans Europe Fund	0.0182	(7)	0.0169	(6)	0.0067	(10)	−0.0444	(69)
AEGON Aandelenfonds	0.0136	(25)	0.0123	(23)	0.0021	(72)	−0.0489	(78)
AEX Index Fund	0.0191	(3)	0.0176	(3)	0.0054	(29)	−0.0556	(84)
AH Vaste Klanten Fonds	0.0138	(24)	0.0133	(22)	0.0092	(1)	−0.0108	(47)

APPENDIX (*continued*)

Fund name	$a = 0.5$		$a = 1$		$a = 5$		$a = 25$	
Alrenta	0.0065	(58)	0.0063	(56)	0.0048	(37)	−0.0024	(38)
Amvabel	0.0033	(85)	0.0024	(88)	−0.005	(87)	−0.042	(66)
Andere Beleg-gingsfonds Het	0.0077	(51)	0.0075	(45)	0.0055	(27)	−0.0041	(42)
Asian Tigers Fund	0.003	(88)	−0.0003	(98)	−0.0264	(96)	−0.1567	(95)
AXA Aandelen Nederland	0.0172	(9)	0.016	(8)	0.0064	(12)	−0.0416	(65)
AXA Actief Beheer	0.012	(32)	0.0116	(28)	0.0086	(2)	−0.0063	(44)
Bary Netto Rentefonds De	0.0019	(94)	0.0019	(93)	0.0019	(75)	0.0018	(16)
Beleggingsfonds Voor Medici	0.0121	(30)	0.0114	(29)	0.0066	(11)	−0.0178	(52)
Columbia Securities	0.0141	(23)	0.0123	(23)	−0.0024	(83)	−0.0757	(88)
Delta Lloyd Donau Fonds	0.0089	(44)	0.0028	(84)	−0.0461	(100)	−0.2907	(100)
Delta Lloyd Mix Fonds	0.0087	(45)	0.0084	(41)	0.0062	(17)	−0.0048	(43)
Delta Lloyd Rente Fonds	0.0077	(51)	0.0075	(45)	0.0064	(12)	0.0008	(29)
Engels–Hollandse Beleggings Tr	0.0182	(7)	0.008	(43)	−0.0737	(103)	−0.4824	(103)
European Assets Trust	0.0112	(36)	0.0073	(48)	−0.0243	(94)	−0.1823	(96)
European City Estates	0.0012	(101)	−0.001	(100)	−0.0183	(93)	−0.1047	(93)
Finles Collectief Beheer Fds	0.011	(37)	0.0105	(34)	0.0064	(12)	−0.0144	(49)
First Mexico Income Fund	0.0103	(40)	0.0055	(61)	−0.0334	(98)	−0.2277	(98)

APPENDIX (*continued*)

Fund name	$a = 0.5$		$a = 1$		$a = 5$		$a = 25$	
Fortis Amerika Fds small caps	0.0072	(53)	0.0059	(59)	−0.0047	(86)	−0.0578	(85)
Fortis Azie Fonds	0.0001	(102)	−0.0041	(102)	−0.0377	(99)	−0.2053	(97)
Fortis Europa Fds Small Caps	0.0116	(34)	0.0105	(34)	0.002	(73)	−0.0406	(64)
Fortis OBAM	0.0169	(11)	0.0155	(13)	0.0046	(40)	−0.0501	(79)
Fortis Obligatie Dividend Fond	0.0055	(66)	0.0054	(63)	0.0047	(39)	0.0008	(29)
Friesland Dividend Fonds	0.0059	(65)	0.0058	(60)	0.0053	(32)	0.0029	(4)
Friesland Rentegroei Fonds	0.0042	(76)	0.0041	(73)	0.0039	(51)	0.0028	(6)
Generale Bank Oblig Dividfds	0.0054	(69)	0.0052	(65)	0.004	(49)	−0.0018	(37)
Generale Bank Oblig Waardefds	0.0037	(82)	0.0036	(79)	0.003	(63)	−0.0003	(35)
GIM Global Convertible Fund	0.0078	(50)	0.0073	(48)	0.0035	(59)	−0.0155	(50)
GIM Real Estate Equity Fund	0.0043	(75)	0.0034	(81)	−0.0039	(85)	−0.0404	(63)
Holland Europe Fund	0.0168	(13)	0.0156	(10)	0.0058	(22)	−0.0431	(67)
Holland Fund	0.016	(17)	0.0149	(16)	0.0057	(24)	−0.0402	(61)
Holland Obligatie Fonds	0.0066	(57)	0.0065	(53)	0.0056	(26)	0.0009	(28)
Holland Pacific Fund	0.0014	(100)	−0.0003	(98)	−0.0141	(91)	−0.0832	(91)
Holland Selectie Fonds	0.0126	(26)	0.0121	(25)	0.0083	(4)	−0.0108	(47)
ING Bank Dutch Fund	0.0192	(2)	0.0178	(2)	0.0071	(6)	−0.0463	(75)

APPENDIX (*continued*)

Fund name	$a = 0.5$		$a = 1$		$a = 5$		$a = 25$	
ING Bank Geldmarkt Fonds	0.0019	(94)	0.0019	(93)	0.0019	(75)	0.0017	(20)
ING Bank Global Fund	0.0155	(18)	0.0142	(17)	0.0044	(43)	−0.0451	(70)
ING Bank Obligatie Fonds	0.0068	(55)	0.0066	(52)	0.0055	(27)	−0.0001	(33)
ING Bank Rentegroei Fonds	0.0047	(71)	0.0046	(68)	0.0041	(48)	0.0016	(21)
ING Bank Spaardividend Fonds	0.0028	(89)	0.0028	(84)	0.0027	(65)	0.0025	(9)
Intereffekt Japanese Warrants	−0.0111	(104)	−0.0264	(104)	−0.1491	(104)	−0.7622	(104)
IS Himalayan Fund	0.0104	(39)	0.0039	(76)	−0.0484	(101)	−0.3097	(101)
J.I. Emerging Markets Bond Fd	0.0036	(84)	0.002	(90)	−0.0112	(90)	−0.0771	(90)
J.I. International Bond Fund	0.0065	(58)	0.0063	(56)	0.0046	(40)	−0.0039	(41)
Japan Fund	0.0016	(98)	−0.004	(101)	−0.0494	(102)	−0.2761	(99)
Liquirent	0.0019	(94)	0.0019	(93)	0.0019	(75)	0.0018	(16)
Lombard Odier EMS Plus Rente	0.0099	(43)	0.0097	(37)	0.0081	(5)	0.0001	(31)
MeesPierson Euro Liq Fonds	0.0019	(94)	0.0019	(93)	0.0019	(75)	0.0018	(16)

APPENDIX (*continued*)

Fund name	$a = 0.5$		$a = 1$		$a = 5$		$a = 25$	
MeesPierson Oblig Groei Fonds	0.0033	(85)	0.0032	(82)	0.0029	(64)	0.0013	(25)
Mondibel	0.0053	(70)	0.0052	(65)	0.0043	(45)	0.0001	(31)
Obligatie Beleggingspool	0.0065	(58)	0.0064	(54)	0.0058	(22)	0.0029	(4)
Ohra Aandelen Fonds	0.0185	(5)	0.0172	(5)	0.0062	(17)	−0.0486	(77)
Ohra Liquiditeiten Groeifonds	0.0023	(92)	0.0023	(89)	0.0023	(70)	0.002	(13)
Ohra Obligatie Dividendfonds	0.0068	(55)	0.0067	(50)	0.006	(19)	0.0025	(9)
Ohra Obligatie Groeifonds	0.0046	(72)	0.0046	(68)	0.0042	(46)	0.0026	(8)
Ohra Total Fonds	0.0123	(28)	0.0118	(26)	0.0084	(3)	−0.0087	(46)
Opbouwfonds Voor Medici	0.015	(19)	0.0137	(18)	0.0037	(55)	−0.0462	(74)
Optimix	0.0106	(38)	0.0099	(36)	0.0042	(46)	−0.024	(54)
Orange Fund	0.0168	(13)	0.0156	(10)	0.0064	(12)	−0.0398	(60)
Postbank Aandelenfonds	0.0146	(22)	0.0136	(21)	0.0051	(35)	−0.0371	(58)
Postbank Beleggingsfonds	0.0085	(47)	0.0082	(42)	0.0063	(16)	−0.0034	(40)
Postbank Vermo-gensgroeifonds	0.0031	(87)	0.003	(83)	0.0027	(65)	0.0011	(26)
Rentalent	0.0044	(73)	0.0043	(71)	0.0038	(53)	0.0011	(26)
RG Aandelen Mixfund	0.0101	(41)	0.0096	(38)	0.0054	(29)	−0.0155	(50)
RG America Fund	0.0183	(6)	0.0167	(7)	0.0032	(62)	−0.0638	(86)
RG Divirente Fund	0.0041	(78)	0.004	(75)	0.0037	(55)	0.0023	(11)
RG Europe Fund	0.0165	(16)	0.0152	(14)	0.0046	(40)	−0.0482	(76)

APPENDIX (*continued*)

Fund name	$a = 0.5$		$a = 1$		$a = 5$		$a = 25$	
RG Florente Fund	0.0028	(89)	0.0028	(84)	0.0027	(65)	0.0021	(12)
RG Obligatie Mixfund	0.0061	(64)	0.006	(58)	0.0049	(36)	−0.0002	(34)
RG Pacific Fund	0.004	(80)	0.002	(90)	−0.0146	(92)	−0.0972	(92)
RG Rente Mixfund	0.0044	(73)	0.0044	(70)	0.0039	(51)	0.0018	(16)
Rolinco	0.0119	(33)	0.0106	(32)	0.0002	(80)	−0.0518	(80)
Rorento	0.0069	(54)	0.0067	(50)	0.0052	(33)	−0.0026	(39)
Sarakreek	−0.0112	(105)	−0.0268	(105)	−0.1515	(105)	−0.7752	(105)
Schroder European Property Fd	0.0125	(27)	0.0118	(26)	0.0068	(8)	−0.0185	(53)
SNS Obligatie Dividendfonds	0.0055	(66)	0.0055	(61)	0.0052	(33)	0.0037	(1)
SNS Obligatie Groeifonds	0.0039	(81)	0.0039	(76)	0.0037	(55)	0.0028	(6)
Stewart Holding (WP)	0.0167	(15)	0.0152	(14)	0.0034	(60)	−0.0555	(82)
TG Netto Geldmarket Fonds	0.0016	(98)	0.0016	(97)	0.0015	(79)	0.0015	(22)
Tokyo Pacific Holdings	−0.0041	(103)	−0.0064	(103)	−0.0245	(95)	−0.1154	(94)
Uni-Invest	0.0121	(30)	0.0107	(31)	−0.0003	(82)	−0.0555	(82)
Van Lanschot Global Equity Fd	0.015	(19)	0.0137	(18)	0.0038	(53)	−0.0456	(71)
VastNed Offices/ Industrials	0.0114	(35)	0.0106	(32)	0.0044	(43)	−0.0267	(56)
VastNed Retail	0.0082	(49)	0.0075	(45)	0.0022	(71)	−0.0246	(55)

APPENDIX (*continued*)

Fund name	$a = 0.5$		$a = 1$		$a = 5$		$a = 25$	
VHS Onroerend Goed Mij	0.0393	(1)	0.0315	(1)	−0.0308	(97)	−0.3425	(102)
VIB	0.0064	(63)	0.0054	(63)	−0.0031	(84)	−0.0456	(71)
VPV HollandHaven	0.0122	(29)	0.0111	(30)	0.0025	(68)	−0.0403	(62)
VPV International Geldmkt Fds	0.0026	(91)	0.0026	(87)	0.0025	(68)	0.002	(13)
VSB Mix Fund	0.01	(42)	0.0096	(38)	0.0069	(7)	−0.0069	(45)
VSB Obligatie Groeifonds	0.0037	(82)	0.0036	(79)	0.0033	(61)	0.0015	(22)
Wereldhave	0.0085	(47)	0.0076	(44)	0.0002	(80)	−0.0365	(57)
World Property Fund	0.0055	(66)	0.0039	(76)	−0.009	(89)	−0.0734	(87)

Chapter 11

Building a mean-downside risk portfolio frontier

GUSTAVO M. DE ATHAYDE

11.1 INTRODUCTION

The dissatisfaction with the traditional notion of variance as the measure of risk is becoming a common feature of financial markets all over the world. The main argument against the use of variance is that it makes no distinction between gains and losses. In fact, in Markowitz's original work (1952) he argues for other measures of risk. Two ways are suggested. The first would be to include higher moments. This has been approached by a few authors, like Ingersoll (1975), Kraus and Litzenberger (1976), among others. However the complete formal characterization of the portfolio frontier with higher moments has not been done since Athayde and Flôres (1999). In this chapter the portfolio set with higher moments and all of its features are presented.

The second way that Markowitz proposed was to use what he called semi-variance. That is the sum of the squares of negative deviations from the mean, divided by the total number of observations:

$$\frac{1}{n} \sum_{i=1}^{n} [\text{Min}(r_i - \mu, 0)]^2 \qquad (11.1)$$

The great advantage of the use of semi-variance over variance is that it does not include positive gains, so what is considered as risk takes into account only negative deviations. However, one may be led to the wrong conclusion that minimizing downside means minimizing only negative deviations. This common mistake becomes even clearer if the distributions we are dealing are symmetric, like the normal curve. In this case minimizing variance and semi-variance will lead to the same problem. The only case that justifies the use of semi-variance is when the presence of skewness is observed.

That leads us back to the problem of adding moments. Although the approach to use higher moments is far more complete than the use of semi-variance, the popularity of the latter is larger, maybe because it measures risk in one number, while the use of variance, skewness and possibly kurtosis would give us three different values to capture risk. In terms of portfolio frontier, we will be dealing only with two dimensions, rather than three or four, and make the analysis simpler (although not so efficient if compared to the multi-dimensioned three or four moment portfolio frontier).

Finding the portfolios with minimum semi-variance is not an easy task. This is due to the fact that we don't have a fixed number to represent the downside risk of an asset. For instance, if we have acquired a single asset, then its semi-variance will be given by negative deviations, while if we short sell this asset, then we will have to deal with positive deviations (because now the risk is for the asset to go up). Thus what will be used to construct its semi-variance depends on whether we are short or long.

The problem becomes even more complex when we're dealing with more than one asset. Suppose we have a given portfolio P_0. To compute the semi-variance of this portfolio we have to take into consideration only the observations that were negative deviations. If we change a little the weights of this portfolio, creating a new portfolio P_1, some observations in which the former portfolio was negative might become positive, and vice-versa. Thus they will have to be included or excluded from the downside risk of portfolio P_1. Therefore the set of observations that will be taken into account when building the semi-variance of this portfolio will be function of the portfolio weights, making the problem more difficult to handle that in the case of minimizing variance.

For instance, we have two assets, with zero mean. On one day, one has a return of 1%, and the other of -1%. If the weight of the first asset is more (less) than $1/2$, the portfolio's return will be positive (negative), and therefore excluded (included) in the semi-variance of the portfolio.

The definition of semi-variance becomes even more complicated in terms of the cross product. By semi-covariance, which of the following terms are we referring to?

$$\frac{1}{n}\sum_{i=1}^{n}[\text{Min}(r_a^i - \mu_a, 0)][\text{Min}(r_b^i - \mu_b, 0)]$$

$$\frac{1}{n}\sum_{i=1}^{n}[\text{Min}(r_a^i - \mu_a, 0)](r_b^i - \mu_b)$$

$$\frac{1}{n}\sum_{i=1}^{n}(r_a^i - \mu_a)[\text{Min}(r_i^b - \mu_b, 0)]$$

$$\frac{1}{n}\sum_{i=1}^{n}\text{Min}[(r_a^i - \mu_a)(r_b^i - \mu_b), 0]$$

Even if we pick any of the definitions above, it should be clear that there is no such thing as a well-behaved positive definite semi-variance matrix, that we can pre and post multiply by the vector of weights of any portfolio and get its respective semi-variance. Therefore the minimization problem becomes much more complicated, because the set of observations that will be taken into account is endogenous to the weights of the portfolio in question.

Nevertheless, one common approach used in the market is to approximate what would be a semi-variance matrix by:

$$
\begin{bmatrix}
\frac{\sigma_{11}{}^*}{\sigma_{11}} & 0 & \cdots & 0 \\
0 & \frac{\sigma_{22}{}^*}{\sigma_{22}} & \ddots & \vdots \\
\vdots & \ddots & \ddots & 0 \\
0 & \cdots & 0 & \frac{\sigma_{kk}{}^*}{\sigma_{kk}}
\end{bmatrix}^{1/2}
\begin{bmatrix}
\sigma_{11} & \sigma_{12} & \cdots & \sigma_{1k} \\
\sigma_{21} & \sigma_{22} & \cdots & \sigma_{2k} \\
\vdots & \vdots & \ddots & \vdots \\
\sigma_{k1} & \sigma_{k2} & \cdots & \sigma_{kk}
\end{bmatrix}
$$

$$
\times
\begin{bmatrix}
\frac{\sigma_{11}{}^*}{\sigma_{11}} & 0 & \cdots & 0 \\
0 & \frac{\sigma_{22}{}^*}{\sigma_{22}} & \ddots & \vdots \\
\vdots & \ddots & \ddots & 0 \\
0 & \cdots & 0 & \frac{\sigma_{kk}{}^*}{\sigma_{kk}}
\end{bmatrix}^{1/2}
$$

where $\sigma_{ii}{}^*$ is the semi-variance of asset i.

This formula gives us a symmetric positive definite matrix. The semi-variances will be on this matrix diagonal. It is feasible to find a portfolio that pre and post multiplies this matrix that gives us the minimum value of this function, which is not the minimum semi-variance. Depending on the correlations and other characteristics of the assets in question these minima can differ by an enormous amount.

Before we go on, we must define downside risk (DSR). The latter is a generalization of semi-variance:

$$
\text{downside risk} \Rightarrow \frac{1}{n}\sum_{i=1}^{n}[\text{Min}(r_i - \mu, 0)]^k \tag{11.2}
$$

Where k is any power you can choose (when $k = 1$, it should be considered the absolute value of the term in brackets), and μ is a chosen benchmark (not necessarily the mean).

11.2   THE MEAN-DSR PORTFOLIO FRONTIER: THE BIVARIATE CASE

Let us assume that we have two risky assets, a and b, and we want to find the optimal portfolio that gives us the minimum downside risk. To start, let us consider the case where $k = 2$ (if the benchmark is the mean of the portfolio, than we will be dealing with semi-variance).

Consider one observation t_0 of these two assets. The portfolio return will be given by:

$$r_p = wr_a^0 + (1 - w)r_b^0$$

The value of w at time t_0 that makes the portfolio return equal to the benchmark μ is given by:

$$w_0 = \frac{\mu - r_b^0}{r_a^0 - r_b^0} \tag{11.3}$$

If we had only this observation, assuming that $r_a^0 > r_b^0$, the DSR of this portfolio will be given by:

$$\text{DSR}(w) = [w(r_a^0 - r_b^0) - (\mu - r_b^0)]^2, \quad \text{if } w < w_0; \quad \text{and } 0 \text{ otherwise}$$

$$\text{DSR}'(w) = 2[w(r_a^0 - r_b^0) - (\mu - r_b^0)](r_a^0 - r_b^0) < 0, \quad \text{if } w < w_0;$$
$$\text{and } 0 \text{ otherwise}$$

$$\text{DSR}''(w) = 2(r_a^0 - r_b^0)^2 > 0, \quad \text{if } w < w_0; \text{ and } 0 \text{ otherwise}$$

The function is illustrated in Figure 11.1.

Consider now another observation, t_1. Suppose that $r_a^1 > r_b^1$, and that $w_1 < w_0$. If we take only this observation in consideration, its DSR will be given by Figure 11.2, just like in the former case.

When we will be computing the DSR of our portfolio with these two observations, we will be adding these two semi-parabolas, so that the new curve will be like Figure 11.3.

The new DSR will be given by:

$$\text{DSR}(w) = \sum_{i=0}^{1} [w(r_a^i - r_b^i) - (\mu - r_b^i)]^2, \quad \text{if } w < w_1$$
$$[w(r_a^0 - r_b^0) - (\mu - r_b^0)]^2, \quad \text{if } w_1 < w < w_0$$

$$0, \quad \text{otherwise}$$

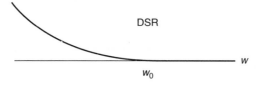

Figure 11.1

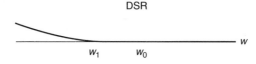

Figure 11.2

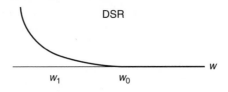

Figure 11.3

The first derivative is given by:

$$\text{DSR}'(w) = 2\sum_{i=0}^{1} [w(r_a^i - r_b^i) - (\mu - r_b^i)](r_a^i - r_b^i) < 0, \text{ if } w < w_1$$

$$2[w(r_a^0 - r_b^0) - (\mu - r_b^0)](r_a^0 - r_b^0) < 0, \text{ if } w_1 < w < w_0$$
$$0, \text{ otherwise}$$

The concavity is given by:

$$\text{DSR}''(w) = 2\sum_{i=0}^{1} (r_a^i - r_b^i)^2 > 0, \text{ if } w < w_1$$

$$2(r_a^0 - r_b^0)^2 > 0, \text{ if } w_1 < w < w_0$$
$$0, \text{ otherwise}$$

As can be seen from above, the function is monotonically decreasing with respect to w. The most important aspect however is that once we cross the point w_1 the concavity changes, and we start to deal with a new parabola. The convexity decreases with w. For some specific regions the convexity is fixed, until a new parabola is formed as we cross one of the critical points w_0 or w_1. If we keep adding more and more observations in which $r_a > r_b$, the curve will become steeper and steeper as we decrease w.

Consider now the situation in which we only have observations in which $r_a < r_b$. The curve will look exactly like the former, but increasing with w, becoming steeper and steeper, as we will be adding more and more semi-parabolas, like Figure 11.4.

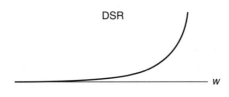

Figure 11.4

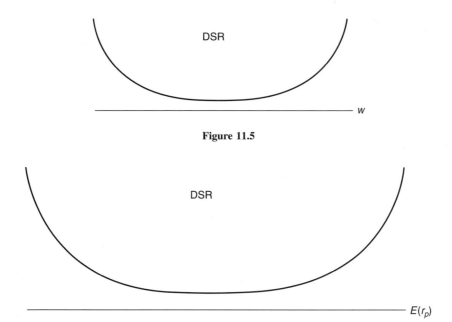

Figure 11.5

Figure 11.6

When we include all of observations, those that in which $r_a > r_b$ and $r_a < r_b$, the whole DSR will be a curve, as in Figure 11.5.

The expected return of the portfolio will be given by:

$$E(r_p) = wE(r_a) + (1 - w)E(r_b) \iff w = \frac{E(r_p) - E(r_b)}{E(r_a) - E(r_b)}$$

Thus, since we have a linear relation between w and $E(r_p)$, we may conclude that the shape of the set DSR $\times E(r_p)$ will be like Figure 11.6.

As has been shown, this curve is made on segments of parabolas, each one becoming steeper and steeper as we move toward the extremes, in either direction. The more observations we have, the more parabolas will appear and the smaller the segment of each will become. The changes in the convexity, when we move from one parabola to another, will become more frequent and smoother. In the limit case, where we will have an infinite number of observations, each of these parabolas will degenerate to a single point, creating a continuous smooth changing in the convexity of the curve.

11.3 THE ALGORITHM

Suppose we want to find the portfolio weights that give us the minimum DSR (the vertex of the curve above). We start with a portfolio w_0 (which is not necessarily the same as the one in equation (11.3) above), and calculate its downside risk. We select only the set of observations S_0 that contains negative deviations. Consider the following curve given by:

$$\sigma_0^2 = \sum_{i \in S_0} (r_i - \mu)^2, \quad \text{where } r_i = w r_a^i + (1 - w) r_b^i \tag{11.4}$$

It should be clear from the last section that for a small neighbourhood of w_0, the set of days with negative deviations remain the same as S_0, without adding or taking out any observation, remaining on the same parabola. When w becomes very different from w_0, some days will enter and some will go away when we compute the downside risk of w (because we have moved to another segment of a different parabola in the DSR curve). In this case the curve that describes the downside risk and σ_0^2 will become more and more different. However for small changes on w, if the set of negative deviations is still given by S_0, the two curves will coincide.

The second step is to find a portfolio w_1 that minimizes σ_0^2. Note that this problem is analogous to minimizing variance, implying that this curve is a convex well-behaved function whose minimum is easily obtained. In this case it will be given by:

$$w_1 = \frac{\displaystyle\sum_{i \in S_0} (r_a^i - r_b^i)(\mu - r_b^i)}{\displaystyle\sum_{i \in S_0} (r_a^i - r_b^i)^2}$$

Once we find w_1, we compute its DSR, creating a new set of observations S_1, that have only negative deviations of w_1 with respect to the benchmark μ. In the neighbourhood of w_1, the DSR will coincide with the following parabola:

$$\sigma_1^2 = \sum_{i \in S_1} (r_i - \mu)^2, \quad \text{where } r_i = w r_a^i + (1 - w) r_b^i \tag{11.5}$$

We will then minimize (11.5) with respect to w. The solution is given by:

$$w_2 = \frac{\displaystyle\sum_{i \in S_1} (r_a^i - r_b^i)(\mu - r_b^i)}{\displaystyle\sum_{i \in S_1} (r_a^i - r_b^i)^2} \tag{11.6}$$

From w_2 we will separate the new set of observations with negative deviations S_2, construct a new parabola that take into consideration only the observations in S_2, minimize it with respect to w, finding w_3, that will give us a new set S_3, and so on. The algorithm will stop when $S_t = S_{t+1}$, which will be the unique minimum DSR. Once we found the minimum for that specific set of observations, it will not be necessary to change the set of observations. We will have achieved our objective.

Consider the example in Figure 11.3. We have three possible situations:

(1) If we had started with $w \geq w_0$, the DSR would be null, so we would stop right there.

(2) If we had started with $w_1 \geq w > w_0$, we would have the parabola given by $[w(r_a^0 - r_b^0) - (\mu - r_b^0)]^2$. The minimum point would be given by w_0. The DSR on this point is zero. The next step would be given by the case above.

(3) If we had started with $w < w_1$, we would have the parabola given by $\sum_{i=0}^{1} [w(r_a^i - r_b^i) - (\mu - r_b^i)]^2$. The minimum point would be given by somewhere in between w_1 and w_0. The next step would be given by the case above.

In order to extend the last example – which was very trivial – consider Figure 11.7, in which we have three parabolas, each one representing a segment of the DSR, which is given by the thick black line. It is easy to see that no matter which parabola we pick from the start, if we follow the proposed algorithm, we will end up in P_3. The minimum of this parabola is also the minimum of DSR, guaranteeing the convergence.

For instance, if our initial guess of w is very low, we will select the observations in such a way that we will start at P_1. Once we find the w that minimizes this parabola, we will select a new set of observations that are negative, ending up with a new parabola P_3. Again, we will find the portfolio w that minimizes this parabola. However, after this portfolio is found, the new set of observations whose deviations are negative is the same as before, so we will remain at P_3, and the minimum DSR (which coincides with the minimum of P_3) is achieved.

The same goes for the case in which our initial guess of w is high. In this situation, we would have started at P_3 and on the next iteration, be driven to P_3.

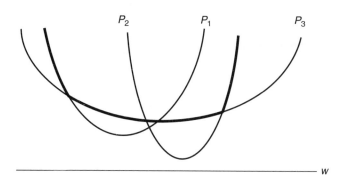

Figure 11.7

If we have started on P_3, only one iteration would be necessary to achieve the minimum.

11.4   THE MULTIVARIATE CASE

The procedure for the multivariate case is analogous to the former. Let's say we have n assets. We will start with a given portfolio, w_0. Then we select the set S_0 of observations in which this portfolio w_0 had negative deviations. Then we construct the following positive semi-definite matrix:

$$[M_0] = \sum_{i \in S_0} \begin{bmatrix} r_a^i \\ r_b^i \\ \vdots \\ r_n^i \end{bmatrix} [\, r_a^i \quad r_b^i \quad \cdots \quad r_n^i \,]$$

where r_j^i means the excess return (actual return minus the benchmark) of asset j on date i.

The next step is to find the portfolio w_1 that solves the following problem:

$$\text{Min}[w]'[M_0][w] \, s.t. \, [w]'[1] = 1,$$

where $[1]$ is a vector of 1s.

The solution to the problem will be given by:

$$[w_1] = \frac{[M_0]^{-1}[1]}{[1]'[M_0]^{-1}[1]}$$

If $[M_0]$ is non-invertible, this means that we will have few observations, and that will be possible to find a portfolio that will give us a null DSR. This is not an interesting case: it does not mean there is no DSR, it only means that the sample in question is poor, leaving us with few degrees of freedom.

With the new portfolio w_1 we will collect the set of observations S_1 that contains only negative excess returns of portfolio w_1. We will now form a new positive semi-definite matrix $[M_1]$:

$$[M_1] = \sum_{i \in S_1} \begin{bmatrix} r_a^i \\ r_b^i \\ \vdots \\ r_n^i \end{bmatrix} [\, r_a^i \quad r_b^i \quad \cdots \quad r_n^i \,]$$

The next step is to find the portfolio w_2 that solves the following problem:

$$\text{Min}[w]'[M_1][w] \, s.t. \, [w]'[1] = 1$$

The solution to the problem will be given by:

$$[w_2] = \frac{[M_1]^{-1}[1]}{[1]'[M_1]^{-1}[1]}$$

From then on, we will form a new matrix $[M_2]$ collecting only the negative observations of portfolio w_2.

The iterations will stop when the matrix $[M_T]$ will be the same as $[M_{T+1}]$. The solution will be given by:

$$[w_T] = \frac{[M_T]^{-1}[1]}{[1]'[M_T]^{-1}[1]}$$

This portfolio will give us the minimum DSR. In terms of the portfolio frontier, this will represent the vertex of the curve. In order to build the portfolio frontier, we will have to find some other points on the efficient set. Since we are interested in points with a higher expected return than the vertex, we shall fix an expected return a bit higher than the minimum downside risk portfolio above. So the new recursive minimization procedure will be given by:

$$\text{Min}[w]'[M]\{w]s.t.[w]'[1] = 1 \quad \text{and} \quad [w]'[e] = E(r_p)$$

where $[e]$ is the vector of expected returns.

Like in the former case, we will start with a given portfolio, select only its negative deviations, construct a new matrix M_0 with these observations, make the minimization above, and find a new portfolio. Again, select its negative observations, construct a matrix M_1, repeat the minimization with M_1, find a new portfolio, select its negative deviations, and so on. After we have achieved the convergence, after T iterations, the minimum downside risk portfolio with expected return given by $E(r_p)$ is given by:

$$[w_p] = \frac{AE(r_p) - B}{AC - B^2}[M_T]^{-1}[e] + \frac{C - BE(r_p)}{AC - B^2}[M_T]^{-1}[1] \qquad (11.7)$$

where

$$A = [1]'[M_T]^{-1}[1], \quad B = [e]'[M_T]^{-1}[1], \quad C = [e]'[M_T]^{-1}[e]$$

It should be noted that for small changes in the expected return, the matrix we will end up with remains unchanged. Pre-multiplying equation (11.7) by $[w_p]'[M_T]$:

$$\sigma_{p^2}{}^* = \frac{A(E(r_p))^2 - 2BE(r_p) + C}{AC - B^2}$$

The equation above shows us that while the final matrix does not change, downside risk will be a parabola on the expected return, just like in the bivariate case. However, if we change the expected return a lot, we will end up with a new matrix, and therefore a new parabola. Thus, like in the bivariate case, the portfolio frontier will be described as a sequence of segments of different parabolas.

This result is expected because since the portfolio frontier is a convex combination of several bivariate cases, each one is like Figure 11.6. One interesting aspect is that the more assets are used, the smoother will be the portfolio frontier in question, creating a similar effect as if we were adding more observations.

Since this algorithm is a series of standard minimization procedures, adding linear constraints, like not exceeding a given amount of a given asset, or not allowing short sales, are still valid. For these minimizations of quadratic functions subject to linear constraint, any simple algorithm, like Newton–Raphson's can be used.

To construct the portfolio frontier then, we shall start with the simplest problem: Minimize downside risk. From that point, we will get the vertex of the curve, and the other points of the portfolio frontier will be constructed using the procedure above, each time with a higher expected return. The only recommendation is that we should use the minimum downside risk portfolio as a warm start for the next point (the one with a higher expected return). After this point is achieved, after all the iterations suggested above, this portfolio should be used as a warm start for the next point, with an even higher expected return, and so on.

Since the matrix $[M_T]$ will differ for frontier portfolios with very different expected returns, we will not have the traditional two-fund separation property. Looking at equation (11.7), it would only happen if we had a fixed matrix $[M_T]$, like in the variance case. However, since it will change as we move along for higher expected returns, this property will be violated. We will have only a local two-fund separation (while the matrix does not change). As we add more assets, or more observations, this matrix will be changing more frequently, until in the limit case, we will have a given matrix (and a 'collapsed' parabola) for every point in the frontier.

11.5   ASSET PRICING

In this section, we will provide a new version of the CAPM, which had already been derived by Bawa and Lindenberg (1977). The only difference is that we will make use of the properties of the frontier shown in the last sections to construct the formula.

Consider a portfolio z that has a zero cross-DSR with a frontier portfolio p:

$$\frac{1}{n} \sum_{i=1}^{n} [\text{Min}(r_p^i - \mu, 0)](r_z^i - \mu) = 0$$

If we pre multiply equation (11.7) by $[z]'[M_T]$, we will have:

$$0 = \frac{AE(r_p) - B}{AC - B^2} E(r_z) + \frac{C - BE(r_p)}{AC - B^2}$$

Substituting in equation (11.7) it becomes:

$$[w_p] = \frac{AE(r_p) - B}{AC - B^2} [M_T]^{-1} ([e] - E(r_z)[1]) \tag{11.8}$$

If we pre multiply the equation above by $[p]'[M_T]$, we will have:

$$\sigma_{p^2}{}^* = \frac{AE(r_p) - B}{AC - B^2} (E(r_p) - E(r_z))$$

Consider now a given portfolio i. If we pre multiply equation (11.8) by $[i]'[M_T]$, we will have:

$$\sigma_{ip}{}^* = \frac{AE(r_p) - B}{AC - B^2} (E(r_i) - E(r_z)), \quad \text{where } \sigma_{ip}{}^* = \sum_{j \in S_T} (r_i^j - \mu)(r_p^j - \mu)$$

Comparing the two equations above, we will see that:

$$E(r_i) - E(r_z) = \frac{\sigma_{ip}{}^*}{\sigma_{pp}{}^*} (E(r_p) - E(r_z)) \tag{11.9}$$

This means that any asset or portfolio i can be expressed as this version of the CAPM for any portfolio p of the portfolio frontier. The only difficulty in transforming it into a CAPM is that we do not have the two-fund separation property to guarantee that the market portfolio is an efficient portfolio.

Let us consider now the case where we also have a riskless asset, so that our problem now becomes:

$$\text{Min}[w]'[M][w] s.t. E(r_p) - ([w]'[e] + (1 - [w]'[1])r_f)$$

After all the iterations, the solution will be given by:

$$[w_p] = \frac{E(r_p)}{[d]'[M_T]^{-1}[d]} [M_T]^{-1} [d], \quad \text{where } [d] = [e] - [1]r_f \tag{11.10}$$

If we pre multiply the equation above by $[p]'[M_T]$, we will have:

$$\sigma_{pp}{}^* = \frac{E(r_p)}{[d]'[M_T]^{-1}[d]} (E(r_p) - E(r_z))$$

Consider now a given portfolio i. If we pre multiply equation (11.10) by $[i]'[M_T]$, we will have:

$$\sigma_{ip}{}^* = \frac{E(r_p)}{[d]'[M_T]^{-1}[d]} (E(r_i) - E(r_z))$$

Comparing the two equations above, we will see that:

$$E(r_i) - E(r_f) = \frac{\sigma_{ip}^{*}}{\sigma_{pp}^{*}}(E(r_p) - E(r_f)) \tag{11.11}$$

As in the former case, we will not have a fixed coefficient because the final matrix is endogenous to the expected return desired. This will make the so-called Capital Market Line convex in our case. Bawa and Lindenberg (1977) have also shown this property for the continuous case. They have also shown that when the target is in fact the risk-free return r_f, then two-fund separation will be obtained.

11.6 A NON-PARAMETRIC APPROACH

In this section we will make use of a more sophisticated estimation of DSR, in which we estimate the density of the returns using kernels. A kernel estimation of one point can be seen as a weighted average of the observations, in which the weight given to each observation decreases with its distance from the point in question. A kernel estimation of some return r_t of a given asset or portfolio is given by:

$$\hat{r}_t = \frac{\sum_i r_i K\left(\frac{r_i - r_t}{h}\right)}{\sum_i K\left(\frac{r_i - r_t}{h}\right)} \tag{11.12}$$

where $K(x)$ is a function that decreases with x. The term h is chosen in order to penalize the distance between r_t and r. It is not hard to see that the estimations $\hat{r}_t$ will tend to be smoother than the original series r_t.

The new estimation of the DSR is given by:

$$\text{DSR} \Rightarrow \frac{1}{T}\sum_{t=1}^{T}[\text{Min}(\hat{r}_t - \mu, 0)]^n \tag{11.13}$$

Let's work now on the classic case where $n = 2$. Again, we will begin in the bivariate case. In the latter the DSR curve had some segments in which there was a constant concavity, because they belonged to the same parabola. In our new case, this will not occur. Even if we set a new portfolio w_1 that is very close to w_0, although the set of observations that are positive and negative might remain the same, there will be slight change in the concavity, due to the changes in the kernel weights. In other words, the kernel estimation will make the concavity of curve change continuously and provide us with a smoother estimate of the portfolio frontier, instead of those abrupt changes in concavities followed by regions of constant concavities.

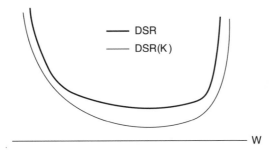

Figure 11.8

Figure 11.8 illustrates this aspect. DSR is the curve constructed with the first method proposed, while DSR(K) is the kernel estimation. It can be seen that the kernel estimation resembles what would be the curve when we have an infinite number of observations. It would also be expected that the kernel estimation curve would tend to be a little below the first one, because we are dealing with smoother estimation of returns, and consequently offsetting a little some extremes effects.

How does the algorithm work in this case? Just like in the previous sections, we will start with some portfolio w_0, then we will make a non-parametric estimation of all the returns $\hat{r}_0^t$ of this new portfolio:

$$\hat{r}_0^t = \frac{\sum_i r_0^i K\left(\dfrac{r_0^i - r_t}{h}\right)}{\sum_{t=1}^{T} K\left(\dfrac{r_0^i - r_t}{h}\right)} \tag{11.14}$$

For the estimation of the returns of each single asset, we shall follow the same procedure, but we will use the same (kernel) weights of the portfolio w_0:

$$\hat{r}_a^t = \frac{\sum_i r_a^i K\left(\dfrac{r_0^i - r_t}{h}\right)}{\sum_{t=1}^{T} K\left(\dfrac{r_0^i - r_t}{h}\right)}, \quad \hat{r}_b^t = \frac{\sum_i r_b^i K\left(\dfrac{r_0^i - r_t}{h}\right)}{\sum_{t=1}^{T} K\left(\dfrac{r_0^i - r_t}{h}\right)} \tag{11.15}$$

Consider S_0 to be the set of the estimated excess returns of w_0 that were negative. The first minimization will be given by:

$$\text{Min} \sum_{t \in S_0} (\hat{r}_t - \mu)^2, \quad \text{where } \hat{r}_t = w\hat{r}_a^t + (1 - w)\hat{r}_b^t$$

Let's call the portfolio that solves this problem w_1. The next step will be the non-parametric estimation of the returns of this portfolio:

$$\hat{r}_1^t = \frac{\sum_i r_1^i K\left(\frac{r_1^i - r_t}{h}\right)}{\sum_{t=1}^{T} K\left(\frac{r_1^i - r_t}{h}\right)}$$

And then, the new estimations of the returns of each single asset:

$$\hat{r}_a^t = \frac{\sum_i r_a^i K\left(\frac{r_1^i - r_t}{h}\right)}{\sum_{t=1}^{T} K\left(\frac{r_1^i - r_t}{h}\right)}, \quad \hat{r}_b^t = \frac{\sum_i r_b^i K\left(\frac{r_1^i - r_t}{h}\right)}{\sum_{t=1}^{T} K\left(\frac{r_1^i - r_t}{h}\right)} \qquad (11.16)$$

Consider S_1 to be the set of the estimated excess returns of w_1 that were negative. The second minimization will be given by:

$$\text{Min} \sum_{t \in S_1} (\hat{r}_t - \mu)^2, \quad \text{where } \hat{r}_t = w\hat{r}_a^t + (1 - w)\hat{r}_b^t \text{ with } \hat{r}_a^t \text{ and } \hat{r}_b^t$$

given by equation (11.16)

From then on, we will follow the same procedure. In contrast to the previous case, in which we would stop the algorithm when $S_p = S_{p+1}$. In this case, we should continue the iterations because even with the same set of observations selected, the kernel estimations will differ for every new portfolio found. Nevertheless, it should be noted that the changes in the portfolio, and consequently on DSR, will be smaller for each iteration. Thus, we should set a convergence limit in which, if the changes in the portfolio are smaller than the limit, we will stop the iterations.

For the multivariate case, we will start with a portfolio w_0, then we will make a non-parametric estimation of the returns $\hat{r}_0^t$ of this new portfolio, just like in the former case:

$$\hat{r}_0^t = \frac{\sum_i r_0^i K\left(\frac{r_0^i - r_t}{h}\right)}{\sum_i K\left(\frac{r_0^i - r_t}{h}\right)}$$

Following that, we will make estimations of the returns of each single asset j on date t:

$$\hat{r}_j^t = \frac{\sum_i r_j^i K\left(\dfrac{r_0^i - r_t}{h}\right)}{\sum_i K\left(\dfrac{r_0^i - r_t}{h}\right)}$$

From that, we will select the dates when the estimated returns of portfolio w_0 had negative excess returns. Let's call this set of observations S_0. Then we shall construct the following positive semi-definite matrix:

$$[\hat{M}_0] = \sum_{i \in S_0} \begin{bmatrix} \hat{r}_a^i \\ \hat{r}_b^i \\ \vdots \\ \hat{r}_z^i \end{bmatrix} [\hat{r}_a^i \quad \hat{r}_b^i \quad \cdots \quad \hat{r}_z^i]$$

The first task will be to find a portfolio w_1 that solves the following problem:

$$\text{Min}[w]'[\hat{M}_0][w] \, s.t. [w]'[1] = 1$$

The solution will be given by:

$$[w_1] = \frac{[\hat{M}_0]^{-1}[1]}{[1]'[\hat{M}_0]^{-1}[1]}$$

Then, we will make a non-parametric estimation of the returns $\hat{r}_1^t$ of this new portfolio:

$$\hat{r}_1^t = \frac{\sum_i r_1^i K\left(\dfrac{r_1^i - r_t}{h}\right)}{\sum_i K\left(\dfrac{r_1^i - r_t}{h}\right)}$$

Following that, the new estimations of the returns of each single asset j on date t will be given by:

$$\hat{r}_j^t = \frac{\sum_i r_j^i K\left(\dfrac{r_1^i - r_t}{h}\right)}{\sum_i K\left(\dfrac{r_1^i - r_t}{h}\right)}$$

From that, we will construct a new positive definite matrix, taking into consideration only the observations in which $\hat{r}_1^t < \mu$. Let's call this set of observations S_1:

$$[\hat{M}_1] = \sum_{i \in S_1} \begin{bmatrix} \hat{r}_a^i \\ \hat{r}_b^i \\ \vdots \\ \hat{r}_z^i \end{bmatrix} [\hat{r}_a^i \quad \hat{r}_b^i \quad \cdots \quad \hat{r}_z^i]$$

The second task will be to find a portfolio, w_2, that solves the following problem:

$$\text{Min}[w]'[\hat{M}_1][w] \, s.t. [w]'[1] = 1$$

The solution will be given by:

$$[w_2] = \frac{[\hat{M}_1]^{-1}[1]}{[1]'[\hat{M}_1]^{-1}[1]}$$

Then we will make a non-parametric estimation of the returns $\hat{r}_2^t$ of this new portfolio, and follow the same procedure as before. The iterations should stop when the changes in the portfolio become neglectable, or simply smaller than a pre-established limit.

In order to construct a portfolio frontier, we shall use the same procedure as in the former sections, but making use of estimated returns of the assets. The problem becomes computationally more complex, since for every iteration, we will have new estimations of returns for every asset, due to the changes in the kernel weights, for every time we alter the portfolio. As already mentioned, the portfolio frontier will be a smoother curve than the former case.

One may ask why shouldn't we make a non-parametric estimation of the whole joint, multivariate distribution of all the assets and construct the portfolios from there, instead of all this series of univariate non-parametric estimations? A proper answer is given by the so-called 'curse of dimensionality'. The latter shows that the more dimensions we add to a multivariate non-parametric estimation, the less efficient our estimators will become. Therefore, it is more recommended to form a portfolio and make the non-parametric estimation of its returns rather than estimating the whole joint distribution of all the assets returns and form a portfolio.

As far as asset pricing is concerned, the results are the same as before. The only difference is that in the non-parametric methodology, σ_{ip}^* and σ_{pp}^* are calculated using $\hat{r}_t$ instead of r_t.

11.7 CONCLUSION

In this chapter we have provided an algorithm to minimize portfolios DSR. Properties of the portfolio frontier, such as convexity, were demonstrated. Asset pricing relations were also derived, with and without a risk-free asset. Finally, a non-parametric approach was presented to calculate DSR, as well as an algorithm to optimize it, and construct a non-parametric portfolio frontier.

REFERENCES

Athayde, G. and Flôres, R. (1999) A CAPM with higher moments: theory and econometrics, Ensaios Econômicos, no. 317, EPGE/FGV, Rio de Janeiro.

Bawa, V. and Lindenberg, E. (1977) Capital market equilibrium in a mean-lower partial moment framework, *Journal of Financial Economics*, 5.

Ingersoll, J. (1975) Multidimensional security pricing, *Journal of Financial and Quantitative Analysis*, December.

Kraus, A. and Litzenberger, R.H. (1976) Skewness preference and the valuation of risk assets, *Journal of Finance*, 31.

Markowitz, H. (1952) Portfolio selection, *Journal of Finance*, 6.

Chapter 12

FARM: a financial actuarial risk model

ROBERT S. CLARKSON

12.1 INTRODUCTION

12.1.1 Objectives

The primary objective of this chapter is to construct a measure of financial risk that can explain real world behaviour and lead to the attainment of better standards of financial risk management by individuals, financial institutions and government institutions.

The secondary objective is to provide solid foundations on which to build an actuarial theory of finance.

12.1.2 Actuarial approaches to risk

Actuaries first came to prominence as financial experts through their ability to measure and manage mortality risk in the life assurance and pension fund contexts. The foundation work for this expertise was the empirical investigation set out in Halley (1693), which describes the construction of the first 'scientific' life table.

Some actuaries then applied their mathematical and practical skills to general insurance, and in the process developed a new 'risk theory' covering loss functions and the probability of ruin.

The actuarial profession responded to the upsurge in interest in financial risk during the 1980s by setting up AFIR (Actuarial Approach for Financial Risk) as the finance section of the International Actuarial Association. However, although AFIR has now been in existence, and running international colloquia, for more than ten years, no dominant single approach to financial risk has emerged. Instead, colloquium papers have typically reflected a wide spectrum of approaches to risk, with papers following the risk methodologies of financial economics tending to become more frequent over recent years.

12.1.3 Expected utility

The expected utility approach pioneered by Bernoulli (1738, 1954) and later developed along rigorous mathematical lines by von Neumann and Morgenstern (1944) is one of the cornerstones of present day economic science and is perhaps the most widely used theoretical framework for human choice under conditions of uncertainty and risk.

Utility theory has been severely criticized by many eminent economists and its predictions are in many well-documented cases markedly inconsistent with observed real world behaviour.

12.1.4 Neural mechanics of physical risk

The starting point in the derivation of the Financial Actuarial Risk Model (FARM) is the recognition that in the assessment of risk of any type the human mind acts as an analogue computer rather than as a digital computer, with the strength of the risk perception neural response being determined almost instantaneously at a subconscious level rather than as a time-consuming quantitative computation. A corollary is that the neural mechanics of financial risk, where the unwanted outcomes are financial distress or financial ruin at the personal or corporate level, will be identical to the neural mechanics of physical risk, where the unwanted outcomes are injury or death.

It should be possible to translate how the human mind assesses and manages physical risk and then to translate this into a model of financial risk.

12.1.5 Structure of the chapter

If FARM is to have any claim to generality, it should be consistent with the broad conceptual guidelines suggested by eminent economists and be able to account for real world behaviour that is anomalous in the context of alternative approaches. Accordingly, section 12.2 discusses perceptive observations by various eminent economists and also a number of instances of 'anomalous' behaviour.

The construction of the new and more general theory of risk falls into two parts. Section 12.3 follows the approach first suggested in outline in Clarkson (1989) and describes the construction of a theory of financial risk that represents an extension of the framework described in Clarkson (1989, 1990).

Three levels of application of the FARM are then described. Section 12.5 discusses elementary applications including the resolution of paradoxes relating to behaviour that is clearly anomalous within the paradigm of financial economics. Section 12.6 applies the FARM to the 'equities versus bonds' debate, and section 12.7 discusses some wider implications of the FARM as a guide to prudent financial behaviour.

12.2 ANOMALIES AND INCONSISTENCIES

12.2.1 Observations by Adam Smith

In his *Wealth of Nations*, Smith (1776, 1976) observes how the 'absurd presumption in their own good fortune' on the part of most people leads to behaviour that is blatantly inconsistent with the 'rational behaviour' cornerstone of present day economics:

> *The chance of gain is by every man more or less overvalued, and the chance of loss is by most men under-valued.*

Smith cites the popularity of lotteries, where the expected payout is always well below the price of a ticket, as a classic example of the overvaluation of gains. It is salutary to note that in January 1999 the Chairman of the US Federal Reserve used the phrase 'lottery mentality' in connection with his 'irrational exuberance' warning that the aggregate market capitalization of Internet-related stocks was vastly in excess of what could be justified by the likely aggregate future profits of the industry. Also, in the first week of January 2000, when major stock markets experienced sharp setbacks after the 'new millennium' euphoria of December 1999, the Governor of the Bank of England warned that it was very easy for stock markets to become seriously overvalued.

As his flagship example of how most people undervalue risk as a result of 'thoughtless rashness and presumptuous contempt', Smith cites the failure of many people to insure against serious wealth-destroying hazards such as fire and shipwreck, even although appropriate insurance cover is often readily available at reasonable cost. He also refers to a 'nice calculation' on a probabilistic basis whereby risk may be reduced to an acceptable level through what would today be called self-insurance:

> *When a great company, or even a great merchant, has twenty or thirty ships at sea, they may, as it were, insure one another. The premium saved upon them all may more than compensate such losses as they are likely to meet with in the common course of chances.*

This provides our first pointer towards a new measure of risk, namely that risk cannot be eliminated completely but must be brought down below some small value that is deemed acceptable.

Smith begins his discussion of the determinants of wages and profit by observing that the theoretical state of equilibrium that would result from every man's self-interest to 'seek the advantageous and to shun the disadvantageous' does not in fact occur, largely because of factors that exist only 'in the imaginations of men'. This is perhaps the first documented evidence of what might today be called 'systematic irrationality'.

In the context of commodity prices (of which stock market prices are perhaps the most important present day examples), Smith observes that, rather than always being close to what he called their 'natural' (or equilibrium) value, the observed market prices often differ markedly from these 'natural' prices:

> *The natural price, therefore, is, as it were, the central price, to which the prices of all commodities are continually gravitating. Different accidents may sometimes keep them suspended a good deal above it, and sometimes force them down even somewhat below it. But whatever may be the obstacles which hinder them from settling in this centre of repose and continuance, they are constantly tending towards it.*

Smith discusses the annual prices of corn, the most important commodity several hundred years ago, to illustrate the general behaviour of commodity prices. It is instructive to note that his numerical approach of using 10-year moving averages as reference values is identical in principle to the Mean Absolute Deviation analysis of stock market prices described in Plymen and Prevett (1972) and Clarkson (1978, 1981).

12.2.2   Observations by John Maynard Keynes

In his much earlier *Treatise on Probability*, Keynes (1921) suggests various ways in which to achieve better understanding of how the human mind perceives probability and risk. In particular, he is strongly distrustful of the marginal utility of wealth approach that Daniel Bernoulli (1738, 1954) relied upon to 'solve' the famous St Petersburg Paradox, and observes that what might be called tacit knowledge, especially regarding Peter's ability to pay Paul and the enormous risk of Paul incurring a serious loss, leads to considerable 'psychological doubt' which makes a purely mathematical approach difficult:

> *We are unwilling to be Paul, partly because we do not believe Peter will pay us if we have good fortune in the tossing, partly because we do not know what we should do with so much money or sand or hydrogen if we won it, and partly because we do not think it would be a rational act to risk an infinitely larger one, whose attainment is infinitely unlikely. When we have made the proper hypotheses and have eliminated these areas of psychological doubt, the theoretical dispersal of what element of paradox remains must be brought about, I think, by a development of the theory of risk.*

Keynes discusses instances of where the human mind appears to ignore the risk when it is below some very small value, and cites an interesting observation by the French philosopher Buffon (1777):

I am thinking of such arguments as Buffon's when he names 1/10,000 as the limit, beyond which probability is negligible, on the grounds that, being the chance that a man of 56 taken at random will die within a day, it is practically disregarded by a man of 56 who knows his health to be good.

12.2.3   Observations by von Neumann and Morgenstern

In von Neumann and Morgenstern (1944), the foundation work of modern utility theory, it is assumed that human choice under conditions of uncertainty and risk is based on 'rational behaviour' as defined by a set of seemingly innocuous utility axioms. Even the authors themselves had serious doubts about the validity of certain of the axioms, particularly (3:C:b), but they concluded that this axiom was 'plausible and legitimate, unless a much more refined system of psychology is used than the one now available for the purposes of economics'.

The authors also observed that 'the common individual, whose behaviour one wants to describe, does not measure his utilities exactly but rather conducts his economic activities in a sphere of considerable haziness'. Despite this admission that 'rational behaviour' as defined by their utility axioms was more likely to be the exception rather than the rule in the real world, they expressed their belief that at some future date the benefits of their utility approach might be significant:

Once a fuller understanding of economic behaviour has been achieved with the aid of a theory which makes use of this instrument, the life of the individual might be materially affected.

Many eminent economists of the day, such as Friedman, Malinvaud, Samuelson and Savage, were highly critical of the von Neumann and Morgenstern utility axioms.

12.2.4   Observations by Maurice Allais

By far the most powerful attack on the highly mathematical approach of utility theory was from Allais (1953), who argues that there is no single-valued function (such as a value of expected utility) which can provide an accurate guide as to how deliberative choices are made by 'reasonable' men. He accordingly concludes that the expected utility maxim cannot be regarded as the criterion of rational behaviour.

The now famous 'Allais Paradox' is a counterexample Allais used to support his rejection of the expected utility maxim. When given the choice between receiving £1 m with certainty or of receiving nil, £1 m and £5 m with probabilities of 0.01, 0.89 and 0.1 respectively, most subjects choose the former, but when given the choice between receiving nil or £1 m with probabilities of 0.89 and 0.11 respectively or of receiving nil or £5 m with probabilities of 0.9 and 0.1 respectively, most of the same subjects choose the latter. Such a combination of choices is inconsistent with any expected utility function. Reference will be made at the end of this section to the following similar but less contrived choice. A businessman has sought your actuarial advice as to whether or not he should put his entire working capital of £1 m at risk for a business opportunity which will lead either to a profit of £80 000 with probability 0.95 or to a loss of all £1 m of his working capital with probability 0.05, giving an expected profit of £26 000.

In his Nobel Lecture, given on 9 December 1988, Allais (1989) suggests that his paradox demonstrates what he calls 'the preference for security in the neighbourhood of certainty'.

Allais (1954) draws attention to the very serious dangers of building an apparently rigorous mathematical theory on simplifying assumptions that have no real world relevance, and accordingly he suggests that only those who have extensive practical experience gained over a period of many years should attempt to formulate economic models.

12.2.5   Observations by William Sharpe

Sharpe (1970) investigates utility theory as a plausible framework for the implementation of the Markowitz (1959, 1991) mean-variance approach to portfolio selection, and observes that, of the various possible utility curves that have been proposed, 'Only one is completely consistent with choices based solely on expected return and standard deviation of return: the assumption that utility is a quadratic function of wealth.' However, on investigating the implications of using a quadratic utility function, he discovers some serious inconsistencies and draws the following conclusions:

> *In some instances, investors will be concerned with more than the expected return and standard deviation of return. In such cases a quadratic utility curve will imperfectly approximate an investor's actual utility curve. If portfolios with radically different prospects are considered by an investor, too much reality may be omitted if his decision is assumed to depend only on expected return and standard deviation of return.*

Despite these serious inconsistencies, Sharpe suggests that the use of a utility curve may still be justified if it is assumed that investors choose amongst portfolios of roughly similar risk. However, in many suggested applications of utility theory, such as whether or not to insure against the risk of a serious financial loss, the risk levels of the scenarios being compared differ enormously.

12.2.6   Attempted generalizations of expected utility

Until the late 1970s, most economists believed that agents were rational and that expected utility provided a highly satisfactory framework for human choice under conditions of uncertainty and risk. However, by the early 1980s the volu-minous experimental evidence of axiom violations that had been published over the previous decade, particularly by Kahneman and Tversky (1979) and Grether and Plott (1979), forced economic theorists to attempt to build more complex new theories that could give a better explanation of real world behaviour. Anand (1993), Machina (1987) and Quiggin (1993) have been especially prolific in first of all documenting axiom violations (particularly in the areas of 'independence' and 'transitivity') and then suggesting more and more complex generalized axiomatic approaches.

12.2.7   Absence of an unambiguous basic measure of risk

In virtually all branches of science where a mathematical approach is attempted, an unambiguous basic measure of key attributes is a necessary condition for the subsequent successful development of a body of theory which can accurately describe real world behaviour. In particular, we need to be able to make unam-biguous statements along the lines of 'the value in the case of A is twice the value in the case of B'.

No such unambiguous basic measure exists for financial risk. In particular, standard deviation of return and variance of return are both used as a measure. However, if the standard deviation in the case of *A* is twice that for *B*, the variance for *A* is four times that for *B*. The probability of ruin is also used as a measure of risk, but there is no obvious link between this 'non-parametric' measure and a 'parametric' measure such as variance. Furthermore, the Risk Assessment and Management for Projects (RAMP) methodology, which has been put forward jointly by the UK actuarial profession and the Institution of Civil Engineers as a basic framework for practical risk management, does not incorporate an explicit numerical measure of risk.

12.2.8   Behavioural finance

Over the past decade or so, numerous economists and psychologists have estab-lished a new branch of economic science, namely behavioural finance, which studies behavioural patterns that might be regarded as 'systematic irrationality' under mainstream theories of finance where 'rational behaviour' is an essential cornerstone.

The four most familiar behavioural finance traits are 'framing and coding', where observed behaviour differs depending on how the relevant information is presented to the subject, 'over-confidence', as first diagnosed by Adam Smith, 'over-reaction bias', which would explain the 'excess volatility' documented by Shiller (1989) and others, and 'myopic loss aversion', where subjects choose high risk courses of action despite the availability of convincing evidence as to the existence of more profitable courses of action that also involve lower risk.

12.2.9   Myopic loss aversion

Any financial disadvantage resulting from the first three of these four behavioural traits could be mitigated to a considerable extent by the availability of more detailed information, presented in as impartial a manner as possible. Myopic loss aversion, however, is a much more deeply ingrained wealth-destroying behaviour trait. A classic physical risk example is a refusal to fly for either business or pleasure purposes, despite the existence of vast amounts of statistical evidence showing that going by car is vastly more risky, in terms of deaths per passenger mile, than flying with a recognized airline.

The classic financial risk example is a preference on the part of many investors for long-term investment in bonds rather than equities, despite very strong evidence that the likelihood of equities outperforming bonds increases to near certainty as the investment horizon increases. This equities versus bond question is discussed in detail in section 12.6.

12.2.10   The Tversky paradox

Tversky (1990) questions the absolutely fundamental assumption that individuals are 'risk-averse' in the generally accepted sense of preferring, for a given expected value, the choice which involves the lowest uncertainty of return, as measured, for example, by the standard deviation or variance of return. If investors have the choice between a gain with certainty of £85 000, or an 85% chance of gaining £100 000 and a 15% chance of gaining nothing, most will choose the former, certain, outcome which is inconsistent with standard theory.

Suppose now that investors have a choice between losing £85 000 with certainty, or an 85% chance of losing £100 000 and a 15% chance of losing nothing. Most people will 'gamble' and choose the latter, which is inconsistent with standard theory.

12.2.11   A 'risk equals uncertainty' paradox

An insurance company with assets at present of 100 requires assets at some future date of 110 or more to achieve what it regards as a satisfactory return on capital, and will be insolvent if assets have a value of 105 or less at that future date. The company can invest either in asset class A which will give 105 with certainty, or in asset class B which will give 110 or 115 with equal probability.

The paradox here is that textbooks on stochastic calculus as applied to finance, such as Lamberton and Lapeyre (1996), define asset class A as the 'risk-free' asset and asset class B as 'risky', in that it involves an uncertain outcome. Common sense shows that it is asset class A that is (pathologically!) risky, whereas asset class B is risk-free in that the criterion of a satisfactory return on capital is achieved with certainty.

12.2.12   The other St Petersburg paradox

Bernoulli (1738, 1954) applies the logarithmic utility approach that he used to 'solve' the St Petersburg Paradox to the case of a merchant shipping goods from St Petersburg to Amsterdam. He can sell his cargo for 10 000 ducats if the ship arrives safely, but there is a probability of 0.05 that the ship and cargo are lost at sea, with the requisite insurance cover being available for a premium of 800 ducats, which the merchant regards as outrageously high. Bernoulli asks what other wealth the merchant should possess for it to be rational for him to choose not to insure. Bernoulli obtains the answer of 5843 ducats, and is very pleased with his approach:

> *Though a person who is fairly judicious by natural instinct might have real-ized and spontaneously applied much of what I have here explained, hardly anyone believed it possible to define these problems with the precision we have employed in our examples. Since all our propositions harmonize perfectly with experience it would be wrong to neglect them as abstractions resting on precarious hypotheses.*

Taking one ducat as being equivalent to £100, this example is identical to that in section 12.2.4, namely whether or not a businessman should put his entire working capital at risk for a business opportunity which will lead either to a profit of £80 000 with probability 0.95 or to a loss of all £1 m of his working capital with probability 0.05, giving an expected profit of £26 000. Even with other wealth of around £600 000, the equivalent of Bernoulli's computa-tion, most actuaries would strongly discourage the businessman from taking up the opportunity. The obvious corollary is that Bernoulli's logarithmic utility approach must after all be based on 'precarious hypotheses'.

12.3   PHYSICAL RISK IN SPORTS

12.3.1   Severity of consequences of an adverse occurrence

Consider the consequences of a serious hang-gliding accident, such as equip-ment failure, as a function of the height above ground at which the accident

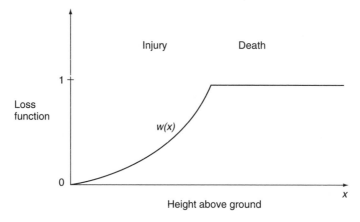

Figure 12.1

occurs. From a height of only a few feet, this might result in no injury or nothing worse than a sprained ankle, but from several hundred feet or more death would be almost certain. If we use the same range as for probability to represent the 'loss function', we have 0 for no injury, 1 for death, and the general pattern shown in Figure 12.1 with $w(x)$ increasing with the severity of injury in the intermediate zone between no injury and death.

Suppose now that we classify the intermediate injuries into five broad categories – minor injury, moderate injury, serious injury, very serious injury and permanent incapacity. The human mind not surprisingly perceives the negative consequences of imminent death as being effectively infinite, with the result that lesser degrees of physical damage are 'discounted' at a very high rate. Accordingly, we can, as a first guess, calibrate the severity function $w(s)$ by using a factor of 10 between each reference point from minor injury up to death, giving the values shown below.

Severity	Consequence	$w(s)$
0	No injury	0
1	Minor injury	0.00001
2	Moderate injury	0.0001
3	Serious injury	0.001
4	Very serious injury	0.01
5	Permanent incapacity	0.1
6	Death	1

12.3.2 Equivalent probability of death

We can now, for example, say that for a given probability of death the perception of risk within the human mind is equivalent to that for serious injury when the associated probability is one thousand times as high. The function $w(s)$ introduces a measure of equivalence between widely differing outcomes, namely death and varying degrees of injury, that could not previously be combined mathematically to produce an overall value for risk.

In ski mountaineering, a very risky sport, there are two dominant adverse occurrences, namely a bad fall and an avalanche. For each of these, we can first of all estimate the probability of an adverse occurrence taking place and then, given that it does in fact take place, estimate the probabilities (which will clearly sum to 1) for each outcome from no injury up to death. In an obvious notation we can now obtain the value of risk as:

$$R = p(n)p(n, s)w(s)$$

where $p(1)$ and $p(2)$ are the respective probabilities of a bad fall and avalanche and $p(2, 6)$ is, for example, the probability that an avalanche, if it occurs, will lead to death. The generalization to a larger number of adverse occurrences is obvious. This measure of risk R can be called, for obvious reasons, the 'equivalent probability of death', with the minimum value of 0 corresponding to no possibility of injury or death and the maximum value of 1 corresponding to imminent death with certainty.

12.3.3 Estimation procedures

The Poisson distribution is ideal for representing the severity function, with the value of 0 corresponding to no injury, 1 corresponding to minor injury, and so on up to 6 or higher corresponding to death. Since the mean of the Poisson distribution is equal to the variance, only one parameter has to be estimated for each adverse occurrence.

The following values of the probability of an adverse occurrence (for typical daily participation), of the associated Poisson parameter, and of the resulting values of risk are set out in Clarkson (1989), and are based not on comprehensive empirical data but on a combination of personal observation and 'intelligent guesswork'.

Sport	*Adverse occurrence*	*Daily rate*	*Poisson parameter*	*Daily risk* $\times 10^6$
Wind-surfing	Falling off board	5	0.01	0.5
Ski-ing	Bad fall	2	0.1	3.1
Rapid river canoeing	Capsize in rapids	1 in 5	0.5	13.8
Ski-mountaineering	{ Bad fall	2	0.2 }	106.4
	{ Avalanche	1 in 1000	3 }	
Hang-gliding	Fall to ground	1 in 5000	7	142.6

12.3.4   Royal society (1992) risk study

An investigation into fatality rates in sports as part of a wider study of risk by the Royal Society of London covers two of the five sports for which risk values are estimated above. The corresponding values, after appropriate standardization, are shown below.

Sport	Clarkson (1989) Daily risk $\times\ 10^6$		Royal Society (1993) Deaths per day $\times\ 10^6$
Ski-ing	3.1	$\begin{cases} 3.5 \\ 6.5 \end{cases}$	USA, 1967–68 France, 1974–76
Hang-gliding	142.6	$\begin{cases} 100-325 \\ 375 \end{cases}$	USA, 1978 UK, 1977–79

The close agreement in the case of the USA experience is quite remarkable, given the totally different methodologies used. The higher values for ski-ing in France and for hang-gliding in the UK are not surprising, but space does not permit a fuller discussion here.

12.3.5   Personal threshold of maximum acceptable risk

Different individuals have different tolerances of the level of physical risk in sports. We can first of all observe that for each individual there is a personal threshold of acceptable risk and then, given that ski-mountaineering is towards the top end of the risk spectrum, take 0.0001 per day as an 'upper guideline' value, possibly around the 90th percentile, for the maximum acceptable limit.

Many individuals regard skiing, where avalanches and collisions with trees or other skiers have given rise to many highly publicized fatalities in recent years, as 'far too risky'. In the light of the estimated risk values in sections 12.3.3 and 12.3.4, the seemingly very low value of 0.000001 per day, equivalent to a chance of one in a million of being killed, can be taken as a plausible 'lower guideline' value, corresponding perhaps to the 10th percentile.

12.3.6   Indifference curves and axioms of choice

There is clearly a risk, however small, in all day-to-day activities. But most people are prepared to fly on normal passenger aircraft for business or holiday purposes, and virtually everyone is prepared to travel by car, without giving any thought to the physical risk involved. Such travel decisions are thus made solely on the basis of other criteria such as cost, convenience and reliability. This accords with the observation by Buffon (1777) that the human mind ignores risk completely when its perceived value is very small. In potentially risky sports it is therefore reasonable to assume that very low levels of perceived risk will be ignored completely.

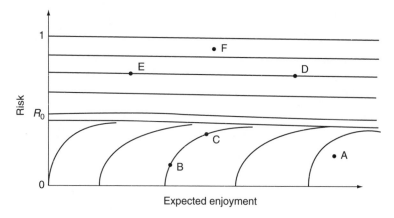

Figure 12.2

Suppose now that for every available sporting activity we can make a quantitative estimate E of 'expected enjoyment' in addition to our 'equivalent probability of risk' estimate R. Then the above discussion suggests that the situation can be portrayed by patterns of indifference curves in the $E–R$ diagram of the type shown in Figure 12.2.

Above R_0, the indifference 'curves' are essentially horizontal lines, while below R_0 they are asymptotic to vertical lines for very low risk, have continuous and decreasing gradient as risk increases, and are asymptotic to the horizontal line $R = R_0$ as risk increases towards R_0.

The four simple rules required to determine preference and optimality can be illustrated by the points A, B, C, D, E and F in Figure 12.2. If at least one point has a risk value below R_0, the preferred point is A, the one to the right of the most indifference curves, whereas B and C, lying on the same indifference curve, are equally preferable. Otherwise, both D and E, lying below more indifference lines, are preferred to F, whereas – regarding the 'horizontal' indifference lines as having infinitesimally small negative gradient – D is preferred to E.

It is obvious that transitivity is preserved under these preference and optimality rules, even although the situation is two-dimensional rather than one-dimensional as in the case of expected utility.

12.3.7　Summary of the quantification of physical risk

(1) Identify all possible adverse occurrences than can lead to injury or death.
(2) For each adverse occurrence, identify the probabilities $p(n)$ and $p(n, s)$ as defined in section 12.3.2.
(3) Identify the appropriate severity weighting function $w(s)$ as defined in section 12.3.1.

(4) Calculate the values of risk as defined in section 12.3.2.
(5) Calculate the values of expected enjoyment.
(6) Identify the value of R_0, the maximum acceptable value of risk, and appropriate indifference curves for values of risk below R_0.
(7) Use the preference rules in section 12.3.6 to identify the activity that is optimal on risk/expected enjoyment considerations.

12.3.8   The reality of physical risk

Explicit quantitative evaluation along the lines summarized in section 12.3.7 is impracticable; the required probability distributions cannot be determined with any precision, and the effective values of $w(s)$ and R_0 are determined at a subconscious level in response to innate self-protection mechanisms (such as a fear of heights) or to previous practical experience. Accordingly, the quantification of physical risk is put forward as an assumption of how the human mind *should* perceive risk and determine optimality.

Most of the examples below are very brief summaries of some of those discussed in Clarkson (1999).

12.3.9   Over-confidence

Although nearly all participants in potentially risky sports accept their 'beginner' status when they first take part and only tackle more difficult challenges after they have acquired – generally under expert tuition and supervision – an understanding of the basic skills, it is only human nature that some individuals will be over-confident about their abilities and accordingly underestimate the true level of risk.

An unfortunate example of this has been the alarmingly high number of fatalities on Scottish mountains in recent years as a result of what has been called the 'Surrey syndrome'. Whereas those living not far distant will simply stay at home if the weather conditions are likely, especially in winter, to make climbing unduly dangerous, those who have come a considerable distance will, on account of the time and expense they have devoted to their planned climbs, be much less likely to abandon their plans in the face of adverse weather forecasts.

12.3.10   Innate failsafe behaviour

Many people, when encountering a sport for the first time, will say to themselves 'this looks great fun, but it is too risky for me!' However, after observation over a sufficiently long period and assuming that no accidents have occurred, they will often adopt the quite different mental attitude that the inherent level of risk is sufficiently low for them to be able to participate without undue worry.

This in many ways answers the question discussed in section 12.2.2, namely how much further information should we seek out before pursuing a particular course of action. The above answer is to participate only after we have obtained sufficient information for us to be confident that the inherent level of risk is acceptably small.

12.3.11   Over-reaction bias

An actuary whom the author met at the 1994 FARM International Colloquium in the United States had booked, and paid for, an introductory hang-gliding flight. But when he returned for his lesson a few days later he found that, of the three instructors at the company, one had a leg in plaster and another had an arm in a sling, both as a result of hang-gliding accidents in the previous two days. He immediately asked for, and was given, a full refund for the lesson that he now perceived as being foolhardily dangerous.

Such a change of mind is entirely reasonable, even although the accident experience might not – on purely statistical arguments – be inconsistent at a given confidence level with previous average rates. Just as with Einstein's General Theory of Relativity for physical behaviour, human behaviour is not 'absolute' but is very much dependent on 'locality', in this case recent personal experience.

12.3.12   Temporary insanity

Identify the appropriate severity weighting function $w(s)$ as defined in section 12.3.1.

For most people, the joys of sailing soon outweigh the serious discomfort of occasional bouts of seasickness. However, on an overnight yacht race in which the author participated one crew member became so ill and mentally disturbed through seasickness that he attempted to jump overboard to bring an end to his suffering and had to be tied down in the cockpit for his own safety until the gale force winds abated. The following morning he had returned to a normal frame of mind, and he later bought his own yacht.

Seasickness is the result of the human mind shutting down certain physical functions in response to being overwhelmed by contradictory signals from the delicate fluid canal balance system within the inner ear. A useful palliative measure is to help the mind to restore an effective sense of perspective by focusing on the horizon. In acute cases, however, all power of rational thought is lost and temporary insanity results.

12.4   TRANSLATION INTO FINANCIAL RISK

12.4.1   Severity of consequences of an adverse occurrence

For an insurance company, the 'loss function' for hang-gliding portrayed in Figure 12.1 translates into the loss function in Figure 12.3, with the horizontal

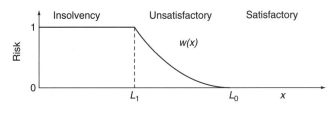

Figure 12.3

axis x being 'assets less liabilities', and the vertical axis again being risk on a scale of 0 to 1.

Below L_1, the outcome is 'insolvency' and the risk value is 1. From L_0 to L_1, the outcome is 'unsatisfactory' and risk follows a smooth curve $w(x)$. Above L_0, the outcome is 'satisfactory' and risk is zero.

For portfolio investment, assuming short positions are not permissible, L_1 corresponds to a portfolio value of nil, while L_0 corresponds to the point above which the outcome is deemed to be 'satisfactory'.

12.4.2 Equivalent probability of financial ruin

Assuming that we know $p(x)$, the probability density function of outcome x, the financial risk $R(x)$ translates into:

$$R(x) = p(x)\,dx + w(x)p(x)\,dx$$

where the first and second terms correspond respectively to 'non-parametric risk' (the probability of financial ruin) and 'parametric risk'. On this formulation, the risk measure $R(x)$ can, for obvious reasons, be interpreted as 'the equivalent probability of financial ruin'.

This framework unifies two existing approaches to risk that are useful in differing application areas. In 'catastrophe' general insurance the 'risk of ruin' component dominates and the parametric component can for most practical purposes be ignored. In portfolio investment, on the other hand, the parametric component dominates. In very high risk investment areas, where short positions may arise, both components may be important.

12.4.3 Formulating the equivalence function

Identify the appropriate severity weighting function $w(s)$ as defined in section 12.3.1.

For portfolio investment, the consequences of losing a given proportion of investment value are far more than twice as serious as losing half that proportion. We can therefore infer that the 'parametric' function $w(x)$ is concave upwards. A highly convenient formulation for $w(x)$ is a power (greater than one) of the proportionate shortfall below L_0 towards L_1. Taking this power as two is not only eminently plausible in that the severity of the consequences quadruples as the shortfall doubles but is also broadly consistent with vast tranches of the financial economics literature in that variance of return and semi-variance can then be regarded as special cases when L_0 is equal to the mean return.

12.4.4   Thresholds of maximum and minimum risk

In the case of a financial company the threshold of maximum risk for which the value of risk attains its maximum value of 1 can normally be taken as the value of financial outcome below which insolvency results. For an individual, the threshold below which bankruptcy results will normally be appropriate.

For the threshold L_0 above which risk is zero it will normally be appropriate to use either the current value of wealth or net assets, or the minimum future value that is deemed to be satisfactory. Where, however, a higher value is available with certainty under one of the available choices, then this higher value should be used. For instance, if the choice for an individual with negligible current wealth is between receiving £1 m with certainty and receiving either nil or £3 m with equal probability, £1 m is the appropriate value for L_0. This means that L_0 and hence the value of risk is not absolute but may depend on the available choices.

12.4.5   Maximum level of acceptable risk

We can use the uncertain outcome under the first half of the Allais Paradox to begin the calibration. The probability of 0.01 of receiving nothing as against being able to receive £1 m with certainty involves a risk of 0.01 which can, on the basis of the experiments carried out by Allais, be taken as being in excess of the risk that nearly all 'reasonable' individuals would accept. This suggests 0.005 as a plausible guess as to an 'upper guideline' value that might correspond to the 90th percentile.

A probability of ruin of 0.001, one in a thousand, is generally regarded as a very prudent risk of ruin criterion. This suggest 0.001 as a plausible guess as to a 'lower guideline' value that might correspond to around the 10th percentile.

12.4.6   Indifference curves and axioms of choice

Replacing 'expected enjoyment' by 'expected return', section 12.3.6 translates into the indifference curves and axioms of choice framework in the context of financial risk.

12.4.7   Over-confidence

The essentially short term neural response mechanism of the perception of risk, combined with the relatively long time scales of episodes of economic and stock market behaviour, suggests that in the face of apparently attractive investment opportunities far too little weight will be paid to historical evidence of similar scenarios that led to serious losses. Accordingly, over-confidence through an underestimation of the true level of risk is likely to be a not uncommon feature of stock market behaviour at a collective level. Classic examples are the 'nifty fifty' boom in US growth stocks during the 1960s, the Poseidon nickel boom of 1969, and the meteoric rise in Japanese equities in the late 1980s.

12.4.8 'Lack of confidence' and 'myopic loss aversion'

As with unfamiliar risky sports, most people have an innate awareness that certain financial or investment opportunities may be 'too risky' for them until they have investigated the risks in sufficient detail. To begin with such a refusal to participate might be described as understandable and laudable 'lack of confidence'. However, once more background information is available, the relatively short-term neural response mechanism for the perception of risk can be expected to attach too little weight to relevant long-term data. This leads to 'myopic loss aversion', the classic example of which is a refusal to contemplate long-term investment in equities even although all the UK and US data show that the probability of equities outperforming bonds increases to near certainty as the investment horizon increases.

12.4.9 Over-reaction bias

The human trait of trying to find causes for events, particularly those involving adverse consequences, means that financial reporting tends to give undue prominence to negative background factors when stock market prices have been falling. Accordingly, the neural response nature of the perception of risk will tend to amplify the recent trend, particularly when it is downwards.

12.4.10 Temporary financial insanity

The obvious financial risk parallel to the sea-sick yacht crew member who tried to jump overboard is the 'flight to liquidity' that occurs at the bottom of a bear market, when some investors try to sell at any price, no matter how far below any realistic long term value, to escape from the mental anguish of a seemingly endless series of price falls.

12.5 APPLICATIONS

12.5.1 The Allais Paradox

Assume, as is implicit, that any other wealth of the subjects can be ignored. Then for the first pair of choices, A and B, say, £1 m is available with certainty if A is chosen and thus L_0 is £1 m, and the obvious choice for L_1 is nil. Clearly the value of risk is nil for choice A. For choice B, the only shortfall below £1 m is the outcome of nil, which corresponds to L_1 with probability 0.01; the value of risk is thus 0.01×1, i.e. 0.01. Since this value is greater than the higher guideline value for maximum acceptable risk, namely 0.005, A is chosen in preference to B, agreeing with the choice of most subjects.

For the second pair of choices, C and D, say, no value higher than nil is available with certainty, and hence L_0 is nil, and the value of risk is zero for both C and D. Since D has by far the higher expected value, namely £0.445 m as against £0.1 m D is chosen is preference to C, again agreeing with the choice of most subjects.

A subject with enormous existing wealth, such as £1 bn, would perceive the risk in B to be negligible and would accordingly choose B on account of the higher expected value, namely £1.39 m as against £1 m. It is interesting to calculate what other wealth a subject should possess for the risk under choice B to be equal to either the lower or the upper guideline value of maximum acceptable risk. For other wealth W (in millions of pounds), L_0 is now $1+W$, L_1 is still nil, and the proportionate shortfall is $1/(1+W)$ if nil occurs under choice B.

Using the square of the proportionate shortfall as the parametric risk function, we have:

$$0.01(1/1 + W)^2 = R_0$$

which gives $W = 2.16$ when $R_0 = 0.001$ and $W = 0.41$ when $R_0 = 0.005$. These values of £2.16 m and £0.41 m for subjects with low and high risk tolerances respectively seem eminently sensible. Accordingly, a subject with existing wealth comfortably in excess of the appropriate minimum value would be expected to choose B in preference to A.

This extension of the Allais Paradox corresponds exactly to the thought experiment at the beginning of Bernoulli (1738, 1954), namely the deduction that, if a very poor man had somehow obtained a lottery ticket that would pay either 20 000 ducats or nil with equal probability, he would be unwise not to sell it for 9000 ducats, whereas a very rich man would be unwise not to buy it for 9000 ducats. The corresponding values of existing wealth for maximum acceptable risk are 195 000 ducats when $R_0 = 0.001$ and 81 000 ducats when $R_0 = 0.005$; again these values seem eminently reasonable.

12.5.2   The Tversky Paradox

Assume, as is implicit, that the level of existing wealth is less than £85 000, so that a loss of either £85 000 or £100 000 leads to financial ruin. Then a loss of

£85 000 with certainty has 1 as the risk value, whereas the alternative, namely either a loss of £100 000 with probability 0.85 or a loss of nil with probability 0.15 has 0.85 as the value of risk, taking L_0 as the value of existing wealth. Since both values of risk are vastly in excess of any acceptable level, the latter will be chosen as having the lower, though still dangerously high, value of risk. This is in accord with Tversky's experiments.

It can easily be shown that, no matter how high the level of existing wealth, the value of risk is always lower on the latter, uncertain, scenario. Since the expected value is the same in both cases, the uncertain scenario would always be chosen by FARM.

12.5.3 A 'risk equals uncertainty' paradox

In the paradox described in section 12.2.11, $L_0 = 110$ and $L_1 = 106$. Investment in asset class A, which gives 105 with certainty, has a risk value of 1, whereas investment in asset class B has a risk value of nil and also a higher expected value, namely 112.5. Investment in asset class B, which involves the uncertain scenario, is the blindingly obvious choice under the FARM.

An immediate corollary is that any so-called 'theorem' relating to financial risk that has been derived using stochastic calculus is likely to be dangerously unsound, since in the abstract world of stochastic calculus asset class A would in the case of the present example be the 'risk-free' asset.

12.5.4 The other St Petersburg Paradox

With W as the level of other wealth over and above the 10 000 ducats expected from the safe arrival of the ship at Amsterdam, the choice is between $W + 10 000$ with certainty if insurance is taken out, or $W + 10 800$ with probability 0.95 and $W + 800$ with probability 0.05 if insurance is not taken out. Taking $L_0 = W + 10 000$ and L_1 as nil, and using the square of the proportionate shortfall as the parametric risk measure, we obtain $W = 55 054$ for $R_0 = 0.001$ and $W = 19 093$ for $R_0 = 0.005$. Hence the value of other assets must be in excess of 55 054 ducats or 19 093 ducats for a merchant with low or high risk tolerance respectively before the option of not insuring the ship can be contemplated.

Since the corresponding minimum wealth value of 5843 ducats that Bernoulli derives using his logarithmic utility function is very significantly lower than even the value of 19 093 ducats using the higher guideline value of acceptable risk under the FARM, it is difficult to avoid the conclusion that the use of a logarithmic utility function in financial risk investigations may often lead to dangerously unsound conclusions, in this case an equivalent probability of financial ruin of 0.020, four times the suggested upper guideline of maximum acceptable risk.

12.5.5   Comparing profiles of financial outcomes

On the present management strategy, strategy A, the financial outcome of an insurance company follows a normal distribution with mean 5 and variance 2. The value of 2, around two standard deviations below the mean, is seen as the minimum satisfactory outturn and hence is equivalent to L_0. L_1 is zero, since insolvency will occur for an outcome lower than this. The management of the company wish to investigate, subject to an over-riding requirement of the risk of insolvency not exceeding 0.001, the merits of adopting an alternative management strategy, strategy B, where the financial outcome corresponds to a normal distribution with mean 6 and variance 2.5.

Using the square of the proportionate shortfall as the measure of parametric risk, the values of risk are as below:

Strategy	Probability of ruin	Parametric risk	Total risk
A	0.0002	0.0018	0.0020
B	0.0001	0.0005	0.0006

Strategy B is accordingly chosen in preference to strategy A, since the expected value is higher, the value of total risk is very significantly lower, and the insolvency risk constraint is satisfied very comfortably.

This example has been chosen to correspond to Example 1.1 of the actuarial risk textbook (Bowers *et al.*, 1986), where an exponential utility function is used to 'prove' that the distribution $N(5, 2)$ has a higher value of expected utility than the distribution $N(6, 2.5)$, and hence is preferable, the heuristic justification being that the more diffuse nature of the distribution $N(6, 2.5)$ is a highly adverse factor.

To investigate this further example of an expected utility approach giving the opposite result to that obtained using the new 'equivalent probability of ruin' theory, consider what might be called a 'pseudo-utility' function $u(x)$ defined as follows:

$$u(x) = \begin{array}{ll} x & x \geq L_0 \\ x - \lambda w(x) & L_1 < x < L_0 \\ x - \lambda & x \leq L_1 \end{array}$$

with $w(x)$ having the properties of a parametric risk weighting function as described in section 12.4, L_0 and L_1 being the thresholds of zero and maximum risk respectively, and λ being a constant. Then if $p(x)$ is the probability density function of the financial outcome x, we can express the integral $U(x)$ of 'expected pseudo-utility' as:

$$U(x) = \int_{-\infty}^{\infty} u(x)(px)\, dx = \int_{-\infty}^{\infty} xp(x)\, dx - \lambda \int_{-\infty}^{L_1} p(x)\, dx$$

$$+ \int_{L_1}^{L_0} w(x)p(x)\, dx = E(x) - R(x)$$

where $E(x)$ is the expected value of x, and $R(x)$ is the value of risk under the FARM approach.

Since this expression appears to correspond, with λ interpreted as a Lagrange multiplier, to the utility theory solution where the indifference curves in the E − R diagram are straight lines with constant positive gradient, it might appear at first sight that expected utility could give the same results as the FARM, at least as a good first approximation. This is not the case, for two reasons. Firstly, under the FARM the indifference curves in the E − R diagram do not have constant positive gradient. Below the threshold of maximum acceptable risk they are asymptotic to vertical straight lines for very low values of risk, with the gradient decreasing to zero as risk increases towards the threshold of maximum acceptable risk. Above this threshold they are essentially horizontal straight lines. Second, the shape of the 'pseudo-utility' function is rectilinear, with the same positive gradient, both below L_1 and above L_0, as shown in Figure 12.4, whereas all standard utility curves have continuous gradient and convexity and hence, outside the range L_1 to L_0, follow the general shapes

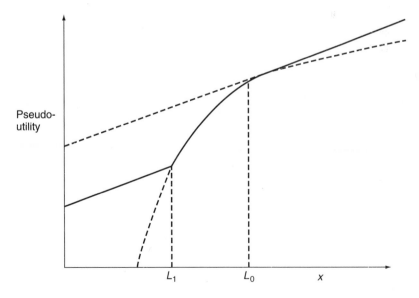

Figure 12.4

shown by the dotted curved lines. The FARM can thus predict that standard utility functions will often lead to unsound conclusions, with in particular an exponential utility function – which tends to minus infinity very rapidly as x decreases – attaching a pathologically high weighting to minuscule levels of downside risk that are of no real world significance.

12.5.6   Risk assessment and management for projects (RAMP)

The RAMP initiative, a joint undertaking of the Faculty and Institute of Actuaries and of the Institution of Civil Engineers, is a formal framework for risk management in which all reasonably practicable scenarios by which risk can be eliminated or reduced or transferred are investigated before coming to a reasoned choice as to which scenario best meets the risk and return requirements of the sponsor.

The FARM encapsulates this seeking out of additional information (in accordance with the extension of Bernoulli's second maxim as discussed in section 12.2.2) and can also be used as a structured framework for the identification of the optimal solution once further necessary information has been elucidated.

12.5.7   Application of RAMP to the Allais Paradox

Having been offered the choice between A, namely receiving £1 m with certainty, and B, namely receiving nil, £1 m or £5 m with probabilities 0.01, 0.89 and 0.1 respectively, we can investigate the possibility of transferring the risk inherent in B through insurance. Suppose that for £15 000, 50% above the 'pure' premium, we can obtain insurance of £1 m for the 0.01 probability of receiving nil under B. Then B, with the associated insurance, gives £985 000 with probability 0.9 and £4 985 000 with probability 0.1. Taking, as before, L_0 as £1 m and L_1 as nil, the value of risk under B as modified by insurance is $0.015^2 \times 0.9$, i.e. 0.0002, assuming that the measure of parametric risk is the square of the proportionate shortfall.

Since this risk value is very significantly below the lower guideline value of maximum risk, namely 0.001, and the expected value is much higher than for A, namely £1.385 m as against £1 m, most subjects might now prefer B (as modified by the addition of insurance) to A.

12.5.8   A new resolution of the St Petersburg Paradox

An inherent feature of FARM is that individuals will take into account 'tacit knowledge', i.e. knowledge acquired either first hand through practical experience or second hand through education or reading, and held at an essentially subconscious level, when assessing choices amongst different scenarios. In the case of the St Petersburg Paradox, the legend of the wise man who asked his king for one grain of rice for the first square of a chess board, two grains for the second square, four grains for the third square, and so on, comes readily to mind. The king thought that such a reward for services well rendered was trivial in the extreme, whereas the weight of rice for all 64 squares of the chess board was of the order of many thousands of millions of tons.

Suppose that Paul knows that Peter has certified wealth of at least 16 ducats. Then if Peter has to pay Paul up to 16 ducats, we can expect him to pay this with certainty. But if he has to pay 32 ducats, 64 ducats, 128 ducats, and so on, plausible probabilities of Paul receiving payment might be 0.5, 0.25, 0.125, and so on, reducing by a factor of two each time, in which case Paul's expectation is $\frac{1}{2} + \frac{1}{2} + \frac{1}{2} + \frac{1}{2} + \frac{1}{2} + \frac{1}{4} + \frac{1}{8} + \frac{1}{16} + \dots$, which is 3 ducats rather than being infinite. Similarly, if Peter has certified wealth of at least 128 ducats or 1024 ducats, realistic appraisals of Paul's expectation would be 4.5 ducats and 6 ducats respectively. If, however, the role of Peter is played by a soundly financed company or by a government agency (e.g. a national lottery) payment can be assumed to be made with certainty, but for obvious prudential reasons there will be a limit, possibly very high, to the amount that can be paid out. It is interesting to note that a highly popular television game show in the UK offers cash prizes that increase by around a factor of two up to £1 m for correct answers to general knowledge questions. If we take one ducat as being equivalent to £100 and assume a maximum payout of £100 × 10^{15}, i.e. £3.28 m, then the expected value of the payout (ignoring diminishing marginal utility of wealth) is £800. Since houses, yachts, classic cars and other expensive items can readily be bought by a winner of the maximum prize regardless of his or her previous level of wealth, diminishing marginal utility of wealth is unlikely to be of any significant importance until perhaps £1 m is reached, so that allowance for this effect will reduce the expectation only slightly, possibly to an equivalent of around £750.

Consider now the maximum price that Paul should pay, on risk considerations alone, to enter this constrained version of the St Petersburg Paradox, where the possible payouts are £100, £200, £400, and so on up to £3.28 m. For values of £1000, £10 000 and £100 000 as Paul's existing wealth (these correspond to the values of 10 100 and 1000 ducats used by Bernoulli) the maximum amount is shown in the table below for both the lower and the higher guideline value of maximum acceptable risk. The amounts in brackets are those in excess of the upper limit of £750 obtained above. Also shown are the values of Paul's expectation (if he already owns the entitlement to the gamble) and of the purchase price he should pay (if he does not already own it) using the logarithmic utility approach pioneered by Bernoulli.

	Maximum under FARM		Logarithmic utility	
Paul's wealth	Low risk	High risk	Expectation	Purchase price
(£)	(£)	(£)	(£)	(£)
1 000	145	200	304	285
10 000	495	(920)	438	430
100 000	(3450)	(7420)	588	551

Two important conclusions can be drawn. First, the acute counterparty risk when Peter is an individual and the limited liability 'cap' that will apply otherwise ensure that in real life the expectation is so modest that declining marginal utility of wealth is of little significance. Second, when Paul's wealth is at the lowest of the three levels investigated, Bernoulli's logarithmic utility 'solution' leads to a dangerously high level of risk on the new 'equivalent probability of financial ruin' basis, namely 0.019, which is almost four times the suggested higher guideline value of 0.005 for the maximum acceptable level of risk.

12.6   THE 'EQUITIES' VERSUS GILTS DEBATE

12.6.1   Testing the conventional wisdom

It is generally accepted, by many actuaries as well as by nearly all financial economists, that equity investment, while having a higher expected return than fixed-interest investment, involves a higher level of risk. The FARM allows this conventional wisdom to be tested.

Since the principal aim of long-term investment is to maintain or exceed the purchasing power of money, we can take for UK investments the threshold of zero risk as the change in the Retail Price Index (RPI) over the period. Taking the threshold of maximum risk as an end-period investment value of nil, the risk value is then the square of the proportionate shortfall (if any) of the total return below the return on the RPI. For instance, if investment of 100 gave an end period value of 114 whereas the RPI increased 20% over the period, the proportionate shortfall is 0.05 and the risk value is the square of this, i.e. 0.0025.

12.6.2   The UK experience from 1918 to 1998

The most comprehensive data source for UK investment returns is the annual Barclays Capital (formerly BZW) Equity-Gilt Study. Using these data for total returns after reinvestment of gross dividends, average risk values were calculated for UK equities and conventional long-dated gilts (British Government

Table 12.1 *UK equities and gilts from 1918 to 1998*

Duration in (years)	Risk		1974 contribution	
	Equities	Gilts	Equities (%)	Gilts (%)
1	0.0104	0.0052	40.6	19.9
2	0.0126	0.0106	53.0	20.4
3	0.0143	0.0139	44.6	20.9
4	0.0145	0.0162	32.7	12.2
5	0.0155	0.0189	35.7	11.9
6	0.0142	0.0231	46.5	11.0
7	0.0125	0.0278	37.1	11.4
8	0.0095	0.0313	29.8	10.2
9	0.0071	0.0350	48.0	9.1
10	0.0076	0.0391	39.6	8.2
15	0.0032	0.0571	100.0	7.0
20	0	0.0767	–	7.7

securities) for all available durations (from 1918 to 1998) of 1 to 10 years and 15 and 20 years. In the case of equities, a very prominent feature is the contribution to the total risk that arises from the period ending December 1974, which represented the bottom of a very severe bear market. The average risk values and the 1974 percentage contributions are shown in Table 12.1.

The (geometric) average real (i.e. inflation-adjusted) rates of total return from 1918 to 1998 are 8.0% pa for equities and 2.4% for gilts.

For equities, risk increases up to a maximum of 5 years and then decreases to around 50% of this maximum at 10 years and to around 20% of this maximum at 15 years. The risk at 20 years is zero, indicating that at this duration the real total return was never negative. For gilts, risk increases steadily with duration, being below the equity value at 1 and 2 years, virtually identical to it at 3 years, and higher than it at all longer durations. At 10 years the risk on gilts is more than five times that on equities, and at 15 years it is almost twenty times that on equities. A remarkable feature of the risk on gilts is that the values at 10, 15 and 20 years are almost exactly two, three and four times the value at 5 years, mirroring the linear increase with time exhibited by the variance of a pure diffusion process.

12.6.3 Unconventional wisdom

These results lead to the unconventional conclusion that equities are less risky than gilts for investment horizons of four years or longer. Given also the higher average returns, equities are accordingly the vastly superior asset class to investment horizons of four years or longer.

It is often recommended that, if an individual invests mainly in equities while in paid employment, he or she should switch into the supposedly 'less risky' asset class of fixed interest bonds on retirement. Unless there were significant fixed liabilities (such as having to repay a mortgage) within the first few years of retirement, any such recommendation would – on the basis of the above results – represent bad advice.

12.6.4   The academic literature

As a result of a prevalence of the simplistic 'risk equals uncertainty of return' teaching of financial economics and the indisputably higher variability of equity returns, the academic literature is pervaded with articles which foster the notion that equities are riskier than bonds, even when the investment horizon is fairly long. An excellent article setting out the opposite viewpoint is Thaler and Williamson (1994) in the twentieth anniversary issue of the *Journal of Portfolio Management*. Using data from the Ibbotson Associates Yearbook, it is shown that the likelihood of US equities outperforming bonds increases to near certainty as the investment horizon increases.

The article by Nobel Laureate Paul Samuelson (1994), in the same issue of the *Journal of Portfolio Management*, attempts to dismiss as 'unscientific' articles such as those of Thaler and Williamson (1994) which use empirical data to justify the message of 'buy and hold equities for sure-thing long-term performance'. In an end-note, Samuelson makes the comment:

> *No-one can prove to me that I am too risk-averse. Long-run risk (in equities) is not ignorable.*

In the context of the risk results set out above for UK equities and bonds and the virtually identical risk results that could be derived for US equities and bonds, continued adherence by academics to the notion that long-term risk on equity investment is significant would amount to a classic instance of 'myopic loss aversion' in a scientific context.

12.7   WIDER CAPITAL MARKET IMPLICATIONS

12.7.1   The hurst exponent and mean absolute deviation analysis

Harold Edwin Hurst (1880–1978) spent almost his entire working career as a hydrologist in Egypt struggling with the problem of reservoir control. As Peters (1991) observes:

> *An ideal reservoir would never overflow; a policy would be put in place to discharge a certain amount of water each year. However, if the influx from the river were too low, then the reservoir level would become dangerously*

low. The problem was: What policy of discharges could be set, such that the reservoir never overflowed or emptied?

Hurst (1955) describes how the range of the reservoir level fluctuated around its average level; if successive influxes were random (i.e. statistically independent) this range – as with standard deviation in the Black–Scholes option pricing model – would increase over time in line with the square root of time. Hurst obtained a dimensionless statistical exponent by dividing the range by the standard deviation of the observations, and hence his approach is generally referred to as rescaled range (R/S) analysis. By taking logarithms, we obtain the Hurst exponent H from the equation:

$$H \log(N) = \log\left(\frac{R}{S}\right) + \text{constant}$$

where N is the number of observations and R/S is the rescaled range. In practice the best way to obtain an estimate of H is to find the gradient of the log/log plot of R/S against N. In strict contrast to the 'statistical mechanics' independence value of 0.5 for H, Hurst found not only that for almost all rivers the exponent was well in excess of 0.5 (0.9 for the Nile!) but also that for a vast range of other quite distinct natural phenomena, from temperatures to sunspots, the estimates of H clustered very closely around the value of 0.71, indicating the existence of a powerful 'long-term memory' causal dependence.

The 'over-reaction bias' effect predicted in section 12.4.9 from the corresponding behaviour in potentially risky sports can be expected to generate a powerful 'long-term memory' effect. Share prices which have been driven by 'over-reaction bias' to extreme values either above or below what Adam Smith would call their 'natural values' will tend to revert towards these 'natural values' rather than follow an essentially random progression from the extreme values, thereby giving rise to a Hurst exponent significantly in excess of 0.5.

Peters (1991) and others have shown that equity market indices and the price series of individual equity shares do indeed exhibit Hurst exponents well in excess of 0.5, with typical values of around 0.7. Such behaviour is anomalous in the context of the mainstream 'rational behaviour' teachings of financial economics but is a prediction of the new general theory of risk and the associated underlying patterns of real world investor behaviour.

In the Mean Absolute Deviation analysis approach described in Plymen and Prevett (1972) and Clarkson and Plymen (1988), the multiplier value of 1.6 that was found to work best for equity price series in practice is significantly lower than the theoretical value of 2 implied by statistical independence. There is a strong (and obviously numerically inverse) correspondence to the Hurst exponent being significantly in excess of 0.5. Furthermore, if we regard 'over-reaction bias' as a 'momentum' effect superimposed on a mean-reverting 'value' effect, the resultant equity price dynamics would approximate to a sine wave, the optimal Mean Absolute Deviation multiplier value of which is 1.57, in very close agreement with the empirically obtained value of 1.6.

12.7.2   Pension fund investment strategy

There are very strong parallels between reservoir control and pension scheme funding, where the investment return corresponds to the influx of water from unpredictable levels of rainfall within the catchment area, while the difference between payments to beneficiaries and contributions from employer and employees corresponds to the controlled level of discharge of water from the dam. The pension funding problem is to find a reasonably stable strategy that does not lead either to excess surplus (the dam overflowing) or to financial or regulatory insolvency (the reservoir emptying). Assuming that there are no significant short-term liabilities, and ignoring for the moment any relevant solvency regulations, the investment horizon is very long and it is blindingly obvious from the risk and return results set out in section 12.6.2 that, if equities and long-dated fixed interest stocks are the only two available asset classes, then the 'natural' investment strategy is 100% equities.

A Hurst exponent of around 0.7 for equities means that, just as Hurst found for reservoir control, financial control policies which use only means and standard deviations estimated from past data will seriously understate the extremes of investment value that will occur. Accordingly, mean-variance analysis could give dangerously unsound results.

Another formalized mathematical approach which could give rise to highly unsatisfactory results is utility theory. Well-intentioned attempts to encapsulate a balance between funding level and insolvency risk using a standard type of utility function may, for the reasons set out in section 12.5.5, magnify the insolvency risk out of all proportion and force the sponsor into an unnecessarily low equity exposure and, accordingly, an unnecessarily high funding rate.

The crucial difference between FARM, which suggests 100% equities as the 'natural' investment strategy, and the financial economics approach, which suggests 100% fixed interest as the 'matched' position, corresponds very closely to the two different world views in the 'risk equals uncertainty of return' paradox described in sections 12.2.11 and 12.5.3. In the pension fund investment strategy context, this paradox can be translated into the following question that the scheme actuary might ask the chief executive of the sponsoring company:

Which would you prefer: 100% investment in fixed interest, which means that in theory the actuarial liability and the asset value are highly correlated over the short term, or – for a significantly lower funding rate which will translate into immediate and continuing higher profits and earnings per share for your company – 100% investment in equities, which involves higher asset value volatility that does not in any way threaten the long-term solvency of your scheme?

12.7.3 Solvency regulations

It is natural for governments and regulatory bodies to try to put in place rules intended to reduce the financial risk to which members of the public are exposed. However, FARM recognizes that, on occasions such as during 1974, investors will act 'irrationally' and drive equity share prices to unrealistically low values that do not in any way affect the satisfactory long term returns that will be achieved. If the basic solvency test for an insurance company or pension fund relates purely to market values with equities being classed as 'more risky' than bonds or cash, a strong decline in equity prices, once established, could become self-feeding in the same way as resulted from margin calls in the Wall Street Crash of 1929. The well-intentional rules would be potentially destabilizing and could vastly increase the inherent level of financial risk.

12.7.4 Stochastic investment models

The risk values described in section 12.6.2, as corroborated by a Hurst exponent significantly in excess of 0.5, show that the statistical behaviour of equity prices over periods of up to five years cannot be used to extrapolate equity price behaviour into the indefinite future. In particular, the value of risk as measured against an appropriate benchmark (such as an increase in line with either price or salary inflation) will, as a result of the 'long-term memory' effect that is consistent with behavioural finance conclusions, increase to a maximum at around four or five years and then decrease steadily thereafter. However, the most widely used stochastic investment models within the actuarial profession, and in particular the Wilkie (1984, 1986, 1995) model, follow an autoregressive approach that takes no account whatsoever of this crucial 'long-term memory' effect. Within such models, the risk on equity investment, as measured on the 'equivalent probability of financial ruin' basis of the FARM, will increase steadily with duration rather than reflecting the real world behaviour of decreasing from around five years onwards. This distortion will lead to a very significant overestimation of the long-term risk of equity investment, and accordingly to the recommendation of unnecessarily low levels of equity investment.

The absence of statistical independence between successive annual equity returns will, mainly as a result of 'over-reaction bias', often cause estimates of expected returns on the basis of recent history to be either far too high or far too low. The oil industry analogy just over two decades ago comes readily to mind: in the aftermath of the two very traumatic 'oil shocks', the projection models used by some major oil companies did not allow for the possibility of future oil prices falling below the then current value of 40 dollars per barrel.

12.8 CONCLUSION

In Clarkson (1996) it is suggested that a new and essentially actuarial theory of finance might before long offer a better scientific framework for prudent financial management than the general teachings and methodologies of what has become known as financial economics. Since the management of risk is absolutely central to prudent financial behaviour, the FARM framework set out in this chapter will hopefully be a step in that direction.

REFERENCES

Allais, M. (1953) Le comportement de l'homme rationnel devant le risque: critique des postulats et axiomes de l'école Americaine, *Econometrica*, 21.

Allais, M. (1954) L'outil mathématique en economique, *Econometrica*, 22.

Allais, M. (1989) An outline of my main contributions to economic science, Nobel Lecture, December 9, 1988, Les Prix Nobel, Stockholm.

Anand, P. (1993) *Foundations of Rational Choice under Risk*, Oxford: Clarendon Press.

Bernoulli, D. (1738, 1954) Specimen theoriae novae de mensura sortis. *Commentarii Academiae Scientiarum Imperialis Petropolitanea*, 5. English translation in *Econometrica*, 22 (1954).

Booth, P. Chadburn, R. Cooper, D. Haberman, S. and James, D. (1999) *Modern Actuarial Theory*, London: Chapman & Hall/CRC.

Bowers, L.N., Gerber, H.U., Hickman, J.C., Jones, A.J. and Nesbitt, C.J. (1986) *Actuarial Mathematics*, Society of Actuaries.

Buffon, J. (1777) *Essai d'arithmétique morale*, Supplément a l'Histoire Naturelle, 4.

Clarkson, R.S. (1978) A mathematical model for the gilt-edged market, *Transactions of the Faculty of Actuaries*, 36; and *Journal of the Institute of Actuaries*, 106.

Clarkson, R.S. (1981) A market equilibrium model for the management of ordinary share portfolios, *Transactions of the Faculty of Actuaries*, 37; and *Journal of the Institute of Actuaries*, 110.

Clarkson, R.S. (1989) The measurement of investment risk, *Transactions of the Faculty of Actuaries*, 41; and *Journal of the Institute of Actuaries*, 116.

Clarkson, R.S. (1990) The assessment of financial risk, *Transactions of the 1st AFIR International Colloquium*, Paris, 2.

Clarkson, R.S. (1991) A non-linear stochastic model for inflation, *Transactions of the 2nd AFIR International Colloquium*, Brighton, 3.

Clarkson, R.S. (1996) Financial economics – investment actuary's viewpoint, *British Actuarial Journal*, 2.

Clarkson, R.S. (1999) Artificial intelligence and stockmarket success, *The Staple Inn Actuarial Society*, May.

Clarkson, R.S. and Plymen, J. (1988) Improving the performance of equity portfolios, *Journal of the Institute of Actuaries*, 115; and *Transactions of the Faculty of Actuaries*, 41.

Daykin, C.D., Pentikainen, T. and Personen, M. (1994) *Practical Risk Theory for Actuaries*, London: Chapman & Hall.

Grether, D.M. and Plott, C.R. (1979) Economic theory of choice and the preference reversal phenomenon, *American Economic Review*, 69.

Halley, E. (1693) An estimate of the degrees of mortality, *Philosophical Transactions of the Royal Society of London*, 17.

Hurst, H.E. (1955) Methods of using long-term storage in reservoirs, *Proceedings of the Institution of Civil Engineers*, Part 1 (5).

Kahneman, D. and Tversky, A. (1979) Prospect theory, *Econometrica*, 47.

Keynes, J.M. (1921) *A Treatise on Probability*, London: Macmillan.

Keynes, J.M. (1936) *A General Theory of Employment, Interest and Money*, London: Macmillan.

Kuhn, T.S. (1970) *The Structure of Scientific Revolutions*, Chicago: The University of Chicago Press.

Kuhn, T.S. (1977) *The Essential Tension: Selected Studies in Scientific Tradition and Change*, Chicago: University of Chicago Press.

Lamberton, D. and Lapeyre, B. (1996) *Introduction to Stochastic Calculus Applied to Finance*, London: Chapman & Hall.

Machina, M.J. (1987) Choice under uncertainty: problems solved and unsolved, *Journal of Economic Perspectives*, 1.

Markowitz, H. (1959) *Portfolio Selection* (2nd edn 1991), Oxford: Blackwell.

von Neumann, J.R. and Morgenstern, O. (1944) *Theory of Games and Economic Behavior*, Englewood Cliffs, NJ: Princeton University Press.

Peters, E.E (1991) *Chaos and Order in Capital Markets*, New York: Wiley.

Plymen, J. and Prevett, R.M. (1972) The computer for investment research, *Transactions of the Faculty of Actuaries*, 33.

Quiggin, J. (1993) *Generalised Expected Utility Theory*, London: Kluwer Academic.

Royal Society of London (1992) Risk: analysis, perception and management, Report of a Royal Society Study Group.

Samuelson, P.A. (1994) The long-term case for equities, *Journal of Portfolio Management*, 21.

Sharpe, W.F. (1970) *Portfolio Selection and Capital Markets*, New York: McGraw-Hill.

Shiller, R.J. (1989) *Market Volatility*, Boston, MA: Massachusetts Institute of Technology.

Smith, A. (1795, 1980) *Essays on Philosophical Subjects. Volume III of the Glasgow Edition of the Works and Correspondence of Adam Smith*, Oxford: Oxford University Press.

Smith, H.A. (1776, 1976) *An enquiry into the nature and causes of the wealth of nations. Volume II of the Glasgow Edition of the Works and Correspondence of Adam Smith*, Oxford: Oxford University Press.

Thaler, R.H. and Williamson, J.P. (1994) College and university endowment funds: why not 100% equities?, *Journal of Portfolio Management*, 21.

Tversky, A. (1990) The psychology of risk.In: *Quantifying the Market Risk Premium Phenomena for Investment Decision Making*, Charlottesville, VA: Institute of Chartered Financial Analysts.

Wilkie, A.D. (1984) Steps towards a comprehensive stochastic investment model, *Occasional Actuarial Research Discussion Paper*, 36.

Wilkie, A.D. (1986) A stochastic investment model for actuarial use, *Transactions of the Faculty of Actuaries*, 39.

Wilkie, A.D. (1995) More on a stochastic investment model for actuarial use, *British Actuarial Journal*, 1.

Source: This chapter was first published in Part 1 of Volume 116 of the Journal of the Institute of Actuaries, pp. 127–178, printed in Great Britain by The Alden Press, Oxford, 1989 and thereafter published in Part 4 of Volume 41 of the *Transactions of the Faculty of Actuaries*, pp. 677–729, printed in Great Britain by Alna Press Limited, Broxburn, West Lothian, 1990.

Appendix

The Forsey–Sortino model tutorial

This tutorial will walk the reader through the steps to install the Forsey–Sortino model on the reader's computer and demonstrate how to use the model to calculate upside potential and downside risk in accordance with procedures established at the Pension Research Institute. We are concerned that the way some people are calculating upside potential and downside risk may substantially under-estimate risk, and over-estimate upside potential. Therefore, *we ask that any output from this model acknowledge that upside potential and downside risk were calculated with the Forsey–Sortino model.*

The demonstration program will help the user gain an understanding of the three parameter lognormal curve and related statistics described in this book. In the US the publisher may be contacted at 800 366 2665 or e-mail: orders@bhusa.com. In the UK call 01865 888180 or e-mail bh.orders@ repp.co.uk.

We strongly recommend you read the book before using this program. Use of this model from any source other than the CD accompanying the book is strictly prohibited. Copies from the original CD may be put on any number of computers in an office that has a copy of the book available to users in that office. Our concern is that people may use the model without understanding what they are doing.

INSTALLATION

If you want to follow the default settings for installation, skip to paragraph 2.

1. To install the F–S model in a directory of your choosing, create the directory now, e.g. create a directory on your C:\ drive and name it 'Downside'. Put the CD in your computer and the program should start. If it does not, go to 'My Computer' on your desktop and access the CD drive. Double click on the folder named Downside and double click on the **setup icon (blue computer)**. At the Welcome screen click OK. Click on **'Change Directory'**. Scroll down to

Downside and click. (The window should look like C:\Downside.) Click OK. At the lognormal setup screen click on the **computer icon** (called a button). The program will install, then click **OK**.

2. To follow the default installation, put the CD in your computer and the program should start. If it does not, go to 'My Computer' on your desktop and access the CD drive. Double click on the folder named Forsey–Sortino and double click on the **setup icon (blue computer)**. At the Welcome screen click OK. At the lognormal setup screen click on the **computer icon** (called a button). The program will install in your program directory in a folder named 'LogNormal'. Click **OK**.

3. Go to the directory where you installed Forsey–Sortino model and double click on the **gold Downside icon**. Figure A.1 will appear.

4. If you see the 'Load Fund' button go to the next paragraph. If you do not see the Load Fund button, your screen settings are too low. Double click the My Computer icon on your desktop screen. Double click the control panel. Double click on Display and click on Settings. Move the setting to the right until 1024 × 768 appears in the window. Save settings and reboot. Go to the Downside directory and click on the Forsey–Sortino icon.

5. Press the 'Load Fund' button. Monthly fund data from the ln.txt text file will load and be shown in the window on the right (see Figure A.2).

6. These are the monthly returns currently on the sample text file. The user can edit this file to add or delete funds with any text editor or spreadsheet

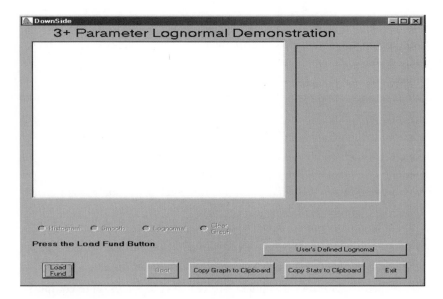

Figure A.1

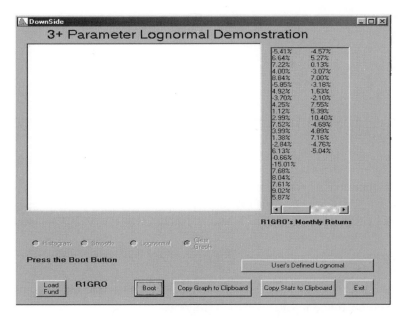

Figure A.2

program in TEXT format (not .exl). Be sure to save the file in text format. All of the returns are in one column (see Figure A.3).

7. The format of the data in this file (Figure A.3) is the name of the fund (e.g. R1GRO) followed by monthly returns as percents with −999 indicating the end of the fund's data. Each name and return is on its own line. This is repeated until all desired funds are included. All data files must be of the same

R1GRO	R1GRO	R1GRO
−5.412	−2.84	−3.18
6.64	6.126	1.63
7.217	−0.66	−2.1
4.002	−15.008	7.55
8.844	7.68	5.39
−5.853	8.04	10.4
4.921	7.607	−4.69
−3.697	9.02	4.89
4.247	5.87	7.16
1.12	−4.57	−4.76
2.99	5.27	−5.04
7.522	0.13	−999
3.99	−3.07	R1VAL
1.38	7	−3.596

Figure A.3

length. Be sure to save edited files as text files. The program will not read a spreadsheet in Excel format.

BOOTSTRAP

8. After a fund's return data is loaded, the bootstrap option becomes available. Press 'Boot' to perform a bootstrap that generates 2500 random annual returns by sampling from the fund's monthly return data. The results are shown in Figure A.4.

9. To view the results of the bootstrap graphically, **click the circle in front of 'Histogram'**, as shown in Figure A.5. The histogram contains a hundred bars with heights representing the number of annual returns falling in the corresponding region. There is a great deal of random fluctuations in these returns.

10. Click on 'Smooth' to see the empirical fit shown in Figure A.6. A histogram of averages based on five adjoining bars is displayed by the Smooth function.

11. Click on 'Lognormal' to fit and graph a three parameter lognormal curve, as described in Chapter 4 by Hal Forsey.

12. The mean for R1GRO is 29.2%. The standard deviation is 24.6%. The extreme value is −208%, meaning the distribution is anchored at −208% and allowed to skew to the right. One standard deviation to the left is 4.5%, and to the right is 53.8%.

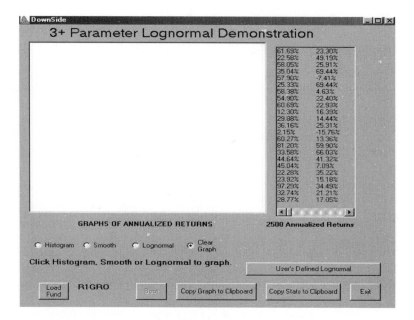

Figure A.4

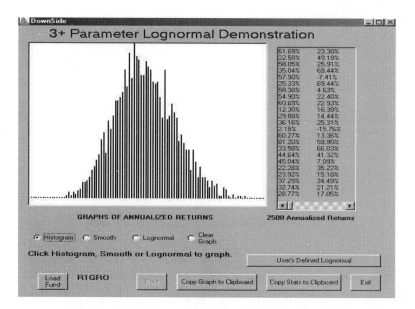

Figure A.5

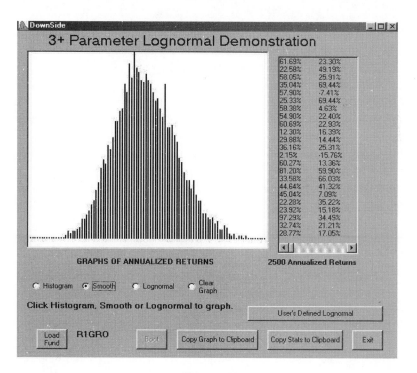

Figure A.6

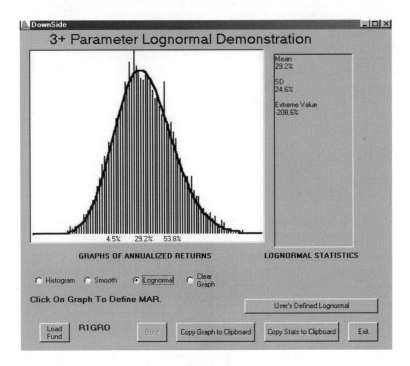

Figure A.7

13. Click on the graph at approximately the point of your MAR as shown by the vertical arrow in Figure A.8.

14. When a lognormal graph is displayed, the user can define an MAR by using the mouse to put the cursor over the MAR and clicking. The arrow in Figure A.8 is pointed at 8.4%, which is also shown in the window to the right of the graph. Additional statistics include the upside potential, downside risk and the probability of doing better than the MAR ($P > MAR$).

15. A displayed graph can be copied to the clipboard by clicking the 'Copy Graph to Clipboard' button.

USER-DEFINED LOGNORMAL

16. Click the User's Defined Lognormal option to define a lognormal model by editing the default mean, standard deviation, or extreme value.

17. The default mean is 23%. Put your cursor on the mean and replace 23 with 18. **Click on the 'Edit Parameters'** bar and the graph will shift. Change the standard deviation to 15, and the extreme value to −25. **Click on 'Edit Parameters'.** One standard deviation to the left is now 3% and to the right is 33%. Click on the graph to mark the MAR and the statistics for that distribution will be shown in the right window.

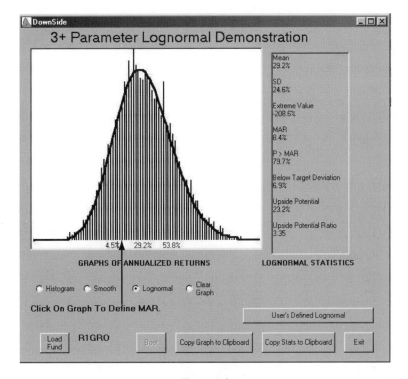

Figure A.8

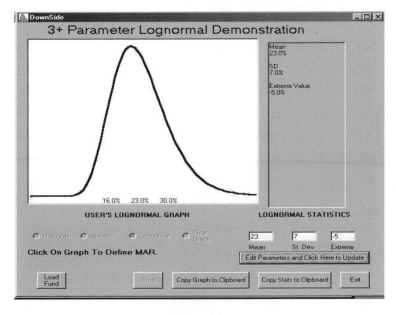

Figure A.9

18. Click on 'Load Fund' and the R1VAL returns appear in the right window. Click on Histogram, Smooth, etc. to generate the statistics for the large value index.

Exit. Click this option to exit the program.

The Excel spreadsheet provided on this disk is a program developed by Neil Riddles and can be accessed by double clicking on the icon. There is no tutorial, but sample data are provided to demonstrate how the program works. Users must provide their own data.

Please do not contact PRI, the authors, or the publisher for assistance if you have difficulty with any of the programs on this disk. There is no charge for these products and none of the parties has the facilities or staff to provide personal assistance. We have made numerous checks to ensure the programs worked before packaging.

Index

Active returns, 83–4, 98–9
Actuarial Approach for Financial Risk
  (AFIR), 212
Actuaries, 212, 234
  for defined benefit plans, 41
  see also Faculty and Institute of
  Actuaries
Adverse occurrences, estimating severity
  of, 220–1, 224, 226–7
AFIR (Actuarial Approach for Financial
  Risk), 212
Air travel, perceived risk in, 219
Allais, Maurice, 216–17
Allais Paradox, 216–17, 229–30, 234
Allocation, asset, see Asset allocation
ALM, see Asset liability management
  (ALM)
Alpha, 4, 10, 77, 84, 178
Alternative investments as a benchmark,
  108
Asset allocation, 24, 75–8, 86–9
  Dutch pension funds, 26–7, 39
  Internet application, 21–3
Asset liability management (ALM),
  26–40
  pension fund liability management,
  27–8
  plan sponsor level, 37–8
  risk, measuring, 32–3
Asset managers, selecting, 41–2
  see also Managers
Asset-only framework, 39
Asset pricing:
  lower partial-moment models, 156–68
  new model for, 204–6

see also Capital Asset Pricing Model
  (CAPM)
Assets, risky and risk free, 220
  in Capital Asset Pricing Model
  (CAPM), 176
  and the Sharpe ratio, 176–7, 178
Asymmetry, 6–8
  of returns, 103, 146
  of risk, 104–5, 152
  see also Skewness; Symmetry
Auxiliary parameters for three parameter
  lognormals, 57
Average downside deviation, 62–3, 96
  comparing managers with, 67–8
  see also Downside deviation
Average weekly earnings as a benchmark,
  108
Axioms of choice, 223–4, 228
  see also Utility axioms

Balzer, L.A., 103, 107, 126–7, 129, 131,
  135, 151
Banks, benchmarks for, 108
Barclays Capital Equity-Gilt Study,
  236–7
Bear markets:
  flight to liquidity in, 229
  self-feeding, 241
  and skewness, 64
Behaviour:
  failsafe, innate, 225–7
  financial, 214–20
  rational, 216, 239
  real world, 213, 218
  research into, 142, 143

Behavioural finance, 13–16, 218–19
Below budgeted return, 108
Below MAR probability (BPROB), 78–9,
    80, 86, 90
    see also Mean-below MAR probability
        (M-BPROB)
Below MAR standard deviation (BTSD),
    86
Below MAR variance (BVAR), 86, 90
    see also Mean-below MAR variance
        (M-BVAR)
Below-target returns, 60
Below-target semi-variance[2], 60
Below target variance, 10
Benchmark relativity, 80–1, 127
Benchmarks, 106, 107–9
    higher order terms, importance of,
        150–1
    and institutional investors' views, 93–4
    investor-specific, 152
    and partial moments, 129, 131, 132,
        134, 143
    and performance measures, 178
    risk relative to, 97–9
    strategic, in ALM framework, 26–40
    variance, skewness and kurtosis
        relative to, 128
Bernoulli, Daniel, 213, 215, 220, 230,
    231–2, 236
Beta, 156, 157–8
    see also Style beta
Bivariate case, mean-DSR portfolio
    frontier, 196–202, 206–8
Black-Scholes option pricing model, 239
Bond managers, measuring performance
    of, 16–17, 31
Bonds:
    compared to equities, 219, 229, 238
    empirical distributions for, 79–80
    proportion of investments in, 75–8,
        86–9
    in retirement, 237–8
Bootstrapping, 12, 51–2, 53–4, 95
    in the Forsey-Sortino model tutorial,
        248–50
Bottom quartile returns as a benchmark,
    108
BPROB (Below MAR probability), 78–9,
    80, 86, 90

    see also Mean-below MAR probability
        (M-BPROB)
BTSD (Below MAR standard deviation),
    86
Buffon, J., 216, 223
Bull markets, skewness and, 64
BVAR (Below MAR variance), 86, 90
    see also Mean-below MAR variance
        (M-BVAR)

Capital:
    loss of, 106, 107
    risk capital, 33, 35
    see also Principal
Capital Asset Pricing Model (CAPM),
    157, 158–60
lower partial-moment capital asset pricing
    models (LMCAPM), 156–68
    and Markowitz portfolio theory, 176
    mean-variance capital asset pricing
        models (MVCAPM), 156, 167
    new version of, 204–6
    performance measures developed from,
        178
CAPM, *see* Capital Asset Pricing Model
    (CAPM)
Capping indexing, 35–6
Catastrophic events, 77, 78, 80
    see also Ruin
Clients, diversity of, 93
Coefficient of kurtosis, 121
Coefficient of skewness, 121
Coherent determinants of pension fund
    policy, 36–7
Commodity prices, 215
Completeness of risk measures, 54,
    110–11, 112, 113, 114
    relative semi-variance, 130
Confidence:
    lack of confidence, 229
    over-confidence, 214, 219, 225, 228–9
Conservatism, downside focus implies, 70
Consultants, investment, 41–3, 45
Continuous formula for downside risk,
    60–2, 70
Contributions:
    defined contribution funds, benchmarks
        for, 108

premium contributions (Dutch pension funds), 27–8, 29–30, 36, 37–8
Conventional moment-based measures, 120–8
Covariance of stocks and bonds, 17
Cubic penalties, 138, 141–2, 150, 153
Cumulative probability distributions, 116–18, 152
 lognormal cumulative distribution function, 58
Customizing risk calculations, 93–4
 see also Mass-customization

Data gathering, 46
DB, *see* Defined benefit (DB) plans/funds
Death, equivalent probability of, 221–2
Decreasing marginal utility, 126–7
 of downside returns, 135–6
 of upside returns, 134–5, 141, 142, 144
 in logarithmic functions, 149
Default risk, 38
Defined benefit (DB) plans/funds, 41
 benchmarks for, 108
 liabilities in, 107
 targets for, 69
 using MAR, 78, 85
Defined contribution funds, benchmarks for, 108
Demographic trends and pension plans, 28
Discounted downside risk, 33, 35, 36–7
Distributional assumptions, 156, 157
Distributions, *see* Probability distributions
Dominance, *see* Stochastic dominance models
Downside deviation, 60, 71, 179
 lognormal formulas based on, 55, 58
 performance measures based on, 178–80
 see also Average downside deviation
Downside frequency, 62–3, 96, 97
 comparing managers with, 67–8
 relevance to investors, 85

Downside kurtosis, 139
Downside magnitude, 96
Downside marginal utility, 134
 decreasing, 135–6
Downside returns, 153
 and asymmetry, 104–5, 146
 PMPT models, 60
 variance is inaccurate for, 126
Downside risk (DSR), 9–21, 60–2
 in asset pricing models, 156
 calculating, 94–5
  software and tutorial for, 245
 continuous formula versus discrete, 60–2
 definition, 10–11, 196
 discounted, 33, 35, 36–7
 for goal relative performance measurement, 49
 for Internet advice, 21–3
 and MAR, in portfolio management, 24
 mean-downside risk portfolio frontier, 194–211
  bivariate case, 196–202, 206–8
  multivariate case, 202–4, 208–10
  non-parametric approach, 206–10
 for pension plan shortfalls, 30–1, 32–3, 39
 portfolio manager's view, 93–100
 slow adoption of, 99–100
 and standard deviation compared, symmetrical distributions, 70–1
 statistics from, 95–7
 and utility functions, 140–2, 234
Downside semi-variance, 143, 144, 149
Downside utility, unified theory of, 104, 131–51
 fourth order, 139–40
 second order, 135–7
 special cases, 142–6
 third order, 138
Downside variance, 64, 135–6
DSR, *see* Downside risk (DSR)
Dutch mutual funds, 180–5, 187–93
Dutch pension funds, ALM-frameworks for, 26–40
Dutch triangle, 28–32

Efficiency ratio, 96
Equities:
    exhibit Hurst exponents, 239–40
    long term view and risk, 236–8,
        239–41
    in pension funds, 26–7, 240–1
    reluctance to invest in, 219, 229, 238
    see also Stock market; Stocks
Equity funds, comparisons with, 180, 181
Equity managers, measuring performance
    of, 16–17, 31
Equivalence functions, formulating,
    227–8
Equivalent probability of death, 221–2
Equivalent probability of ruin, 227,
    231–2, 241
ERISA, 41
Estimation, 151–2, 222
EU, *see* Expected utility (EU)
Excess return, 4
    in information ratio, 80–1, 89–90
    using the M-BVAR index, 90
Excess volatility, 219
Expected enjoyment, quantifying, 224,
    228
Expected return:
    mean-DSR portfolio frontier
        bivariate case, 199
        the multivariate case, 203
    in the Sharpe ratio, 178
Expected shortfall, 113–15, 130, 152
    RLPM^1 as, 129, 130
Expected utility (EU), 4–5, 125–6, 213
    attempted generalizations, 218
    comparing to FARM approach, 232–4
    from utility function optimization,
        140–2
    and *IR*, 81–3
    and the Sharpe ratio, 85
    see also Utility theory
Ex post performance, *IR* for, 83–4
Extreme value of annual returns, 54–5,
    56
    formulas for, 57–8

Faculty and Institute of Actuaries, 234
Failsafe behaviour, innate, 225–7
FARM (financial actuarial risk model),
    212–44

Financial actuarial risk model (FARM),
    212–44
Financial behaviour, anomalies and
    inconsistencies in, 214–20
    see also Behaviour
Financial outcomes, comparing two,
    232–4
Financial planners, a new paradigm for,
    41–50
Financial planning paradigm, 43–6
Financial risk, 212–14
    models of, 226–9
        applications, 229–36
    see also Risk
Financial ruin, 218, 227, 228, 230–2, 241
First moment, 4, 121
    see also Mean
First order stochastic dominance, 5,
    117–18, 152
First order utility, 134
Fishburn, Peter, 9, 10, 157, 159, 160,
    172–3, 174
Fishburn utility function, 170, 172–3,
    174, 180, 184–5
Fixed interest investments, 236
    in pension fund investment strategies,
        240–1
    see also Bonds; Gilts; Interest-bearing
        funds; T-bills
Forecasting, 44, 49
Formulas for three parameter lognormal,
    57–8
Forsey-Sortino model tutorial, 245–52
401(k) plans, 41, 44, 46, 69
Fourth moment, 121, 128
    see also Kurtosis
Fourth order downside utility, 139–40
Fourth order leakage sensitivity, 148
Fourth order risk aversion, 148
Fourth order terms, 138–40, 148, 153
    logarithmic utility leakage, 150
Fourth order upside utility, 138–9
Fouse index, 12, 170, 179
    rankings, 182, 183–4, 185
Fouse, W., 12
Framing and coding (behavioural finance
    trait), 219
Fund managers, benchmarks for, 107–8
    see also Managers

Gain, overestimating, 214
  see also Upside returns
Gaussian distributions, *see* Normal
  distributions
Gilts (British Government securities),
  236–8
Goals:
  for 401(k) plan investors, 69
  analyses of, in investment planning,
    43, 44, 45, 46, 49
  and downside risk, 24, 62, 94
  see also Target rate of return

Hang-gliding, risk in, 220–1, 222, 223
Higher moments, 194–5
Higher order terms, 140, 141, 142
  importance of, 148–51, 153
High growth funds, 90
  see also Returns
High returns, psychological devaluation
  of, 137
  see also Returns
Histograms:
  bootstrapping produces, 52
  describing, with lognormal curves,
    53–4
Human mind, 213, 225
  see also Behaviour; Insanity,
    temporary; Perception of risk;
    Psychology of risk
Hurst exponents, 238–40
Hurst, Harold Edwin, 238, 239

Independence, data, in bootstrapping, 52,
  95
Indexing, 27, 28, 29, 34–5
  and sponsor's solvency, 37–8
Indifference curves, 223–4, 228, 232
Individual accounts, a new paradigm for,
  41–50
Inflation:
  beating, as a goal, 69
  compensation for, in Dutch pension
    plans, 27, 29

keeping up with, 78, 85, 87–9, 107
  see also Indexing
Information ratio (*IR*), 4, 80–5
  for excess return, 89–90
  misleading nature of, 74
  as a performance measure, 178
Information, risk assessment with,
  219–20, 225–6, 234
Injuries, perceived probability of,
  220–2
Innate failsafe behaviour, 225–7
Insanity, temporary, 226, 229
Insolvency risk, 232
  see also Solvency
Installing demonstration program,
  245–8
Institutional investors, risk and, 93–4
Institution of Civil Engineers, 234
Insurance:
  actuaries in, 212
  failure to take up, 214
  risk of ruin component, 227
  solvency of companies, 241
  transferring risk through, 234
Interest-bearing funds, comparisons with,
  180, 181
  see also Bonds; Fixed interest
    investments; Gilts; T-bills
International Actuarial Association, 212
Internet, 21–3
  downside risk freeware available on,
    99
  for mass-customization, 46
Internet-related stocks, 214
Investment, alternative, 108
Investment consultants, 41–3, 45
Investment performance, *see* Performance
  measures
Investment policy, 43
Investment portfolio, determination of,
  38–9
  see also Portfolios
Investment risk, 103–55
  conventional moment-based measures,
    120–8
  nature of risk, 104–15
  see also Risk
Investment strategy, pension funds,
  29–31, 38–9, 240–1

Investors:
  institutional investors, and risk, 93–4
  investor-specific risk, 109, 130, 152
  retail investors, 93–4
Investor-specific risk, 109, 130, 152
IR, see Information ratio (*IR*)
Irrationality, systemic, 215, 218–19
  see also Rational behaviour

Japanese stock market, 70, 95
Jensen, Michael C., 4, 178
Jump discontinuities, 127, 133, 142, 147

Kernel estimations, 206, 207
Keynes, John Maynard, 215–16
Kurtosis, 121, 128
  downside kurtosis, 139
  relative lower partial, 129, 131
  upside kurtosis, 139

Lack of confidence, 229
  see also Over-confidence
Leakage, *see* Upside utility leakage
Leptokurtic distributions, 121
Liabilities:
  after retirement, uncertainty in, 47–8
  as a benchmark, 107
  matching, 69, 71(note 7)
  see also Asset liability management (ALM)
Lifestyle goals, financial planners focus on, 43, 44, 45
  see also Goals
Linear utility functions, 171, 172
LMCAPM (Lower partial-moment capital asset pricing models), 156–68
Location-scale (LS) family, 156
Logarithmic utility functions, 146–51, 153
  Bernoulli uses, 220, 231–2, 236
Lognormal cumulative distribution function, 58
  see also Cumulative probability distributions
Lognormals:
  describing histograms with, 53–4
  fitting portfolios with, 56

in the Forsey-Sortino model tutorial, 250–2
software, 57
three parameter, 15–16, 51–8, 60–1, 95, 245, 248–50
Long-term memory causal dependence, 239, 241
Loss, underestimating, 214
  see also Downside returns
Lotteries, 214
Lower partial-moment capital asset pricing models (LMCAPM), 156–68
Lower partial moments, 10
  relative (RLPMs), 129–31
  see also Downside risk
LS family, *see* Location-scale (LS) family

Maclaurin series expansion, 132, 154(note 10)
Magnitude, downside, 96
Magnitude of loss, 85
  maximum shortfall for, 111–12
  and risk perception, 115
Management structure, three-tiered, for pension plans, 29–32
Managers:
  asset managers, selecting, 41–2
  comparing and ranking, 66–8
  fund managers, benchmarks for, 107–8
  measuring performance
    against MAR, 31–2
    bond and equity, 16–17, 31
  portfolio managers, 93–100, 169
MAR, *see* Minimal acceptable return
Marginal utility, 126–7, 172, 215
  downside, 134
    decreasing, 135–6
  upside, 134
    decreasing, 134–5, 141, 142, 144, 149
Market orientation of performance measures, 42
Markowitz, Harry, 3, 9, 10–11, 145–6
  and quadratic utility functions, 171–2
  suggested other risk measures, 85, 122, 130, 194
MAR preferences, 86
MAR risk, 86

Mass-customization, 46
  see also Customizing risk calculations
Maximum acceptable risk, 223, 228,
  231–2, 233, 234
  and existing wealth, 230
  in long term investment, 236
Maximum shortfall, 111–12, 152
M-BPROB (Mean-below MAR
  probability), 86, 87–9
M-BVAR (Mean-below MAR variance),
  86, 89–90, 91
Mean, 4, 121
  and three parameter lognormals, 54–5,
  56
  see also Mean-variance
    framework/model (M-V)
Mean Absolute Deviation analysis,
  239–40
Mean-below MAR probability
  (M-BPROB), 86, 87–9
Mean-below MAR variance (M-BVAR),
  86, 89–90, 91
Mean-BVAR (Mean-below MAR
  variance), 86, 89–90, 91
Mean-downside risk portfolio frontier,
  194–211
  bivariate case, 196–202, 206–8
  multivariate case, 202–4, 208–10
Mean-relative semi-variance portfolio
  construction, 143–4
Mean-variance capital asset pricing
  models (MVCAPM), 156, 167
Mean-variance framework/model (M-V),
  3–8
  assumptions, 176
  evaluation of mutual funds with,
    89–90, 91
  fund allocation, and inflation, 87–9
  for pension fund strategies, unsound
    results from, 240
  portfolio construction, 144–6
  and quadratic utility functions, 170,
    172, 176
  semi-variance measures, 10–11
  and utility theory, 217–18
  and value at risk (VaR), 75
Mean-variance portfolio construction,
  144–6
Median returns as a benchmark, 108

Mesokurtic distributions, 121
Meta-risks, 152
Mind, *see* Human mind
Minimal acceptable return (MAR), 5, 10,
  24, 85–91
  in the demonstration software, 250–1
  downside deviation uses, 179
  for Dutch pension plans, 30–1
  evaluating performance with, 89–91
  failure to achieve, as risk, 74
  formulas based on, 58
  and investors' needs, 93
  lognormals, measurements based on,
    55, 58
  making decisions in, 86–9
  in risk representation, 78–9
Minimum risk, thresholds of, 228
Modern portfolio theory (MPT), 3–4, 59,
  171, 176
Moments, 4, 120–8
  higher moments, 194–5
  partial moments, 131–46
    lower partial-moment capital asset
      pricing models, 156–68
    lower partial moments, 10
    relative lower partial moments
      (RLPMs), 129–31, 153
    special cases, 142–6
    see also Downside risk (DSR)
Morgenstern, O., 213, 216
MPT (Modern portfolio theory), 3–4, 59,
  171, 176
Multidimensionality of risk, 109, 130,
  152
Multivariate case, 202–4, 208–10
Mutual funds:
  evaluation of, 89–90, 91
  financial planners use, 43–4
  for measure comparisons, 180–5
  ranking of, 19–23, 187–93
M-VAR preferences, 86
MVCAPM (Mean-variance capital asset
  pricing models), 156, 167
M-V framework, *see* Mean-variance
  framework/model (M-V)
Myopic loss aversion, 219, 229, 238

Natural price/values, 215, 239
Negative deviations, influence of, 124

Negative returns, 70, 106, 107
 bootstrapping shows potential for, 95
 create jump discontinuities, 132–3, 134
 and utility functions, 134
 see also Downside returns
Negative skew, 121
Netherlands:
 mutual funds, 180–5, 187–93
 pension funds, ALM framework for,
  26–40
Neural mechanics of physical risk, 213
 see also Human mind
Non-linear instruments, 126
Non-linearity:
 of risk, 115, 152
 of risk measures, relative
  semi-variance, 130
 of trading strategies, 124, 126
Non-normal distributions, 124
 analysis of returns for major asset
  classes, 65–6
 empirical distributions of bonds and
  stocks, 79–80
Non-parametric approach, 206–10
Non-stationarity, 125
Normal distributions, 4, 53, 121, 122
 analysis of returns for major asset
  classes, 65–6
 for financial market distributions, 152
 and mean-variance model, 176
 measuring risk with, 75–8
 in Modern Portfolio Theory, 4, 59
 not suitable for investment returns, 94
 Sharpe ratio used for, 68
 see also Mean-variance
  framework/model (M-V)
Numerical positivity for risk measures,
 113

Oil industry analogy, 241–2
Olsen, R.A., 13, 142, 143
Omega excess, 12–13, 18–19
 for self-directed retirement plans, 21–3
Operational level of pension plan
 management, 29, 32
Options, 124, 126
Over-confidence, 214, 219, 225, 228–9
Over-estimating upside potential, 245

Over-reaction bias, 219, 226, 229, 239,
 241
Overvaluation of gains, 214

Parabolas for downside risk, 197–202,
 203–4
Parameters:
 risk aversion parameters, *see* Risk
  aversion parameters
 for three parameter lognormals, 57
 see also Three parameter lognormals
Pareto distribution, 152
Pareto-optimal allocation, 165
Partial moments, 131–46
 lower partial-moment capital asset
  pricing models, 156–68
 lower partial moments, 10
 relative lower partial moments
  (RLPMs), 129–31, 153
 special cases, 142–6
Participants, plan, 27, 28
 age and mobility of, 33
 and risk, 29–30, 32
Peer group analysis, 42
Penalties, 136
 in utility function optimization, 136,
  137, 138, 140, 141–2, 153
 ignoring, 143
 logarithmic utility function, 149, 150
Pension funds:
 case study, 33–7
 developing benchmarks for
  (Netherlands), 26–40
 investment strategy, 240–1
 see also Defined benefit (DB)
  plans/funds; 401(k) plans;
  Retirement plans
Pension Research Institute, 3, 9, 60,
 245
Perception of risk, 59–60, 85, 93–4,
 115
Performance benchmarks, 109
Performance measures:
 absolute versus relative, 16–17
 bond and equity, 16–17, 31

Performance measures: (*continued*)
  financial planners, 44, 45, 46
  investment consultants, 42, 45–6
    goal relative, 49
  peer group analysis, 42
  Post-Modern Portfolio Theory for,
    59–73
  and quadratic utility functions, 182–3
  risk-adjusted, 176–80, 183–4
    and preference functions, 169–70,
      181–3
    and prospect theory value function,
      183–4
  rolling, very large returns disturb, 139
  see also Fouse index; Sharpe ratio;
    Sortino ratio; Upside potential ratio
Performance method 1 (PM1), 89–90
Performance method 2 (PM2), 90
Performance surveys and benchmarks,
  108
Personal threshold of maximum
  acceptable risk, 223
Physical risk, 213, 219, 220–6
Platykurtic distributions, 121
PM1 (Performance method 1), 89–90
PM2 (Performance method 2), 90
PMPT, *see* Post-Modern Portfolio Theory
  (PMPT)
Poisson distributions, 222
Populations, moments refer to, 120
Portfolio construction, 151, 153
  mean-relative semi-variance, 143–4
  mean-variance, 144–6
  problems with very high upside
    returns, 139
  relative mean-relative semi-variance,
    143
  relative mean-RLPM, 142–3
Portfolio frontier, mean-downside risk,
  194–211
Portfolio managers, 93–100, 169
Portfolios:
  fitting to a lognormal, 56
  semi-variance, 195–6
  strategic investment portfolio
    determination, 38–9
Portfolio theory:
  modern (MPT), 3–4, 59, 171, 176
  post-modern (PMPT), 59–73

Positive deviations, influence of, 124
Positive numbers for risk measures, 113
Positive skew, 121, 137–8
Post-Modern Portfolio Theory (PMPT),
  59–73
  in practice, 66–8
  tools of, 60–6
Preference functions, 171–5
  and risk-adjusted performance
    measures, 169–70, 178, 181–93
  see also Fishburn utility function;
    Prospect theory value function;
    Quadratic utility functions; Utility
    functions
Preference rules, 224, 225
Premium contributions (Dutch pension
  funds), 27–8, 29–30, 36, 37–8
Principal, zero MAR protects, 85
  see also Capital
Probability-based risk measures, 109–15
Probability density functions, 110, 111,
  114, 116–17
Probability distributions, 110
  comparing, 116–20
  cumulative, 58, 116–18, 152
  moments of, 120–2
  see also Lognormals; Normal
    distributions; Poisson distributions
Probability of ruin, 218, 228
Probability of shortfall, 109–11, 129, 152
  pension funds, 33, 34–5
Probability weighted function of
  deviations below a specified target
  return, 10
  see also Downside risk
Prospect theory value function, 173–5
  compared to Sharpe ratio, 177, 184–5
  and risk-adjusted performance
    measures, 183–4
  uses reference points, 170
Psychology of risk, 103, 115–16, 152
  see also Human mind
Purchasing power, 35–6

Quadratic penalties, 136
  in utility function optimization, 136,
    137, 141, 153
    logarithmic utility function, 149

Quadratic utility functions, 170, 171–2, 176
  and performance measures, 182–3
  rankings based on, 181, 184–5, 187–93
  Sharpe proposes, 217
Quartic penalties, 140, 141, 153
Quartile boundaries, 121

RA, *see* Risk aversion parameters (RA)
RAMP (Risk assessment and management for projects), 234
Ranking:
  downside risk for, 11, 60
  of mutual funds, 19–23, 181–5, 187–93
  performance measures for, 176
  preference functions for, 176
  risk-adjusted returns for, 66–7
  Sortino ratio for, 64
Rational behaviour, 216, 239
  see also Irrationality
Reality of physical risk, 225
Real returns, 107
Real world behaviour:
  building explanations of, 218
  utility theory inconsistent with, 213
Real world relevance, 6
  utility theory lacks, 217, 234
Reference points:
  downside deviation uses, 179
  preference functions, 170, 172–3, 174
Reference rate, 170
Regulations, solvency, 241
  see also Supervisory bodies
Relative lower partial kurtosis, 129, 131
Relative lower partial moments (RLPMs), 129–31, 153
Relative lower partial skewness, 129
Relative lower partial variance (RLPM^2), 129, 130
Relative mean-relative semi-variance portfolio construction, 143
Relative mean-RLPM portfolio construction, 142–3
Relative semi-variance (RLPM^2), 130
Relativity of risk, 105–9
Representative agents, 157, 158–9, 160, 162, 165–7

Rescaled range (R/S) analysis, 239
Reservoir control, 238–9, 240
Retail investors, 93–4
Retail Price Index (RPI), 236
Retirement:
  liabilities in, 47–8
  types of investment in, 237–8
Retirement plans:
  individual accounts, 46–8
  self-directed, Internet help for, 21–3
  see also Defined benefit (DB) plans/funds; 401(k) plans; Pension funds
Returns:
  asymmetry in, 103, 146
  below-target returns, 60
  for benchmarks, 107–8
    below budgeted return, 108
    bottom quartile returns, 108
    median returns, 108
    real returns, 107
    risk free rate of return, 107
    sector index return, 108
  distributions, 169
  downside returns, *see* Downside returns
  estimating next year's, 51–2, 56
  excess return, 4, 80–1, 89–90
  expected return, 178, 199, 203
  extreme value of, 54–5, 56, 57–8
  high returns, psychological devaluation of, 137
  independence of, and bootstrapping, 52, 95
  minimal, *see* Minimal acceptable return (MAR)
  negative returns, 70, 95, 106, 107, 132–3, 134
  omega excess return, 12–13, 18–19, 21–3
  risk-adjusted returns, 12–13, 66–7, 96
  in style analysis, 12
  target rate of return, *see* Target rate of return
  upside returns, *see* Upside returns

Risk, 104–15
 actuarial approaches, 212
 and asset liability management, 27–8,
  32–3, 36–8
 asymmetry of, 104–5
 downside risk, *see* Downside risk
  (DSR)
 and equities, 26–7, 236–8
 FARM (financial actuarial risk model),
  212–44
 in financial planning paradigm, 45, 46
 financial risk, 212–14, 226–36
 ignoring low, 216, 223
 in investment planning process, 45
 investment risk, 103–55
 investor-specific, 109, 130, 152
 maximum acceptable risk, 223, 228,
  230, 231–2, 233, 234, 236
 multidimensionality of, 109, 152
 non-linearity of, 115, 152
 physical, 213, 219, 220–6
 post-retirement, 47–8, 49
 psychology of, 103, 115–16, 152
 relative to benchmark, 97–9
 relativity of, 105–9
 stakeholders' perspectives, Dutch
  pension plans, 29–30
 standard deviation for, 75–7
 style-adjusted downside risk (SAD), 13
 undervaluing, 214
 value of risk, 222, 225, 229–30, 231,
  232, 233, 234, 236
 value at risk (VaR), 74–80, 113
Risk-adjusted performance measures,
  176–80, 183–4
 downside deviation applied in, 179–80
 and preference functions, 169–70,
  181–93
  consistency of, 181–4
 and prospect theory value function,
  183–4
Risk-adjusted returns, 12–13, 66–7, 96
 see also Returns
Risk assessment and management for
  projects (RAMP), 234

Risk attitudes, 169
 and preference functions, 171, 172–5,
  181
 and risk-adjusted performance ratios,
  179–80
  Sharpe ratio, 177–8
Risk aversion, 134, 136, 141, 143, 219
 and Fishburn utility function, 184
 and preference for second order
  stochastic dominance, 118–19
 and prospect theory value function,
  183–4
 and quadratic utility function rankings,
  182–3
 and risk-adjusted performance
  measures, 170, 182–4, 185
 and utility functions, 171–2, 173, 174,
  175
 and value at risk, 74, 77
Risk aversion parameters (RA), 143–4,
  146–8
 and *IR*, 83
 and rankings, 181, 182, 183, 187–93
Risk benchmarks, 109
Risk capital, 33, 35
Risk equals uncertainty paradox, 219–20,
  231, 238, 240
Risk free rate of return, 107
Riskless rate, 156, 157
Riskless/risk-free assets:
 in Capital Asset Pricing Model
  (CAPM), 176
 compared to risky assets, 220
 and the Sharpe ratio, 178
Risk measures:
 absence of, 218
 completeness of, 54, 110–11, 112,
  113, 114, 130
 probability-based, 109–15
 problems, 124–5
  with standard deviation, 122–3
  with variance, 113, 124, 136
 properties of, 152–3
 skewness as, 128
 utility function basis for, 125–7,
  136–7, 138, 140
Risk perception, 59–60, 85, 93–4, 115
Risk preference functions, *see* Preference
  functions

Risk study, Royal Society's, 223
Risky assets:
 in Capital Asset Pricing Model
  (CAPM), 176
 compared to risk-free assets, 220
 and the Sharpe ratio, 176–7, 178
RLPM^0, 129
 see also Probability of shortfall
RLPM^1, 129, 130
 see also Expected shortfall
RLPM^2, 129, 130
RLPM^3, 129, 131
RLPM^4, 129
 see also Relative lower partial kurtosis
RLPMs (Relative lower partial moments),
  129–31, 153
RMC downside (d_{RMC}), 138, 141, 153
RMC upside (u_{RMC}), 137, 141–2, 150,
  153
RMQ downside (d_{RMQ}), 139–40, 141,
  153
RMQ upside (u_{RMQ}), 138–9, 142, 153
RMS downside (d_{RMS}), 136–7, 141, 149,
  153
RMS upside (u_{RMS}), 137, 141, 153
RMS values, 136
Root Mean Square (RMS) values, 136
Royal Society of London, risk study by,
  223
Ruin, 218, 227, 228, 230–2, 241
 see also Catastrophic events

SAD risk (style-adjusted downside risk),
  13
St Petersburg Paradox, 215, 234–6
 other paradox, 220, 231–2
Samples, moments refer to, 120
Scenarios, market, 56
Second moment, 4, 121
 see also Variance
Second order downside risk aversion, 149
Second order downside utility, 135–7
Second order risk aversion parameters,
  147
Second order stochastic dominance, 5,
  118–20, 152
Second order terms, 134, 135–7, 147,
  149
Second order upside leakage penalty, 149

Second order upside utility, 134
Second order upside utility leakage, 137
Second order utility leakage sensitivity,
  147
Sector index return, 108
Self-directed retirement plans, Internet
  help for, 21–3
 see also Retirement plans
Semi-variance^2, below-target, 60
Semi-variance, 10–11, 60, 194, 196
 downside semi-variance, 143, 144, 149
 Markowitz on, 85, 122, 130, 194
 problems with, 194
 for portfolios, 195–6
 relative (RLPM^2), 130
 see also Mean-relative semi-variance
  portfolio construction; Relative
  mean-relative semi-variance
  portfolio construction
Severity of consequences of an adverse
  occurrence, 220–1, 224, 226–7
Severity functions, 221–2, 224, 226–8
Sharpe ratio (SR):
 for excess return, 89–90
 ignores downside volatility, 66–7
 and *IR*, 85
 rankings, 185
  compared to Fishburn utility
   function, 184
  compared to prospect theory value
   function, 183–4
  compared to quadratic utility
   function rankings, 182
  compared to Sortino ratio, 64, 66–7
 to construct a portfolio of risky assets,
  176–7
 and t-statistic, 85, 178
Sharpe, William, 3, 4, 9, 12, 21, 60, 85,
  217–18
Shortfall:
 average downside deviation shows, 62
 expected, 113–15, 129, 130, 152
 maximum, 111–12, 152
 probability of, *see* Probability of
  shortfall
Sign convention for risk measures, 113

Skewness, 6–8, 121
  comparing managers with, 67–8
  lognormal curves for, 53–4
  relative lower partial skewness, 129
  relative to benchmark, 128
  as a risk measure, 128
  in utility functions, 137–8
  volatility skewness, 63–4, 68
  see also Asymmetry
Ski-ing, risk in, 222, 223
Small-sample problem, 70
Smith, Adam, 214–15, 239
Software:
  Forsey-Sortino model tutorial for, 57,
    245–52
  free, on the Internet for downside risk,
    99
Solvency:
  of pension funds, and contributions,
    27, 29
  of pension plan sponsors, 37–8
  see also Insolvency risk
Solvency regulations, 241
  see also Supervisory bodies
Sortino, F., 12, 60, 61, 69
Sortino ratio, 63–4, 170, 179
  for a portfolio and benchmark
    compared, 97
  rankings, 185
    compared to Fishburn utility
      function, 184
    compared to prospect theory value
      function, 183–4
    compared to quadratic utility
      function rankings, 182
    compared to Sharpe ratio, 66–7
  represents risk-adjusted returns, 96
  shows downside volatility, 66–7
Special cases of the unified utility theory,
    142–6, 153
Sponsors, plan, 27–8
  financial strength of, 28, 37–8
  and funding choices, 240–1
  risks to, 29–30, 32
  use investment consultants, 41
Sports, physical risk in, 220–6
SR, *see* Sharpe ratio (SR)
Stakeholders, pension fund, 27, 29–30,
    32

Standard deviation:
  and downside deviation compared, 179
  and downside risk compared,
    symmetrical distributions, 70–1
  and efficiency ratio, 96
  in information ratio definition, 80–1
  as a measure of uncertainty, not risk,
    122
  in Modern Portfolio Theory, 59
  as a parameter of three parameter
    lognormals, 54–5
  in portfolio fitting, lognormals, 56
  problems with, 67, 75–7, 93, 122–3
    asymmetrical returns, 103
  as a risk measure, 122–3, 218
Statistical significance of active
    management, 83–4
Statistics, downside risk, 95–7
Stochastic dominance models, 4–11, 152
  fail in the risk equals uncertainty
    paradox, 231
  first order, 5, 117–18, 152
  over estimate equity risk, 241–2
  second order, 5, 117–18, 152
Stock markets:
  1974 price fall, 237, 241
  flight to liquidity, 229
  Internet-related stocks, 214
  Japanese stock market, 70, 95
  natural values/prices, 215, 239
  over-confidence in, 228–9
  overvaluation, 214
  see also Bear markets; Bull markets
Stocks:
  empirical distributions for, 79–80
  proportion of investments in, 75–8,
    86–9
  see also Equities
Strategic benchmarks for Dutch pension
    funds, 26–40
Strategic investment portfolio,
    determination of, 38–9
Strategic level, 29–31
Strategy, investment, 29–31, 38–9,
    240–1
Stripped Treasury bond indexes, 70
Style-adjusted downside risk (SAD risk),
    13
Style analysis, 17–18, 20, 67

Style benchmark, 12
Style beta, 13
 see also Beta
Supervisory bodies, pension plan, 27, 38
Symmetry:
 of distributions, 4, 70–1
 implies good outcomes are risky, 59
 in volatility skewness definition, 64
 see also Asymmetry
Systemic irrationality, 215, 218–19

Tacit knowledge, 215, 234–5
Tactical level of pension plan
  management, 29, 31–2
Target rate of return, 9–10, 62, 156, 157
 difficulty in choosing, 69–70
 for downside risk and standard
  deviation compared, 70–1
 and rankings, 66
 social, 165–7
 see also Goals
Tax, 43, 44, 47–8
Taylor series expansions, 125, 127, 145
T-bills, 17, 70
Temporary insanity, 226, 229
TFMS, *see* Two-fund money separation
  (TFMS)
Third moment, 15, 121
 see also Skewness
Third order risk aversion, 148
Third order terms, 137–8, 148, 149–50,
  153
Third order upside utility, 137–8
Third order utility leakage sensitivity, 148
Three parameter lognormals, 15–16,
  51–8, 60–1, 95
 demonstration program for, 245,
  248–50
 formulas for, 57–8
Thresholds, 223, 228
Time:
 indexing, and discounted downside
  risk, 35–7
 and non-stationarity, 125
 and relative semi-variance, 130
 in risk estimation, 12
Treynor ratio, 178
T-statistic, 84
 and the Sharpe ratio, 85, 178

Tutorial, Forsey-Sortino model, 245–52
Tversky, Amos, 115–16, 135
Tversky paradox, 219, 230–1
Two-fund money separation (TFMS),
  157, 162–5, 167, 176
 in new asset pricing model, 205–6
 and portfolio frontiers, 204

Uncertainty:
 estimating next year's, 51–2
 in individual retirement account
  management, 46–8
 modelling with three parameter
  lognormals, 51–8
 risk equals uncertainty paradox,
  219–20, 231, 238, 240
 standard deviation measures, 122
 variance measures, 153
Under-estimating risk in downside risk
  calculations, 245
Undervaluing risk, 214
Unified theory of the utility of upside and
  downside returns, 104, 131–46, 153
 special cases, 142–6
UPR, *see* Upside potential ratio
UP ratio, *see* Upside potential ratio
U-P ratio, *see* Upside potential ratio
Upside kurtosis, 139
Upside marginal utility, 134
 decreasing, 134–5, 141, 142, 144, 149
 rate of change of, 134–5, 137
Upside moments, estimation of, 151–2
Upside potential, 14–15
 lognormal formulas, 55, 58
 maximising, 24
 software and tutorial for, 245
Upside potential ratio (UPR), 15, 55, 58,
  170, 179–80
 ex ante test of, 19–21
 rankings, 185
  compared to Fishburn utility
   function, 184
  compared to prospect theory value
   function, 183–4
  compared to quadratic utility
   function rankings, 182

Upside potential ratio (UPR), (*continued*)
  rankings, (*continued*)
    for self-directed retirement plans,
      21–3
Upside probability, 55, 58
Upside returns:
  asymmetry of, 104–5, 146
  ignoring, 68–9
  Modern Portfolio Theory penalises, 59
  very high, 137, 139, 140, 141
Upside utility leakage, 140–2, 153
  higher order, 139
  logarithmic functions, 147–8, 150
  second order, 137
Upside utility, unified theory of, 104,
  131–51, 153
  fourth order, 138–9
  second order, 134
  third order, 137–8
Upside variance, 64, 134–5
User-defined lognormal in the
  Forsey-Sortino model tutorial,
  250–2
Utility axioms, 216, 218
  see also Axioms of choice
Utility functions:
  Allais rejects, 216–17
  Fishburn, *see* Fishburn utility function
  independence of wealth distribution,
    165–7
  logarithmic, 146–51, 153
    Bernoulli used, 220, 231–2, 236
  and lower partial moment, using upside
    and downside utility, 132–46
  and lower-partial moment capital asset
    pricing models, theory of, 158–67
  modelling preferences with, 171, 172
  quadratic, *see* Quadratic utility
    functions
  for risk-adjusted return, 12
  and two-fund money separation,
    162–4
  and variance as a risk measure, 125–7
Utility leakage sensitivities, 147–8
Utility, partial moments and, 131–46
  special cases, 142–6
  see also Expected utility; Marginal
    utility

Utility theory, 216, 217–18
  inconsistent with real world behaviour,
    213
  and investors' decisions, 13–14
  for pension fund strategies, unsound
    results from, 240–1
  see also Expected utility (EU)

Value of risk, 222, 225, 231, 232, 233
  in the Allais Paradox, 229–30, 234
  in long term investment, 236
Value at risk (VaR), 74–80, 113
  and mean-variance MPT, 75
  representing risk with, 77–8
VaR, *see* Value at risk (VaR)
Variance, 4, 121
  downside variance, 64, 135–6
  problem with, 5–6, 60, 85, 103,
    152–3, 194
  relative lower partial variance
    (RLPM^2), 129
  relative to benchmark, 128
  as a risk measure, 113, 124, 136,
    218
  upside variance, 64, 134–5
  utility function basis for, 125–7
  see also Mean-variance
    framework/model (M-V)
VN-M (von Neumann-Morgenstern
  Axioms), 75, 85
Volatility, mean-variance penalizes, 90
Volatility skewness, 63–4, 68
  see also Skewness
von Neumann, J.R., 213, 216
von Neumann-Morgenstern Axioms
  (VN-M), 75, 85

Wall Street Crash, 241
Wealth:
  existing, 220, 230–1
  marginal utility of, 172, 215
  target level of, 172–3
Wrap programmes, 42

Zero-coupon bonds, 70
Zero MAR, 85
Zero returns, 107, 133, 147
Zeroth order utility, 133–4